Writers and their Background

TENNYSON

LU

Alfred Lord Tennyson: Portrait by Samuel Laurence

(National Portrait Gallery)

Writers and their Background

TENNYSON

EDITED BY D. J. PALMER

LONDON · G. BELL & SONS · 1973

© G. BELL & SONS LTD 1973
PUBLISHED BY G. BELL & SONS LTD
YORK HOUSE, 6 PORTUGAL STREET, LONDON, WC2A 2HL

PRINTED IN GREAT BRITAIN BY
W & J MACKAY LIMITED, CHATHAM

ISBN 0 7135 1744 1

Contents

List of Illustrations

The Contributors

PHILIP DREW
Senior Lecturer in English, University of Glasgow

JOHN DIXON HUNT
Lecturer in English, University of York

JOHN D. JUMP
Professor of English, University of Manchester

JOHN KILLHAM
Senior Lecturer in English, University of Keele

LIONEL MADDEN
Bibliographer, Victorian Studies Centre, University of Leicester

D. J. PALMER
Senior Lecturer in English, University of Hull

M. SHAW
Lecturer in English, University of Hull

SIR CHARLES TENNYSON
Grandson and biographer of the poet

PETER THOMSON
Lecturer in English, University College, Swansea

General Editor's Preface

THE STUDY of literature is not a 'pure' discipline since works of literature are affected by the climate of opinion in which they are produced. Writers, like other men, are concerned with the politics, the philosophy, the religion, the arts, and the general thought of their own times. Some literary figures, indeed, have made their own distinguished contributions to these areas of human interest, while the achievement of others can be fully appreciated only by a knowledge of them.

The series, to which the present volume is an important addition, has been planned with the purpose of presenting major authors in their intellectual, social, and artistic contexts, and with the conviction that this will make their work more easily understood and enjoyed. Each volume contains a chapter which provides a reader's guide to the writings of the author concerned, a Bibliography, and Chronological Tables setting out the main dates of the author's life and publications alongside the chief events of contemporary importance.

The last decade has seen a new and deeper understanding of the Victorian period. No longer is it considered an age of complacency, hypocrisy, and a vulgarity based upon material progress. Instead, we recognize with some sympathy that our grandfathers were wrestling with intellectual and social problems that remain largely unsolved today. Accompanying this change of attitude there has been a steady reassessment of Victorian poetry which has brought a new interest in Tennyson. It gives me great pleasure to welcome to this series a volume devoted to Tennyson, edited by my friend and colleague, Mr D. J. Palmer. The team of scholars and critics he has brought together have produced a most interesting study which, by relating the poet to his age, increases our knowledge of both, and wins for Tennyson himself our sincere admiration.

R. L. BRETT

Abbreviations

CH: *Tennyson: The Critical Heritage,* ed John D. Jump, The Critical Heritage Series (1967).

CPW: *Complete Poetical Works,* ed T. H. Warren, revd. and enlgd. F. Page, Oxford Standard Authors (1953). For quotations from the plays, in Chapter 9 only.

Mem: Hallam, Lord Tennyson, *Alfred, Lord Tennyson: A Memoir,* 2 vol. (1897).

PT: *The Poems of Tennyson,* ed Christopher Ricks, Longmans Annotated English Poets (1969).

Place of publication is London unless otherwise stated.

Editor's Preface

TENNYSON'S LONG poetic career spanned almost the entire Victorian period, and no other English poet of his stature, not even Shakespeare, gained such public prestige in his own lifetime. His relations with the shifting social, spiritual and artistic currents of his age were therefore particularly close, though not always sympathetic. Received by his contemporaries as a spokesman and representative figure in many respects, he was also deeply critical and independent in others. His modern reputation, since Harold Nicolson's brilliantly provocative study of 1923, has largely depended upon attitudes to the Victorian age as a whole and assessments of his place within it, and therefore he is an appropriate subject for a volume in this series.

Today the study of Tennyson and his background has been greatly advanced by two recent works of scholarship, the fine edition of his poetry by Christopher Ricks and the collection of contemporary reviews and criticism edited by John Jump. Present and future Tennyson studies also stand deeply indebted to the energy and dedication of Sir Charles Tennyson, the poet's grandson and his biographer, who has worked with the staff of Lincoln City Library to establish and develop the invaluable collection of material at the Tennyson Research Centre in Lincoln.

In addition to expressing my gratitude to my fellow-contributors to this volume, I should like to thank Professor Brett, the General Editor of this series, for his encouragement, suggestions and patience.

D. J. PALMER

The main events of Tennyson's life	*The main events of literary and intellectual importance in Tennyson's lifetime*	*The main events of historical importance in Tennyson's lifetime*
1809	Tennyson born (6 August) at Somersby, Lincolnshire	Byron, *English Bards and Scotch Reviewers*	Napoleon captures Vienna
1811		J. Austen, *Sense and Sensibility* Shelley, *Necessity of Atheism*	Prince of Wales made Regent
1815	Pupil at Louth Grammar School	Wordsworth, *White Doe of Rylstone* and *Poems* (2 vols)	Battle of Waterloo
1817		Byron, *Manfred* Coleridge, *Biographia Literaria* Keats, *Poems* Death of J. Austen	
1821		Death of Keats	Death of Napoleon
1822		Death of Shelley M. Arnold born	Death of Castlereagh
1824		Death of Byron F. T. Palgrave born	
1827	*Poems by Two Brothers* (April) in collaboration with Charles Tennyson Enters Trinity College, Cambridge	Death of Blake Thomas Arnold, Headmaster of Rugby	Death of Canning
1829	Friendship with Hallam (April) Member of 'The Apostles' (May) Chancellor's Gold Medal for Prize Poem, 'Timbuctoo' (June)	Carlyle, 'Signs of the Times' (in *Edinburgh Review)*	Catholic Emancipation Act
1830	*Poems, Chiefly Lyrical* (June)	Lyell, *Principles of Geology* Cobbett, *Rural Rides*	Death of George IV Accession of William IV Grey Prime Minister Manchester and Liverpool Railway July Revolution in France

1831	Death of Tennyson's father (March) Leaves Cambridge without taking degree Hallam's review of *Poems, Chiefly Lyrical* in *Englishman's Magazine* (August)		First and Second Reform Bills
1832	*Poems* (December, dated 1833) Insanity of brother Edward	Death of Scott Byron, *Works*, ed. Moore (1832–35)	Reform Act
1833	Death of Arthur Hallam (September)	Carlyle, *Sartor Resartus* Browning, *Pauline*	Abolition of slavery in British colonies Oxford Movement begins Factory Act
1834	Falls in love with Rosa Baring	Death of Coleridge Death of Lamb Taylor, *Philip Van Artevelde*	New Poor Law Tolpuddle Martyrs transported
1837	Family moves to High Beech, Epping	Carlyle, *French Revolution* Dickens, *Oliver Twist*	Accession of Queen Victoria
1838	Engagement to Emily Sellwood	Dickens, *Nicholas Nickleby*	Anti-Corn Law League founded Chartist movement
1840	Engagement broken off Family moves to Tunbridge Wells	Browning, *Sordello*	Queen's marriage to Prince Albert
1842	*Poems,* 2 vol (May)	Mudie's Circulating Library	Mines Act Copyright Act Chartist riots
1845	Civil List pension (£200 p.a.)	Disraeli, *Sybil*	Newman becomes Roman Catholic Irish Potato Famine
1846		Dickens, *Martin Chuzzlewit*	Repeal of Corn Laws Railway boom
1847	*The Princess* (December)	George Eliot, *Strauss's Life of Jesus* C. Brontë, *Jane Eyre* E. Brontë, *Wuthering Heights*	Ten Hours Factory Act

1848		Pre-Raphaelite Brotherhood Dickens, *Dombey and Son* Mrs Gaskell, *Mary Barton* Mill, *Principles of Political Economy* Thackeray, *Vanity Fair*	Revolutions in Europe Chartist Petition
1849		Arnold, *Strayed Reveller*	Christian Socialism (F. D. Maurice and C. Kingsley)
1850	*In Memoriam* (published anonymously, May) Marriage to Emily Sellwood (June) Appointed Poet Laureate in succession to Wordsworth (November)	Death of Wordsworth Browning, *Christmas Eve and Easter Day* Carlyle, *Latter Day Pamphlets* Dickens, *David Copperfield* Kingsley, *Alton Locke*	
1851		Kingsley, *Yeast* Meredith, *Poems* Ruskin, *Stones of Venice*	Napoleon III comes to power in France Great Exhibition
1852	Son Hallam born (August) *Ode on the Death of the Duke of Wellington* (November)	Thackeray, *Henry Esmond*	
1853	Moves to Farringford, Isle of Wight	Arnold, *Poems* C. Brontë, *Villette* Mrs Gaskell, *Cranford*	
1854	Son Lionel born (March)	Dickens, *Hard Times* Patmore, *Angel in the House,* Part I	Crimean War
1855	*Maud and Other Poems* (July)	Death of C. Brontë Browning, *Men and Women* Mrs Gaskell, *North and South* Trollope, *The Warden*	Palmerston Prime Minister Florence Nightingale in Crimea Livingstone discovers Victoria Falls
1859	*Idylls of the King* ('Enid', 'Vivien', 'Elaine', and 'Guinevere')	Darwin, *Origin of Species* G. Eliot, *Adam Bede* E. Fitzgerald, *Omar Khayyám* Mill, *On Liberty* S. Smiles, *Self-Help*	

1860	Advises Palgrave on *Golden Treasury*	G. Eliot, *Mill on the Floss* *Essays and Reviews* Patmore, *Angel in the House,* Part II	Unification of Italy
1861		Dickens, *Great Expectations* G. Eliot, *Silas Marner* Mill, *Representative Government* H. Spencer, *Education* Trollope, *Framley Parsonage*	American Civil War Death of Prince Albert
1862	Dedicates new edition of *Idylls of the King* to memory of Prince Albert (January) First audience with the Queen (April)	G. Eliot, *Romola* Meredith, *Modern Love* Ruskin, *Unto This Last*	
1864	*Enoch Arden* (August)	Newman, *Apologia pro Vita Sua* Browning, *Dramatis Personae*	
1868	Building of second home, Aldworth, at Haslemere	Browning, *The Ring and the Book*	Gladstone Prime Minister
1869	Founder member of 'Metaphysical Society' (April) *The Holy Grail and Other Poems* (December, dated 1870)	Arnold, *Culture and Anarchy* Mill, *On the Subjection of Women*	Suez Canal opened Irish Church disestablished
1870		Death of Dickens D. G. Rossetti, *Poems* Newman, *Grammar of Assent*	Franco-Prussian War Elementary Education Act
1872	*Gareth and Lynette* (October)	Death of F. D. Maurice S. Butler, *Erewhon* Hardy, *Under the Greenwood Tree*	
1875	*Queen Mary* (June)	Death of Kingsley	
1876	*Harold* (December, dated 1877)	G. Eliot, *Daniel Deronda* Meredith, *Beauchamp's Career* W. Morris, *Sigurd the Volsung*	Bulgarian atrocities Edison's phonograph

1880	*Ballads and other Poems* (December)	Death of G. Eliot Browning, *Dramatic Idylls* II Hardy, *Trumpet Major*	Transvaal declares itself a republic
1883	Accepts barony	Trollope, *Autobiography*	
1884	*The Cup and the Falcon* (February) *Becket* (December)		Third Reform Bill
1885	*Tiresias and Other Poems* (December)	Meredith, *Diana of the Crossways* Pater, *Marius the Epicurean* Ruskin, *Praeterita*	Fall of Khartoum
1886	*Locksley Hall Sixty Years After* (December)	Gissing, *Demos* Hardy, *Mayor of Casterbridge* Kipling, *Departmental Ditties*	
1889	*Demeter and Other Poems* (December)	Death of Browning Death of G. M. Hopkins Pater, *Appreciations* W. B. Yeats, *Wanderings of Oisin*	London Dock Strike
1892	Death of Tennyson (6 October)	Kipling, *Barrack-Room Ballads* G. B. Shaw, *Widowers' Houses*	

1: Tennyson: A Reader's Guide

LIONEL MADDEN[1]

TEXTS

Old poets fostered under friendlier skies,
Old Virgil who would write ten lines, they say,
At dawn, and lavish all the golden day
To make them wealthier in his readers' eyes;
And you, old popular Horace, you the wise
Adviser of the nine-years-pondered lay,
And you, that wear a wreath of sweeter bay,
Catullus, whose dead songster never dies;
If, glacing downward on the kindly sphere
  That once had rolled you round and round the Sun,
  You see your Art still shrined in human shelves,
  You should be jubilant that you flourished here
  Before the Love of Letters, overdone,
Had swampt the sacred poets with themselves.   (PT, 1322)

ALTHOUGH TENNYSON'S sonnet was finally entitled 'Poets and their Bibliographies', one of several earlier titles—'On publishing every discarded scrap of a Poet'—identifies more precisely the cause of his irritation. He had little sympathy with those who preserved words and sections of poems, 'the chips of the workshop', which he himself had rejected during later reworkings of his material. As he said of collectors of first editions: 'Why do they treasure the rubbish I shot from my full-finish'd cantos?' (*Mem.*, I, 118).

No reader, perhaps, can avoid feeling some instinctive sympathy with

[1] The author gratefully acknowledges financial assistance from the University of Leicester Research Board towards work on this chapter and the Select Bibliography.

Tennyson's firmly expressed dislike of extensive variant readings. Nevertheless, the initial movement towards acceptance of his position may be quickly checked when it is realized how much is lost in the process. Christopher Ricks has shown, in his analysis of 'Tennyson's methods of composition', how hard Tennyson worked at the task of perfecting his works and how frequently in his poems he borrowed from and improved upon his own earlier writings.[1] For a reader interested in the development of Tennyson's poetic technique the 'discarded scraps' may clearly reveal the processes by which a specific poem was made. Equally important, though much less frequent, are the occasions on which Tennyson weakened a poem in order to avoid giving offence to his readers.

If Tennyson professed hostility to the editorial compilation of variant readings, he liked 'those old Variorum Classics—all the Notes make the Text look precious.'[2] Hallam, Lord Tennyson's nine-volume 'Eversley' edition of *The Works of Tennyson Annotated* included notes dictated or approved by the poet. Published in 1907-8 this continued to provide the standard text until 1969 when it was largely superseded as a text by *The Poems of Tennyson* edited by Christopher Ricks in the 'Longmans Annotated English Poets' series. This text is itself based upon the Eversley edition. Since Ricks's edition seems certain to constitute the best scholarly text of Tennyson for some time to come it is necessary to have a clear idea of its aims and its authority.

Ricks's edition collects all the poems published during Tennyson's lifetime, all other poems published since his death by his son Hallam and his grandson Sir Charles Tennyson, and poems which survive in manuscript. Among the scattered poetical manuscripts there is an important manuscript of *In Memoriam* in the research collection in Lincoln. Many early poems are included in a Commonplace Book compiled by J. M. Heath, a friend of Tennyson, during 1832-4, now in the Fitzwilliam Museum in Cambridge. This was described by Sir Charles Tennyson in an article in the *Cornhill Magazine* in 1936.[3] The existence

---

[1] *Proceedings of the British Academy* LII, 1966, 209-30.

[2] *Tennyson and His Friends*, ed Hallam, Lord Tennyson, 1911, 147.

[3] 'J. M. Heath's "Commonplace Book"', *Cornhill Magazine* CLIII, 1936, 426-49.

of some other manuscripts is noted in Ricks's introductions to the poems. The most important collections of poetical manuscripts, however, are contained in the Houghton Library at Harvard University and in Trinity College, Cambridge. The collection at Harvard was sold in 1954 by Sir Charles Tennyson, who was an executor of Hallam, Lord Tennyson. The reasons for Sir Charles's selection of an American library are outlined in his autobiography *Stars and Markets*.[1] The contents of the collection were described by Edgar F. Shannon and W. H. Bond in 1956 in an article in the *Harvard Library Bulletin*.[2]

The collection of manuscripts in Trinity College, Cambridge, includes a manuscript of *In Memoriam* and notebooks containing drafts of poems later published either by Tennyson himself or by Hallam Tennyson in his *Memoir,* his *Materials for a Life of A.T.* and in the Eversley edition. These were deposited by Hallam Tennyson in 1924 on condition that they should not be copied or quoted in perpetuity. This stringent regulation was only relaxed in 1969 after the publication of Ricks's edition. The new regulations, which were introduced largely as a result of the influence of the present Lord Tennyson and Sir Charles Tennyson, were reported in the *Times Literary Supplement* in July 1969. Shortly afterwards Christopher Ricks printed a selection of hitherto unpublished verses and of passages which were not adopted in the published versions of Tennyson's poems.[3] In his introduction to the selection he notes of the Trinity College manuscripts that 'their major importance lies rather in their revelations about the composition of Tennyson's best poems than in their furnishing new unpublished poems'.

Since Ricks's edition of the *Poems* does not aim at a comprehensive treatment but is intended to supply only a selective list of variant readings, the inability to quote extensively from the Trinity College manuscripts does not destroy the value of his work. As Ricks himself justly pointed out in reply to a reviewer in *Victorian Studies,* the publication of his edition was itself one of the causes which helped to bring about the

[1] *Stars and Markets*, 1957, 166–8.
[2] 'Literary manuscripts of Alfred Tennyson in the Harvard College Library', *Harvard Library Bulletin* X, 1956, 254–74.
[3] *TLS* 21 August 1969, 918–22.

relaxation of the restrictions. However, the new regulations should make it possible for him to produce a revision of his work. It is important to emphasise the essentially selective character of Ricks's edition. Although it includes all the hitherto published and unpublished poems, it omits all the plays with the exception of the early *The Devil and the Lady,* written by Tennyson at the age of fourteen and first published by Sir Charles Tennyson in 1930. For the text of the other plays the reader may be referred to the Eversley edition or to the one-volume Oxford edition of Tennyson's *Poems and Plays.* In his editorial treatment of variant readings Ricks is very selective. All differences between the first published text of a poem and the final version in the one-volume 1894 edition or the Eversley edition are recorded but changes in words introduced after the first edition but later withdrawn are only occasionally noted. Manuscript variants are selected according to the importance of the poem, the lapse of time between writing and publication, or the intrinsic significance of the variant.

Despite the inevitable difficulties involved in such a selective edition for the reader who wishes to make an exhaustive study of Tennyson's methods of compostition, Ricks's *Poems* is a magnificent achievement which makes the poems available in one volume and at a price which is not prohibitive for the individual student. Despite his unfortunate inability in this first edition to cite manuscript variants from the Trinity College notebooks, an examination of his introductory notes to such a poem as *Armageddon* indicates how skilfully he has presented valuable and illuminating information about these sources. The poems are arranged as far as possible in chronological order of composition, though, as Ricks notes, many of the poems were written and revised over a very long period of time. Only the *Idylls of the King* and the songs from the plays are printed as groups out of sequence at the end of the volume. There is adequate cross-referencing, relating, for example, the 'O that 'twere possible' stanzas, written in 1833–4, to their appearance in *Maud* in 1855. In addition, the footnotes cite important materials, indicating Tennyson's range of allusion, unconscious reminiscence and parallels which are probably analogues rather than sources.

For all but the most specialist reader, then, Ricks's edition provides an outstandingly valuable text, illustrating in detail the development of the most significant poems and providing texts for many others which were not previously available. If, as he speculates in his introduction, there is one day a complete multi-volume variorum edition—a scholarly labour of love which the liberation of the Trinity College manuscripts has now made possible and desirable—it will lean heavily on the work undertaken for this volume. And, as Gerhard Joseph noted in his review of Ricks's edition, 'the choice of editor for those volumes seems clear enough'.[1]

Life and Personality

The reader's understanding of Tennyson as a literary artist must derive chiefly from a close study of his writings. Tennyson himself attempted to describe his literary history and development in the very revealing poem, 'Merlin and the Gleam', which he wrote in 1889. He attacked the desire for detailed biographies of eminent figures in 'The Dead Prophet'—

> *For since he would sit on a Prophet's seat,*
> *As a lord of the Human soul,*
> *We needs must scan him from head to feet*
> *Were it but for a wart or a mole?* (PT, 1325)

—and in 'To——, After Reading a Life and Letters':

> *Proclaim the faults he would not show:*
> *Break lock and seal: betray the trust:*
> *Keep nothing sacred: 'tis but just*
> *The many-headed beast should know.* (PT, 847)

There can be few readers, however, who will not feel the need for factual information about the actions and events which punctuated his long life. Equally important, most readers will wish to gain an insight into the mysterious secret personality of the man who emerged

[1] *VS* XIII, 1970, 425-7.

from obscurity to become the Victorian embodiment of the Poet figure.

Tennyson's life, though not his work, divides sharply into two periods. His obituary in *The Times* asserted: 'The greatest or most conspicuous men are often the least to be envied; but we should say that few lots were more enviable than his. The son of a clergyman in affluent circumstances, life from the first was made smooth and pleasant to him.'[1] Such an oversimplified view of Tennyson's life failed to do justice to the turmoil of his childhood in Lincolnshire, his youth in Cambridge, his agony at the death of his closest friend, his loss of fortune and his apparent lack of direction or prospects. The first period contrasts with the forty-two years from 1850 during which he was England's Poet Laureate and lived in those great houses which symbolised his success, Farringford on the Isle of Wight and Aldworth on Blackdown.

In his old age Tennyson positively rejected the idea of a long, formal biography of himself. However, he granted his eldest living child, Hallam, permission to undertake a biography, stipulating, as Hallam recorded, that 'the incidents of his life should be given as shortly as might be without comment, but that my notes should be final and full enough to preclude the chance of further and unauthentic biographies' (*Mem.*, I, xii). Hallam, 2nd Lord Tennyson, was forty-five years of age when he published his *Alfred Lord Tennyson: A Memoir* in 1897, five years after Tennyson's death. He was well equipped for the task of writing the biography, having assumed the rôle of Tennyson's secretary in succession to Emily, the poet's wife, when she fell seriously ill in 1874.

The two-volume *Memoir* remains an essential source of information for the student of Tennyson. In addition to factual biographical details it includes selections from correspondence to and from Tennyson, extracts from notebooks and diaries, records of his conversation, and the comments of friends and visitors. The *Memoir* is especially valuable, too, for the interesting light which it casts upon the contemporary reception of Tennyson's works and his very sensitive reaction to

[1] *Times* 7 October 1892, 9.

adverse criticism. If the effect of the *Memoir* is sometimes rather dis-jointed the weakness is inherent in the basic plan adopted for the work and described by Hallam Tennyson in his preface: 'According to my father's wish, throughout the memoir my hand will be as seldom seen as may be, and this accounts for the occasionally fragmentary character of my work'. The *Memoir* is, indeed, rather a collection of source materials than a systematic biography. At the same time Hallam Tenny-son vouches for the essentially trustworthy and accurate nature of his record: 'The anecdotes and sayings here related have been mostly taken down as soon as spoken, and are hence, I trust, not marred or mended by memory, which, judging from some anecdotes of him recently published, is wont to be a register not wholly accurate' (*Mem.*, I, xvi).

Much material which did not find a place in the *Memoir* may be consulted in the four volumes of *Materials for a Life of A.T.* which Hallam Tennyson had privately printed and circulated during 1895 or 1896. The volumes of manuscript notes on which this was based are in the Tennyson Research Centre in Lincoln, which also possesses page proofs of the *Memoir*. Later, in 1911, Hallam Tennyson edited *Tennyson and His Friends*, a collection of essays and reminiscences about Tenny-son and his circle by a variety of contributors. This volume, which usefully supplements the *Memoir*, also prints a number of poems by Tennyson addressed to his friends. In 1893 James Knowles published 'A personal reminiscence' of Tennyson in the *Nineteenth Century*.[1] Des-pite its often distressingly pious and sentimental tone there are further interesting and revealing recollections of Tennyson and his family in H. D. Rawnsley's *Memories of the Tennysons*, first published in 1900.

Tennyson himself was always unwilling to speak of his early ex-periences and for this period Hallam Tennyson was severely hampered by a general lack of documentary evidence. Shortly before the second world war a large collection of family correspondence was discovered at Bayons Manor in Lincolnshire, home first of Tennyson's grand-father and then of his younger son, in whose favour Tennyson's father was largely disinherited and who later took the name of Tennyson d'Eyncourt. This collection, now in the Lincolnshire County Archives,

[1] *Nineteenth Century* XXXIII, 1893, 164–88.

was made available to the poet's grandson, Charles (later Sir Charles) Tennyson, who was already contemplating the possibility of undertaking a new biography of the poet. As a result of the discovery it proved possible to offer a significant reinterpretation of Tennyson's early life and of the strains and terrors at home which influenced the development of his mind and personality.

The discovery of the Bayons Manor correspondence made a new life of Tennyson necessary. Again Tennyson was fortunate in his biographer. His grandson clearly remembered the poet in his later years and had also interviewed many people who remembered him. Since Hallam Tennyson's *Memoir* there had been many reminiscences of Tennyson published and these provided an additional source of information. *Alfred Tennyson* (1949) does not attempt to replace the *Memoir* but supplements our knowledge of Tennyson's life and character by the adoption of a completely different method of presentation. Whereas the *Memoir* is essentially a source-book, providing a collection of documents. *Alfred Tennyson* is a much more formal biography written in strict chronological sequence. Sir Charles Tennyson described his aim as 'a straightforward biography; bringing out Tennyson's singular personality as faithfully as I could and covering his domestic and social background and the political, intellectual and religious movements through which he lived, but confining myself to facts and obvious inferences, without any attempt to make good the gaps in the evidence by the exercise of the imagination.'[1] Although the work is certainly essentially factual in its treatment it does succeed also in evoking Tennyson's personality at different periods of his life. The biography eschews colourful description and psychological analysis alike but displays a warm but unbiassed sympathy for Tennyson himself. Inevitably, it repeats many things which are in the *Memoir* but both books deserve to be read, and together they provide very full documentation of Tennyson's life.

The image of Tennyson as a supremely representative Victorian is presented by Joanna Richardson in *The Pre-eminent Victorian: A Study of Tennyson* (1962). Although essentially popular in its intention this book makes good use of original documents, including the manu-

[1] *Alfred Tennyson*, viii.

script diary kept by Tennyson's wife Emily, which she herself described as 'the authority for a good deal of the story of our lives'. The view of typical 'Victorianism' in this study is certainly too simple. Miss Richardson consistently underestimates the strong neurotic forces of darkness and disturbance in Tennyson's personality. Nevertheless, she presents a readable picture of Tennyson as 'a Victorian husband and father, a Victorian philosopher and moralist, a Victorian social figure, a Victorian poet who was, to his contemporaries, the incarnation of poetry and, indeed, of their own higher thinking'.[1] Despite its faults, the book offers a useful corrective to too great an emphasis on Tennyson as a melancholy brooder.

Nowhere is Tennyson's character as the pre-eminent Victorian more apparent than in his relationship as her Poet Laureate to Queen Victoria. The growth and progress of their friendship has been described in *Dear and Honoured Lady*, edited in 1969 by Hope Dyson and Sir Charles Tennyson. The book prints all the correspondence between Queen Victoria and Tennyson, including letters in the Royal Archives in Windsor Castle and in the Tennyson Research Centre in Lincoln.

Of the research collections which furnish materials for the biographer of Tennyson the most important is the Tennyson Research Centre in Lincoln City Library. While the Centre's collection of proofs corrected by the poet and of first and other important editions of his works is certainly important for the textual study of Tennyson, the greatest value of the collection lies in its biographical materials. The Centre contains the libraries of members of the Tennyson family, most notably those of Tennyson himself and of his father, Dr George Clayton Tennyson. There is also a large amount of manuscript material, including household books, publishers' accounts, and a collection of over 12,000 letters. The contents of the Tennyson Research Centre are currently being listed in a three-volume catalogue, *Tennyson in Lincoln*, the first volume of which provides a listing of the libraries of Tennyson and other members of his family. The additional letters, portraits and personal effects of Tennyson displayed in an exhibition in the Usher Gallery in Lincoln are listed and described by Sir Charles Tennyson in a catalogue of the *Tennyson Collection: Usher Gallery* (1963).

[1] *The Pre-eminent Victorian*, 14.

Biographical information about Tennyson's brothers and sisters is provided by Sir Charles Tennyson in 'The Somersby Tennysons'.[1] This essay is based on anecdotes, family traditions and records, and a large group of family letters in the Lilly Library at Indiana University. The essay is followed by a catalogue of the Frederick Tennyson Collection by Rowland L. Collins.

CRITICISM

To open the complete works of Tennyson is to enter the Victorian age itself. There are the emerald-green landscapes, the dewy roses, the pearly-teethed children; the melancholy maidens, the heavy gardens; peasants, at once comic and pathetic, bob and curtsy. Then there is the tea-shop orientalism, the cardboard classicism, the sawdust Arthurianism. There are railways and geology. The silliness and sentimentality are excruciating. We see the flash of moral indignation, and hear the rumble of received opinion: the smoke of double-think drifts obscuringly across the scene. Then suddenly we are brought up sharp by a voice speaking of doubt; there is a vision of fen country on a winter evening; something robust and chuckling digs us in the ribs; finally we hear the assertive trumpets of imperial patriotism and historic endurance. We are confounded by the range, the colour, the self-confidence of it all.[2]

This response to Tennyson, written in 1969 by Philip Larkin, may serve as a reminder of the enormous difficulties of generalising about the state of critical opinion at any specific time. It is certainly paradoxical that Ricks's edition of the *Poems*, with its serious desire to see Tennyson whole and its implicit assertion of his modern relevance, should have been greeted by popular reviews describing him as 'The most Victorian Laureate' or 'Our grandest lollipop man'.

The course of Tennyson's reputation, especially since his death, provides an interesting illustration of the problems involved in critical debate. K. W. Gransden, in his short study of *In Memoriam*, asserts

[1] *VS* VII, Christmas Supplement 1963, 7–55; IX, 1966, 303–5.
[2] *New Statesman* LXXVII, 1969, 363.

justly that 'On the whole, students have been better served by the poet's biographers than by his critics'.[1] Tennyson himself was strongly influenced by contemporary reviews of his work. He was very sensitive to adverse criticism. As James Knowles records: 'All the mass of eulogy he took comparatively little notice of, but he never could forget an unfriendly word, even from the most obscure and insignificant and unknown quarter'.[2]

The extent to which the opinions of reviewers served not merely to irritate Tennyson but to influence his writing of poetry during the first half of his life has been carefully studied by Edgar Finley Shannon in *Tennyson and the Reviewers*. If Shannon's findings indicate that Tennyson did not suffer so much hostility and abuse from contemporary reviewers as has often been supposed, they also reveal that the reviewers 'exerted a continuous pressure upon him to teach more than to delight, to be speculative and analytical rather than poetical.'[3] Contemporary reviews often caused Tennyson to alter sections of his poems but they also exercised a powerful effect upon his choice of subject matter and his impulse towards didacticism.

Tennyson's sensitivity to criticism and its effect upon his poetic career as a whole is discussed by John Jump in his introduction to *Tennyson: The Critical Heritage*. This volume documents the progress of Tennyson's reputation during his lifetime from the reception of *Poems, Chiefly Lyrical* in 1830 to the achievement of that position of 'almost overwhelming prestige which Tennyson was to enjoy throughout the last third of his life'.[4] Despite the hostility of some early reviewers, the widespread reprobation of the obscurity and morbidity of *Maud*, and the complaints from some critics of 'elegant tameness and mannered derivativeness', Jump's selection of contemporary comment enforces the reader's sense of Tennyson's amazing contemporary success.

[1] *Tennyson; 'In Memoriam'*, 1964, 69.
[2] *Nineteenth Century* XXXIII, 1893, 173-4.
[3] *Tennyson and the Reviewers: A Study of his Literary Reputation and of the Influence of the Critics upon his Poetry 1827-1851*, Cambridge, Mass., 1952, 163.
[4] *Tennyson: The Critical Heritage*, 1967, 13.

The inevitable decline in Tennyson's reputation after his death and the subsequent vicissitudes of critical opinion to 1960 are outlined by John Killham in an introductory review of modern criticism in his selection of *Critical Essays on the Poetry of Tennyson*. Killham's selection of essays published since 1936 was itself both an effect and a cause of the increasing appreciation of Tennyson's poetry. In his introductory essay Killham traces Tennyson's posthumous reputation from the early Symbolist attacks of Yeats—the obvious starting-point for modern criticisms of Tennyson—through the biographical studies of Nicolson and Fausset in 1923, the attitudes of neo-classical critics to Victorian poetry in general and Tennyson in particular, and the analyses of Tennyson's poetic adjustment to his age. On the interesting question of Tennyson's relationship to contemporary society Killham sensitively points to E. D. H. Johnson's argument in *The Alien Vision of Victorian Poetry* that 'nearly all Victorian writers were as often as not at odds with their age, and . . . in their best work they habitually appealed not *to*, but *against* the prevailing mores of that age'.[1] Far from being, in any conventional sense, 'the most Victorian Laureate' Tennyson was often obsessed by the incompatibility between his inner vision and the reality of the society in which he was placed.

Two more recent attempts to place Tennyson studies in perspective by combining bibliographical documentation with critical commentary are provided by E. D. H. Johnson in the second edition of *The Victorian Poets: A Guide to Research*, edited by F. E. Faverty (1968) and John Dixon Hunt in *English Poetry: Select Bibliographical Guides*, edited by A. E. Dyson (1971). The more extensive listing in the *New Cambridge Bibliography of English Literature* is, of course, unannotated. Of the guides which offer information about new studies the most useful are probably the narrative and evaluative annual survey in *Victorian Poetry* and the unannotated annual listing in *Victorian Studies*. The *Tennyson Research Bulletin*, while not attempting any complete listing of new work, is especially valuable in providing information about research in progress.

Students of Tennyson find it easy to value the outstanding editorial

[1] *The Alien Vision of Victorian Poetry: Sources of Poetic Imagination in Tennyson, Browning, and Arnold*, Princeton 1952, ix.

contribution of Ricks and the biographical work of Hallam and Sir Charles Tennyson. It is, perhaps, rather more difficult to isolate the major critical contributions from the mass of undistinguished work. There is general agreement, however, that one of the most influential twentieth-century studies was Harold Nicolson's *Tennyson: Aspects of his Life, Character and Poetry*. Nicolson's book, published in 1923, represented an attempt to reinstate Tennyson and to distinguish his real significance from the Victorian adulation and hero-worship. The timing of the book is crucial to our understanding of Nicolson's purpose. The opening sentences perfectly establish the mood of the period: 'We smile to-day at 'our Victorians, not confidently, as of old, but with a shade of hesitation: a note of perplexity, a note of anger sometimes, a note often of wistfulness has come to mingle with our laughter. For the tide is turning and the reaction is drawing to its close'.[1]

Nicolson argues that, by making Tennyson Poet Laureate, the Victorians converted a naturally subjective and lyrical poet into an objective and instructional writer with a 'message'. The key to any understanding of Tennyson's poetic achievement depends upon the recognition of the tension between the private and the public voice, the essentially solitary dreamer and the typical Victorian he became, the lyric poet who was betrayed into official and didactic verse. For Nicolson, Tennyson's poetic strength lies in his lyricism, the characteristic subjects of which are melancholy and fear. It was Tennyson's tragedy that 'he was unable, except in isolated moments, to dissociate his lyrical energies from his other energies—dramatic, narrative, ethical, theological, and didactic'.[2]

Part of the influence of Nicolson's thesis may be ascribed to his persuasive and evocative style. It is often difficult for the reader to distinguish clearly between the rational force of the argument and the sympathetic power of the critic's language. This is especially true when Nicolson evokes Tennyson's melancholy:

> This haunting wail of fear and loneliness piercing at moments through the undertones of *In Memoriam*, echoes a note which runs

[1] Nicolson, 1.
[2] Nicolson, 292.

through all the poetry of Tennyson, and which, when once apprehended, beats with pitiful persistence on the heart. It proceeds
from . . . the uncertain shadow-edges of consciousness in which
stir the evanescent memories of childhood or the flitting shape-
lessness of half-forgotten dreams. It is a cry that mingles with the
mystery of wide spaces, of sullen sunsets or of sodden dawns;
the cry of a child lost at night time; the cry of some stricken
creature in the dark; 'the low moan of an unknown sea'.[1]

It is passages like this which lead a critic such as John Pettigrew, in
Tennyson: The Early Poems, to assert that Nicolson's book 'should be
treated with grave suspicion and read as fiction'.[2] Yet, despite later
critics, the dual image of Tennyson presented by Nicolson has per-
sisted to the present. Philip Larkin, in the review of Ricks quoted
above, states: 'one wonders how the world of English studies regards
the fact that the general reader's image of Tennyson is pretty much as
Harold Nicolson left it in 1923'. Nor is it only the general reader who
retains an image founded upon Nicolson, as may be illustrated by this
passage from Lord David Cecil's introduction to *A Choice of Tennyson's
Verse*, published in 1971:

> The truth is that there were two Tennysons: what may be called
> the fundamental Tennyson, the inspiration of his successes, and
> the superficial, the source of his lapses. The fundamental was in-
> born, the superficial was largely the product of the period in
> which he lived. The fundamental Tennyson was an aesthete and
> a man of heart; tender, vulnerable, passionately affectionate,
> intensely responsive to whatever appealed to his sense of beauty
> and glory and wonder, and with a delicate delighted sensibility
> to the quality of words and the movement of metre. The super-
> ficial Tennyson was a less unusual phenomenon; an intelligent,
> conscientious nineteenth-century Englishman, liberal-minded,
> domestic, seriously concerned with the political and religious
> issues of his time and who shared with his earnest contemporaries
> a strong sense of social responsibility.[3]

The concept of Tennyson as a divided figure has been presented

---

[1] Nicolson, 302.
[2] *Tennyson: The Early Poems*, 1970, 62.
[3] *A Choice of Tennyson's Verse*, 1971, 7–8.

in a number of different forms. W. H. Auden, in *Tennyson: An Intro-duction and a Selection*, made a distinction between Tennyson's fine ear and his defective intellect, between his knowledge of melancholia and his ignorance of everything else: 'he had the finest ear, perhaps, of any English poet; he was also undoubtedly the stupidest; there was little about melancholia that he didn't know; there was little else that he did'.[1]

F. R. Leavis similarly saw Tennyson's poetry as incapable of be-coming strenuously involved in the intellectual and moral issues of the time. Tennyson was, in his view, the willing victim of a false and essentially escapist poetic tradition:

> He might wrestle solemnly with the 'problems of the age', but the habits, conventions, and techniques that he found congenial are not those of a poet who could have exposed himself freely to the rigours of the contemporary climate. And in this he is represen-tative. It was possible for the poets of the Romantic period to believe that the interests animating their poetry were the forces moving the world, or that might move it. But Victorian poetry admits implicitly that the actual world is alien, recalcitrant, and unpoetical, and that no protest is worth making except the protest of withdrawal.[2]

The related idea of Tennyson as a poet who surrendered his spiritual quest to the conventions of his age is found at the end of T. S. Eliot's essay on *In Memoriam*.[3] Eliot argues that after 1850 Tennyson 'turned aside from the journey through the dark night, to become the surface flatterer of his own time'. Although Eliot recognises qualities of 'abundance, variety, and complete competence' which make Tennyson unquestionably a great poet, he nevertheless distinguishes between his 'lyrical resourcefulness' and his inability to write effective narrative poetry. This conception of divided poetic ability prompts Eliot's description of *The Princess* as 'an idyll that is too long' and of *Maud* as 'a few very beautiful lyrics, such as "O let the solid ground", "Birds in the high Hall-garden", and "Go not, happy day", around which the

---

[1] *Tennyson: An Introduction and a Selection*, 1946, x.

[2] *New Bearings in English Poetry*, 1932, 20–1.

[3] Originally published in *Essays Ancient and Modern*, 1936. Reprinted in Killham, *Critical Essays on the Poetry of Tennyson*, 1960.

semblance of a dramatic situation has been constructed with the greatest metrical virtuosity'.

John Killham has observed that, rather than the notion of two Tennysons, 'one would object much less to the idea of twenty Tennysons'.[1] There is considerable justice in the remark. No reader would wish to deny the variety and complexity of Tennyson's achievement but the strict categorisation of his poems into two groups, however the division is organised, must inevitably provoke feelings of dissatisfaction. Certainly this has happened in the critical study of Tennyson where the most recent works have shown a strong desire to emphasize the unity and integrity of his work.

E. D. H. Johnson's attacks upon the image of Tennyson as a conventional Victorian have already been noted. The frequent critical distinction between 'the bard of public sentiments and the earlier poet of private sensibilities' is one of the targets of Jerome Hamilton Buckley's *Tennyson: The Growth of a Poet*, published in 1960. Using the unpublished notebooks and other Tennyson papers in the Houghton Library of Harvard University, Buckley studies the development of Tennyson's poetic sensibility, citing biographical details to indicate the varied influences upon his emotional and intellectual development. Although Buckley acknowledges Tennyson's consummate craftsmanship he is careful always to relate the appreciation of 'style' and 'technique' to the poet's moral and intellectual development: 'his long-sustained dexterity would have been of little avail had it not served the needs of his ever-changing sensibility'.[2] Buckley sees Tennyson as intensely sensitive to the moral, social and scientific mood of his age, a man whose private vision was constantly in fruitful contact with his public knowledge. Such a view of Tennyson gains by a chronological reading of the poems, showing the interrelationships and conflicts in his work.

Despite the interest of Buckley's work as a study of Tennyson's development, he is aware of the need to assess each poem on its own merits:

[1] *Critical Essays on the Poetry of Tennyson*, 9.
[2] Buckley, 254.

And the longer or 'major' poems, no less than the more tightly
unified short lyrics, do achieve an integrity and independence:
In Memoriam runs through a complete cycle of despair and
recovery, meaningful in itself as a way of the soul; *Maud* creates
its own little world, where love is the one antidote to madness;
and the *Idylls* calls into new self-subsistence a mythology in
which a social order rises, flourishes, and declines. Still, for all
their vitality as separate entities, each of these draws freely on the
established conventions of English and classical poetry; each,
taking its new place in literary history, looks knowingly back to
its antecedents in a similar genre. Throughout his career Tennyson maintained a sophisticated acquaintance with the work of his
predecessors as a standard of aesthetic decorum and a counter-
balance to his own necessary innovations.[1]

Buckley's attempt to present a unified view of Tennyson was
followed in 1962 by a further essay in synthesis which sought also to
establish the value of Tennyson's public and official verse. It is unfortunate that Valerie Pitt's *Tennyson Laureate* should virtually ignore
Buckley's work, dismissing it in one sentence with gross over-sim-
plification as little more than a reworking of Nicolson's viewpoint.
It is sad, too, that Miss Pitt's book should have alienated scholars by
its repetitions and its many inaccuracies of fact and quotation. As both
Christopher Ricks and Clyde de L. Ryals noted in reviews of *Tennyson
Laureate*, the author's treatment is not purely critical but relies upon a
chronological survey of Tennyson's development. Ricks noted that
'as literary history it is very inaccurate. Names, initials, titles, and dates,
especially dates—it is as if a gremlin had ambled through pushing them
all askew.'[2]

Despite its errors, however, *Tennyson Laureate* is a stimulating work
which offers useful insights into Tennyson's sensibility, with its precarious balance between the disturbances of emotional insecurity and
the controls of moral determination, and into the interpretation of
specific poems, especially in a long discussion of *In Memoriam* which
pays detailed attention both to its form and process of composition and

[1] Buckley, 254-5.
[2] *Listener* 25 October 1962, 678.

to its religious and scientific impulse. The major purpose of the book, however, lies, as its title suggests, in the defence of Tennyson's laureate poetry, the exploration of his sense of a 'public, prophet's duty' which makes him conscious of public significance even in his more personal insights and experience. Although Tennyson was often at odds with the sentiments of his contemporaries he became 'the voice of a whole period and a phase of culture'. He felt the changes in the fabric of society, the moral disorder and the physical and spiritual poverty behind the successes of commerce and 'progress'. This is not to imply that Tennyson's thought is schematic, although his ideas owe much to Carlyle modified by Burke and F. D. Maurice. The modern reader who recognizes Tennyson's need to express social ideas may nevertheless feel considerable difficulty in accepting much of the official verse. Certainly many of the occasional poems are limited in significance by the specific nature of their themes. Miss Pitt usefully emphasizes Tennyson's characteristic method of generalising the specific to the level of myth and symbol. While the reader may agree with her re-valuation of these poems he may well feel doubt when she declares:

> In these occasional poems Tennyson sums up all he wanted to say in the *Idylls of the King*. For in these he presents the everlasting struggle to maintain dignity and order in the face of attacking forces, and with this the ideal of loyalty and service: all that the Arthurian epic was to represent to the Victorians. Arthur, in a way, was no more than a glorified Wellington. Tennyson's need to do it again arises partly from the deafness and blindness of the public, partly from his perverse attachment to the myth of Arthur. He had always intended to write *the* Arthurian poem, and he did. The failure of this enormous work, for in spite of individual feli-cities and insights it is *as a whole* a failure, is due to the incom-patibility of his purpose and the medium in which he is trying to express it.[1]

No work of Tennyson's has been so strikingly revalued during recent years as the *Idylls of the King*. In many ways this is the crucial work in modern critical approaches to his achievement. The facts of composition and the reactions of contemporary readers to his attempt to

[1] Pitt, 208.

write a 'compact and vertebrate poem' over a period of forty-three
years are summarised by Kathleen Tillotson in her essay 'Tennyson's
serial poem'.[1] This essay emphasizes the foresight and design which
organised the separate instalments and the novelty and strangeness of
the Arthurian material to the ordinary Victorian reader. The interpre-
tations of the poem by F. E. L. Priestley in 'Tennyson's *Idylls*' (1949)
and Jerome Buckley in *Tennyson: The Growth of a Poet* (1960) have
been generally acclaimed. To these must be added three recent important books: Clyde de L. Ryals' *From the Great Deep: Essays on
'Idylls of the King'* (1967), John R. Reed's *Perception and Design in
Tennyson's 'Idylls of the King'* (1970), and Philip J. Eggers' *King Arthur's
Laureate* (1971). All these studies have increased the modern reader's
understanding of the structural and technical features of the *Idylls*, the
allegorical significance of the work, and the moral and social implications of its theme.

Recognition of the value of the work done upon the *Idylls of the King*
should not be taken to imply that the critics have conclusively proved
the poetic greatness of this work to the satisfaction of all readers.
B. C. Southam's recent British Council pamphlet on Tennyson finds
his treatment of the figures unsatisfactory and attacks his 'failing in
dramatic sense which is really an absence of human sympathy'.[2] In an
important review of the second edition of F. E. Faverty's *The Victorian Poets*, Kenneth Allott underlines a central critical confusion between the elucidation of argument and the evaluation of merit. Allott
quotes a statement of Christopher Ricks that 'verbal achievement is an
essential issue *whenever* a poem is quoted' as a protection 'against
supposing—as evidently many do unconsciously suppose—that any
poetic work that allows us to develop an ingenious critical argument is necessarily poetically valuable. In cultivating our Victorian
garden no amount of agreement among ourselves as professional
gardeners will persuade the onlooker that the cabbages are really
roses'. For Allott it is only by forgetting the necessity to evaluate verbal
achievement that 'some critics of Victorian poetry in the 1960s have

[1] Geoffrey and Kathleen Tillotson, *Mid-Victorian Studies*, 1965.
[2] *Tennyson*, 1971, 37.

been able to delude themselves that Tennyson's *Idylls of the King* deserves to be taken as seriously as *In Memoriam*'.[1] Modern academic writing about the Victorian poets often provides all too clear justification for Allott's strictures. Nevertheless, the study of specific poems by Tennyson has produced fine examples of scholarly elucidation which also recognize the necessity for critical evaluation. In his excellent study of *Tennyson and 'The Princess'* John Killham does not make any exaggerated claims for *The Princess*. Although the poem was very successful with contemporary readers, appearing in seventeen editions in its first thirty years, Tennyson himself described it somewhat depreciatorily in 1869: 'though truly original, it is, after all, only a medley'. *The Princess* has generally been little studied or valued by modern critics. Killham's book temperately aims 'to show what went into the making of that poem, not to prove that it is an overlooked masterpiece, but simply to show that the poem, properly understood, is a great deal more valuable than some estimates have allowed'.[2] Killham traces Tennyson's development during the years between his entry to Cambridge and the composition of the poem and examines the background of the feminist controversy in England, the poem's attitudes to evolutionary ideas, and the connection between feminism, science and socialism. He argues that Tennyson is attempting to make his readers think about social questions in an unprejudiced way by presenting artistically some of the beliefs and ideals of their age. Behind the exotic setting and the fantastic fairy-tale qualities of the poem *The Princess* is written with a serious purpose:

> *maybe wildest dreams*
> *Are but the needful preludes of the truth.*

Ralph Wilson Rader's *Tennyson's 'Maud': The Biographical Genesis* (1963) traces Tennyson's involvement, after the death of Hallam, with 'three successive attachments by which he sought an effective substitute for Arthur Hallam': with Rosa Baring, Sophy Rawnsley and Emily Sellwood. Rader argues that in composing his poem of the 'holy power of Love' Tennyson's image of Maud herself represents a complex

---

[1] *VP* VII, 1970, 82–91.
[2] *Tennyson and 'The Princess': Reflections of an Age*, 1958, 2.

fusion of his memories of all three women—'an image through which he retrospectively defined and interpreted the long search for an ideal and idealizing love which he had carried on from the time of Hallam's death to his marriage with Emily Sellwood'.[1] Although Rader, like many readers, finds *Maud* imperfect as a work of art, he emphasizes its biographical significance:

> Biographically, *Maud* is a crucial document. It is Tennyson's purgative recapitulation of the inner and outer circumstances of his tortured early life, a deeply rooted act of spiritual self-definition and affirmation by which, after the commitment initiated by marriage and the Laureateship, he moved from his earlier to his later career; it is the swan song of the bitter and troubled young poet, the inaugural hymn of the Laureate. Having objectified and judged, as accurately as he was able, the experience of his early life, he felt ready, his own salvation secure, to minister to the moral and spiritual needs of mankind at large.[2]

For Rader, the basic artistic weakness of the poem springs from Tennyson's emotional involvement which prevented him seeing his experiences in adequate perspective. Like Valerie Pitt—though he does not work out the theme in detail—Rader sees Tennyson's greatest poetic successes 'in those many poems (I think particularly of the lovely and too much ignored verses of occasion, of celebration, greeting, and elegy) where, as in *In Memoriam*, he speaks not as dark romantic or ancient sage but with the perfect clarity, tact, and grace of the great classical poet that in the truest part of him he was'.[3]

For a survey of critical attitudes to *In Memoriam* the reader may be referred to John Dixon Hunt's introduction to his selection, *Tennyson, 'In Memoriam': A Casebook* (1970). Hunt's selection of criticism should certainly be supplemented by a reading of A. C. Bradley's *A Commentary on 'In Memoriam'* (1900) and by K. W. Gransden's short but very thoughtful critical monograph, *Tennyson: 'In Memoriam'* (1964). Gransden emphasizes Tennyson's intellectual and scholarly interests, his quietism and introversion, reading *In Memoriam* as a domestic

[1] Rader, 98–9.
[2] Rader, 115.
[3] Rader, 121.

poem which represents a 'slow living-through of experience'. More recently the demands of Ricks and Allott for assessments of verbal achievement have been at least partly met by Alan Sinfield's intensive studies of the language of the poem in his essay on 'Matter-moulded forms of speech: Tennyson's use of language in *In Memoriam*'[1]—a discussion of Tennyson's success in describing the mystical and making it actual to the reader—and, more comprehensively, in *The Language of Tennyson's 'In Memoriam'* (1971).

[1] In *The Major Victorian Poets: Reconsiderations*, ed Isobel Armstrong, 1969.

2: Tennyson's Romantic Heritage

D. J. PALMER

The Kraken

Below the thunders of the upper deep;
Far, far beneath in the abysmal sea,
His ancient, dreamless, uninvaded sleep
The Kraken sleepeth: faintest sunlights flee
About his shadowy sides: above him swell
Huge sponges of millenial growth and height;
And far away into the sickly light,
From many a wondrous grot and secret cell
Unnumbered and enormous polypi
Winnow with giant arms the slumbering green.
There hath he lain for ages and will lie
Battening upon huge seaworms in his sleep,
Until the latter fire shall heat the deep;
Then once by man and angels to be seen,
In roaring he shall rise and on the surface die.

(PT, 246)

THIS STRANGE, powerful little poem from Tennyson's 1830 volume, *Poems, Chiefly Lyrical,* is virtually a literal confirmation of T. S. Eliot's judgment that 'Tennyson's surface, his technical accomplishment, is intimate with his depths'.[1] For the dark, mysterious depths which the Kraken inhabits are those of the subliminal self, and the poem symbolically enacts its meaning as the sea-creature is woken, and with the liberation of violent energy, rises to the surface of momentary consciousness. 'The Kraken' is one of many images of imprisoned or isolated life in Tennyson's early poetry, and it reflects the essentially Romantic basis

---

[1] *Essays Ancient and Modern,* 1936, p. 189.

of this poetry in subjective being and the creative process of self-realization. Beginning in the aftermath of the Romantic movement, Tennyson's development, as it is reflected in the volumes of 1830, 1832 and 1842, is a Romantic progression from introverted and inert states of mind towards emancipated consciousness.

The growth of consciousness, and the relationship between the self and the world beyond, are fundamental concerns of Romantic poetry and poetic theory. Wordsworth's belief in the organic sympathy between nature and the mind, Coleridge's theory of imagination, which held that the act of perception was essentially creative, and Keats's quest for poetic identity through sensuous involvement with the plurality of being outside himself, formulate in different ways the Romantic ideal of the mind's capacity to realize itself through imaginative experience of a world-beyond-self. 'The spirit, in all the objects which it views, views only itself,'[1] wrote Coleridge in *Biographia Literaria;* this is not as solipsist as it sounds, for this act of self-consciousness is also conceived as being an extension and development of the self, the creation as well as the discovery of identity.

The aesthetic implications of this self-realization are seen in the characteristically symbolic modes of Romantic poetry: in the sensuous imagery which embodies states of feeling, rather than being purely descriptive, in the subjective use of mythological fable, and in the adoption of a dramatic *persona.* Tennyson employs each of these modes of self-expression. But the ideal of self-realization also has a moral implication, as in Wordsworth's reflection upon his own inner growth in relation to nature, the theme of 'Tintern Abbey' and of *The Prelude,* and in the spiritual odysseys of Coleridge's 'Ancient Mariner' and Shelley's 'Alastor', and in Keats's notion of 'soul-making'.

Tennyson's early poetry is that of aesthetic rather than moral imagination, as his first reviewers pointed out. It expresses subjective states of feeling, and little else. Most of the poems in the 1830 volume, for instance, are mood-paintings and word-pictures of a highly-sensitized, delicately attuned, sometimes febrile sensibility. In particular, there is a series of lyrics evoking different moods through the *personae* of imaginary female figures: 'Claribel', 'Lilian', 'Isabel', 'Madeline' and 'Adeline' are among

[1] *Biographia Literaria,* ed J. Shawcross (1965 edn), 2 vol., 1907, I, 184.

them, and related to this group as poems of dramatic identity are 'Hero and Leander', 'The Merman' and 'The Mermaid'. They foreshadow Tennyson's later development of the dramatic monologues, as well as recalling Keats's idea of the 'camelion poet' who is 'continually in for— and filling some other Body'.[1] But Tennyson's sensibility lacked the disinterestedness of true 'negative capability'. 'All these ladies', he said later, 'were evolved, like the camel, from my own consciousness' (PT, 181). They are vehicles for subjective states of mind, and the most perfectly realized, perhaps because it is also the most intimate with his depths, is 'Mariana'.

The subject of 'Mariana', the girl deserted by her lover to pine alone in 'the moated grange', is taken from Shakespeare's *Measure for Measure*, but Tennyson is not concerned with the love story. Like Wordsworth's *Lyrical Ballads,* and more so, it is a poem in which 'the feeling therein developed gives importance to the action and situation, and not the action and situation to the feeling'.[2] The characteristically Romantic fusion of feeling with perception makes the silent, decaying house and its desolate landscape an embodiment of Mariana's consciousness, in a series of stanzas without any progression or resolution, this itself adding to the effect of monotony and stagnation. Even the poetic frame of the stanza form and its repeated refrain serve to enclose Mariana and shut her in upon herself:

> *All day within the dreamy house,*
>   *The doors upon their hinges creaked;*
>   *The blue fly sung i' the pane; the mouse*
>   *Behind the mouldering wainscot shrieked,*
> *Or from the crevice peered about.*
>   *Old faces glimmered through the doors,*
>   *Old footsteps trod the upper floors,*
>   *Old voices called her from without.*
>   *She only said, 'My life is dreary,*
>   *He cometh not,' she said;*

[1] *The Letters of John Keats 1814–1821*, ed H. E. Rollins, 2 vol., Cambridge, Mass. 1958, I, 378.
[2] *Lyrical Ballads*, ed R. L. Brett and A. R. Jones, 1963, 248.

> *She said, 'I am aweary, aweary,*
> *I would that I were dead!'*
>
> (PT, 190)

Mariana is the first of many Tennysonian maidens who languish in
lonely seclusion: the Lady of Shalott, Oenone and the Soul in 'The
Palace of Art' were to follow in the volume of 1832. Like 'The Kraken',
they express a sense of disengagement from life, the turning of the mind
upon itself. In Mariana's case, the oppressively claustrophobic feeling,
listless yet uneasy, neither wholly still nor capable of any vigorous
movement, brings us to the question of Tennyson's morbidity.

The state of feeling in 'Mariana' can be related to that of two other
poems in the 1830 volume. The first of these is the 'Song', short enough
to be quoted in full:

I

> *A spirit haunts the year's last hours*
> *Dwelling amid these yellowing bowers:*
>   *To himself he talks;*
> *For at eventide, listening earnestly,*
> *At his work you may hear him sob and sigh*
>   *In the walks;*
> *Earthward he boweth the heavy stalks*
> *Of the mouldering flowers:*
>   *Heavily hangs the broad sunflower*
>   *Over its grave i' the earth so chilly;*
>   *Heavily hangs the hollyhock,*
>   *Heavily hangs the tiger-lily.*

II

> *The air is damp, and hushed, and close,*
> *As a sick man's room when he taketh repose*
>   *An hour before death;*
> *My very heart faints and my whole soul grieves*
> *At the moist rich smell of the rotting leaves,*
>   *And the breath*
>   *Of the fading edges of box beneath,*
> *And the year's last rose.*

> *Heavily hangs the broad sunflower*
> *Over its grave i' the earth so chilly;*
> *Heavily hangs the hollyhock,*
> *Heavily hangs the tiger-lily.*
>
> (PT, 215-16)

In this beautifully melodic autumnal lyric, as in 'Mariana', the lonely spirit identifies itself with a stagnant, decaying world. A consciousness almost stifled and overpowered by its own sentience corresponds to the natural world where the dying flowers droop beneath their own weight. The poem yearns towards the oblivion of death; its melancholy is not a regret for the passing of life, but a sigh of weariness from a spirit over-burdened by the sense of its own being.

This theme of the isolated spirit and its longing for a release from the burden of consciousness recurs in 'Supposed Confessions', Tennyson's first experiment with the form of the dramatic monologue. It is some-times said that the ironic attitude implied in the poem's full title, 'Sup-posed Confessions Of A Second-Rate Sensitive Mind Not In Unity With Itself', is not justified by the poem itself; but the speaker's divided state of mind is like that of the Soul in 'The Palace of Art':

> *Deep dread and loathing of her solitude*
> *Fell on her, from which mood was born*
> *Scorn of herself; again, from out that mood*
> *Laughter at her self-scorn.*
>
> (PT, 415)

This is quite consistent with the view that the speaker of 'Supposed Confessions' is a projection of the poet himself, not a device to disguise his identity, but a mode of the neurotic self-division which is the poem's subject. Similarly, the loss of religious faith which the speaker bemoans is a symptom rather than a cause of his state of mind. As is often pointed out, 'Supposed Confessions' anticipates *In Memoriam*, but it does not foreshadow the Victorian crisis of belief. There is no attempt to argue theological issues, or to intellectualize the emotional struggle within the self. Like the other poems of 1830, this is an expression of feeling, not of ideas. It presents a mind that feels its own apartness, and longs with

regressive nostalgia for the unselfconscious security associated with
childhood:

> *Thrice happy state again to be*
> *The trustful infant on the knee!*
> *Who lets his rosy fingers play*
> *About his mother's neck, and knows*
> *Nothing beyond his mother's eyes.*
> *They comfort him by night and day;*
> *They light his little life alway;*
> *He hath no thought of coming woes;*
> *He hath no care of life or death;*
> *Scarce outward signs of joy arise,*
> *Because the Spirit of happiness*
> *And perfect rest so inward is.*
>
> (PT, 198)

'Supposed Confessions' in fact is not a religious poem at all. It concerns the adolescent experience of individuation, when the mind grows
to self-awareness and loses its undifferentiated sense of being one with
the world-beyond-self:

> *I am void,*
> *Dark, formless, utterly destroyed.*
> *Why not believe then? Why not yet*
> *Anchor thy frailty there, where man*
> *Hath moored and rested? Ask the sea*
> *At midnight, when the crisp slope waves*
> *After a tempest, rib and fret*
> *The broad-imbasèd beach, why he*
> *Slumbers not like a mountain tarn?*
> *Wherefore his ridges are not curls*
> *And ripples of an inland mere?*
> *Wherefore he moaneth thus, nor can*
> *Draw down into his vexèd pools*
> *All that blue heaven which hues and paves*
> *The other? I am too forlorn,*
> *Too shaken: my own weakness fools*
> *My judgment, and my spirit whirls,*

> *Moved from beneath with doubt and fear.*
>
> (PT, 200–201)

The sea, with its secret depths and restless, agitated surface, is one of Tennyson's recurrent images of consciousness. And like Mariana, the speaker of 'Supposed Confessions' knows the life-in-death of the mind turned in upon itself:

> *O weary life! O weary death!*
> *O spirit and heart made desolate!*
> *O damnèd vacillating state!*
>
> (PT, 202)

Morbidity is a malady of the Romantic sensibility, in which the mind, instead of feeling its participation in the world outside itself, experiences a negative estrangement. This recoil of the mind upon itself is a failure of the power of imagination to empathise, an intransitive state of joyless inertia for which there is no outlet, except in poetic expression. It might be interpreted psychologically as the proneness to instability and an overburdening of the nervous system which results from the Romantic stress upon the life of intense emotions. The condition is common enough in Romantic poetry. It is there, for instance, in Keats's 'La Belle Dame Sans Merci', in which the 'wretched wight', 'alone and palely loitering', is placed in a landscape of the desolate spirit, where 'The sedge has withered from the lake, And no birds sing'.[1] It is there in the sense of alienation and persecution suffered by the gloomy Byronic hero. Wordsworth and Coleridge recognise the condition as a stage in the growth of consciousness. Coleridge's 'Dejection: An Ode', for instance, begins with a state of mind so listless and withdrawn that sensation barely exists:

> *A grief without a pang, void, dark, and drear,*
> *A stifled, drowsy, unimpassioned grief,*
> *Which finds no natural outlet, no relief,*
> *In word, or sigh, or tear.*[2]

[1] *Poetical Works*, ed H. Buxton Forman, Oxford Standard Authors, 1908, 354.

[2] *Poems*, ed E. H. Coleridge, Oxford Standard Authors, 1931, 364.

But the poem progresses as the mind objectifies its own condition, and a state of feeling becomes an act of self-comprehension, celebrating the autonomy of the mind: 'We in ourselves rejoice'.

Wordsworth's 'Resolution and Independence' begins with the poet sharing unselfconsciously the joyful life of nature, until there is a sudden unbidden shift of consciousness:

> *But, as it sometimes chanceth, from the might*
> *Of joy in minds that can no further go,*
> *As high as we have mounted in delight*
> *In our dejection do we sink as low;*
> *To me that morning did it happen so;*
> *And fears and fancies thick upon me came;*
> *Dim sadness—and blind thoughts, I knew not, nor could name.*[1]

In this state of self-absorption, Wordsworth encounters the Leech-gatherer, and the poem develops as an expansion of awareness, the Leech-gatherer merging with the poet's inner preoccupations until he becomes a figure 'in my mind's eye', and the means to a realization of conscious, and therefore moral, faith in life.

Perhaps the most complete and comprehensive fable of Romantic consciousness, however, is Coleridge's 'Ancient Mariner': the curse that falls upon the Mariner alienates him not only from his shipmates but from all the benevolent forces of nature:

> *Alone, alone, all all alone,*
> *Alone on the wide wide Sea.*[2]

The drought and becalming which he suffers are images of a spiritual attrition akin to that of the forlorn Mariana; his ship rots away as her grange decays, both symbolising the ennervation of the self that knows only its own isolation. But this life-in-death situation is only the intermediate stage of his voyage of consciousness. It begins in an unreflective communion with nature, and it is the unmotivated spontaneous shooting of the albatross that invokes the curse of guilt and alienation, from which

[1] *Poetical Works*, ed T. Hutchinson, revised E. De Selincourt (1965 edn), Oxford Standard Authors, 1936, 155.
[2] *Lyrical Ballads*, ed Brett and Jones, 19.

the Mariner is eventually released by the equally unmotivated and spontaneous blessing of the water-snakes (cousins of the Kraken?), and so he is reintegrated with the spiritual forces of the universe, completing the process of self-realization by telling his own story. 'The Ancient Mariner' might be seen as a Romantic analogue of man's progress from unselfconscious Innocence, to the Fall and the knowledge of good and evil, thence to self-redemption and self-renewal.

A similar progression is traced by Keats in his 'simile of human life':

> I compare human life to a large Mansion of Many Apartments, two of which I can only describe, the doors of the rest being as yet shut upon me—The first we step into we call the infant or thoughtless Chamber, in which we remain as long as we do not think—We remain there a long while, and notwithstanding the doors of the second Chamber remain wide open, showing a bright appearance, we care not to hasten to it; but are at length imperceptibly impelled by the awakening of this thinking principle—within us—we no sooner get into the second Chamber, which I shall call the Chamber of Maiden-Thought, than we become intoxicated with the light and the atmosphere, we see nothing but pleasant wonders, and think of delaying there for ever in delight: However among the effects this breathing is father of is that tremendous one of sharpening one's vision into the heart and nature of Man—of convincing one's nerves that the World is full of Misery and Heartbreak, Pain, Sickness and oppression—whereby This Chamber of Maiden Thought becomes gradually darken'd and at the same time on all sides of it many doors are set open—but all dark—all leading to dark passages—We see not the ballance of good and evil.[1]

Tennyson's morbidity, the melancholy and despondency of 'Mariana'. the 'Song' and 'Supposed Confessions', have much in common with these Romantic experiences of the solitariness of self. What differentiates his state of feeling, however, is its regressiveness, the desire not only to be intimate with his depths but to sink into them, and lose the burden of self-consciousness. He described this tendency in one of the most revealing comments he ever made about himself:

[1] *Letters*, ed Rollins, I, 281.

A kind of waking trance I have frequently had, quite up from boyhood, when I have been all alone. This has generally come upon
me thro' repeating my own name two or three times to myself
silently, 'till all at once, as it were out of the intensity of the consciousness of individuality, the individuality itself seemed to
dissolve and fade away into boundless being, and this not a confused state, but the clearest of the clearest, the surest of the surest,
the wierdest of the wierdest, utterly beyond words, where death
was an almost laughable impossibility, the loss of personality (if so
it were) seeming no extinction but the only true life.

(Mem., I, 320)

The value which Tennyson set upon this quasi-mystical state of trance
is another aspect of his Romanticism: the belief in the power of visionary
imagination for insight into mysteries that perplex the waking mind. It
is similar to 'that blessed mood' described by Wordsworth in 'Tintern
Abbey':

> *In which the burthen of the mystery*
> *In which the heavy and the weary weight*
> *Of all this unintelligible world*
> *Is lightened: that serene and blessed mood,*
> *In which the affections gently lead us on,—*
> *Until, the breath of this corporeal frame*
> *And even the motion of our human blood*
> *Almost suspended, we are laid asleep*
> *In body, and become a living soul:*
> *While with an eye made quiet by the power*
> *Of harmony, and the deep power of joy,*
> *We see into the life of things.*[1]

Yet characteristically Wordsworth owes this visionary state to his sense
of the 'beauteous forms' of external nature, while in Tennyson's case
it is self-induced. For Tennyson, as for Coleridge, the meaning of life
lies within the self; as he declared in old age: 'Yet God *is* love, transcendent, all pervading! We do not get *this* faith from Nature or the
world. If we look at Nature alone, full of perfection and imperfection,
she tells us that God is disease, murder and rapine. We get this faith

---

[1] *Lyrical Ballads*, ed Brett and Jones, 114.

from ourselves, from what is highest within us' (*Mem.*, I, 314). This remark was made at the end of his life, when his spiritual struggles were over, but even in 1830, when they had barely begun, Tennyson intuitively knew 'the only true life' within the self. Two of the 1830 poems, 'The Poet' and 'The Mystic', loftily affirm this visionary power, while a third, 'The Poet's Mind', defies the 'darkbrow'd sophist':

> *Vex not thou the poet's mind*
> *With thy shallow wit:*
> *Vex not thou the poet's mind;*
> *For thou canst not fathom it.*
> *Clear and bright it should be ever,*
> *Flowing like a crystal river;*
> *Bright as light, and clear as wind.*
>
> (PT, 224)

The 'holy ground' of the poet's mind, that inner sanctum of serenity and undifferentiated being, is symbolised as a remote dreamlike paradise in two poems from the 1832 volume. 'The Hesperides' is the song of the daughters of Hesperus, by whose eternal incantation and the vigilance of the dragon the secret of the golden apple, 'the treasure/Of the wisdom of the west', is preserved from loss. And 'The Lotos-Eaters' sing of their haven of peace and careless ease, where they will dwell for evermore, never again setting out across the troubled sea. Yet there is in these two poems a sense of disengagement from life and human sympathies, which reflects a certain ambivalence of attitude. The sacred apple in 'The Hesperides', for instance, is withheld from mankind, since it would make them 'overwise', and 'cure the old wound of the world'; Tennyson knew from his reading in comparative mythology that Hercules, who stole the apples in the original myth, might be interpreted as a prototype of Christ, the second Adam. Similarly, the Lotos-Eaters hardly invite our wholehearted admiration, in their sensual and slothful indulgence; Tennyson's borrowing from the more insidious speeches of temptation in Spenser's *Faerie Queen* suggests that he did not intend us to identify entirely with the attitude of the singers, although the poem is still often read as a piece of unqualified escapism. The changes which Tennyson made in 'The Lotos-Eaters' between 1832 and 1842, as his

Cambridge friend James Spedding pointed out, express 'the first effects of the physical disease upon the moral and intellectual nature' (CH, 144). The ambiguity of 'The Hesperides' and 'The Lotos-Eaters' is a reflection of the critical self-consciousness which Tennyson had developed by 1832. His Cambridge environment, and in particular his friendship among 'The Apostles', that enthusiastically high-minded group of young intellectuals, could not fail to stimulate his sense of poetic vocation, while forcing him to consider in which direction he should pursue it. 'The Apostles' by no means spoke with one voice, but there was a general consensus of opinion which urged him to moralise his song, and to come down from the heights of aesthetic isolation to assume his place in the society of men. The notable dissenter from this point of view was Tennyson's closest friend, Arthur Hallam, who declared in reviewing *Poems, Chiefly Lyrical* in 1831 that 'whenever the mind of the artist suffers itself to be occupied, during its periods of creation, by any other predominant motive than the desire of beauty, the result is false in art' (CH, 35). Hallam's comparison of Tennyson with Keats and Shelley as 'poets of sensation', 'susceptible of the slightest impulse from external nature' (CH, 36), provoked a resumption of the old feud between English bards and Scotch reviewers when *Blackwood's Edinburgh Magazine* and the *Quarterly Review* turned their conservative authority against this latest protégé of 'the Cockney school'. But the more important issue raised by the reviewers of both the 1830 and 1832 volumes was the question of the poet's responsibilities. While Hallam argued that the poet's allegiance was only to his art, the majority of Tennyson's first critics urged him to use his gifts for the moral and spiritual improvement of mankind. Sensibility alone was not enough: the poet should cultivate his intellect, since all true poets are philosophers.

This debate between the advocates of sensibility and those of responsibility, between aesthetic isolation and moral commitment, was a polarization of Romantic attitudes. The Romantic conception of the poet stressed primarily his capacity for deeper feelings and larger sympathies than those of ordinary men, and therefore his sense of commitment to the cause of humanity. Probably the most celebrated Romantic definition of the poet's nature and vocation is Wordsworth's statement in the 1802 Preface to the *Lyrical Ballads:*

What is a Poet? To whom does he address himself? And what language is to be expected from him?—He is a man speaking to men: a man, it is true, endowed with more lively sensibility, more enthusiasm and tenderness, who has a greater knowledge of human nature, and a more comprehensive soul, than are supposed to be common among mankind; a man pleased with his own passions and volitions, and who rejoices more than other men in the spirit of life that is within him.[1]

'The Poet binds together by passion and knowledge the vast empire of human society', said Wordsworth, and even Hallam's idol Keats had affirmed the poet's dedication to his fellow men:

> *Sure not all*
> *Those melodies sung into the world's ear*
> *Are useless; sure a poet is a sage;*
> *A humanist, physician to all men.*[2]

Yet the very capacities that fit the poet for his high vocation also set him apart from society, elevating him to a solitary eminence from where his voice is either not heard, or if heard misunderstood and even spurned by men of coarser sensibilities, as the Romantics found. Wordsworth's 'Essay, Supplementary to the Preface', which he published in the 1815 edition of his *Poems,* argued that the poet must reconcile himself to the indifference or hostility of the public of his day. So Shelley's image of the poet, in his *Defence of Poetry,* was that of 'a nightingale, who sits in darkness and sings to cheer his own solitude with sweet sounds'; but, quite consistently, he also believed that 'Poets are the unacknowledged legislators of the world'.[3]

The tensions implicit in the situation of the Romantic poets broke into open division in the years of Tennyson's development. Hallam accepted the inevitable alienation of the poet, with his refined '*subjective* power', from the tendencies of contemporary society: 'modern poetry, in proportion to its depth and truth, is likely to have little immediate authority over public opinion' (CH, 41). And certainly the post-

---

[1] *Lyrical Ballads*, ed Brett and Jones, 255–6.
[2] *Poetical Works*, ed Forman, 448.
[3] *Shelley's Literary and Philosophical Criticism*, ed J. Shawcross, 1909, 129 & 159.

Romantic period, in which utilitarianism flourished, was out of sympathy with the kind of Romanticism that Hallam stood for; as Bulwer Lytton observed in 1833: 'The genius of this time is wholly anti-poetic. When Byron passed away, the feeling he had represented craved utterance no more. With a sigh we turned to the actual and practical career of life: we awoke from the morbid, the passionate, the dreaming.'[1]

Hallam's fundamental distinction between thought and feeling in poetry was turned the other way in 1834 by Sir Henry Taylor's Preface to his historical drama *Philip Van Artevelde*, which attacked Byron and Shelley for their cultivation of 'fervid feeling and beautiful imagery'[2] at the expense of reason and morality. The success of this work illustrates the spirit of the time, and Tennyson's mixed reaction to it is a measure of the ambivalence in his own poetic aims, as well as of his sturdy independence: 'I close with him in most that he says of modern poetry, tho' it may be that he does not take sufficiently into consideration the peculiar strength evolved by such writers as Byron and Shelley, who however mistaken they may be, did yet give the world another heart and new pulses, and so are we kept going. Blessed be those that grease the wheels of the old world, insomuch as to move on is better than to stand still. But "Philip is a famous man" and makes me "shamed of my own faults"' (*Mem.*, I, 141). Taylor's objection to the gloomy Byronic hero, as 'evidence, not only of scanty materials of knowledge from which to construct the ideal of a human being, but also of a want of perception of what is great or noble in our nature',[3] is a moral judgment on the Romantic susceptibility to morbid introversion. The positivism of post-Romantic attitudes insisted that the poet should be outwardlooking: even Hallam emphasized in the 'poets of sensation', their 'powerful tendency of imagination to a life of immediate sympathy with the external universe' (CH, 37). Reflecting on the Romantic movement as a whole, he saw it as 'an era of painful struggle, to bring our overcivilized condition of thought into union with the fresh productive spirit that brightened the morning of our literature' (CH, 40). This effort

---

[1] *England and the English*, 1833, Book IV Chap. ii. Quoted in Ian Jack, *English Literature 1815–1832*, Oxford 1963, 423.
[2] *Philip Van Artevelde; A Dramatic Romance*, 2 vol., 1834, I, xix.
[3] *Ibid.*, I, xviii.

to re-unite a dissociated sensibility, however, according to Hallam, only intensified the division of mind: 'Hence the melancholy, which so evidently characterizes the spirit of modern poetry; hence that return of the mind upon itself, and the habit of seeking relief in idiosyncrasies rather than community of interest' (CH, 41).

In the post-Romantic period, there is a retreat from the full Romantic faith in the mind's capacity to know itself, a tendency to regard self-consciousness as an unhealthy state of mind. During the same year in which Hallam's essay appeared, for instance, Thomas Carlyle took up this theme in the *Edinburgh Review*:

> Always the characteristic of right performance is a certain spontaneity, an unconsciousness: 'the healthy know not of their health, but only the sick'. . . . We might pursue this question into innumerable other ramifications, and everywhere, under new shapes, find the same truth, which we have so imperfectly enunciated, disclosed, that throughout the whole world of man, in all manifestations and performances of his nature, outward and inward, personal and social, the Perfect, the Great is a mystery to itself, knows not itself; whatsoever does know itself is already little, and more or less imperfect. Or otherwise, we may say, Unconsciousness belongs to pure unmixed life; Consciousness to a diseased mixture and conflict of life and death: Unconsciousness is the sign of creation; Consciousness, at best that of manufacture . . . The state of Society in our days is, of all possible states, the least an unconscious one.[1]

In this context the crisis experienced by John Stuart Mill in 1826, when he was twenty years old, has almost the force of a parable. Brought up as an ardent disciple of utilitarianism, Mill was suddenly prompted to ask himself whether the fulfilment of all his intellectual and social schemes, it if were possible, would make him happy: 'An irrepressible self-consciousness distinctly answered "No"! At this my heart sank within me: the whole foundation on which my life was constituted fell down.'[2] This state of depression lasted until 1828, when Mill discovered the poetry of Wordsworth: 'What made Wordsworth's

[1] 'Characteristics', *Critical and Miscellaneous Essays*, 2 vol., 1888, II, 3–33.
[2] *Autobiography*, The World's Classics, 1924, 113.

poems a medicine for my state of mind, was that they expressed not mere outward beauty, but states of feeling, under the excitement of beauty. They seemed to be a very culture of the feelings, which I was in quest of'.[1] The arid intellectualism of Mill's upbringing certainly confirms Hallam's diagnosis of the ills attending 'our overcivilized condition of thought' and its divorce from the life of feeling, while Mill's recourse to Wordsworth and 'the culture of the feelings' anticipates Matthew Arnold's tribute to Wordsworth's 'healing power'[2] in the 'Memorial Verses' of 1850. In fact, although coming a generation later, Arnold's characterization of the 'modern' spirit deals essentially with the same sense of lost spontaneity of feeling which Hallam, Carlyle and Mill complain of: 'The predominance of thought, of reflection, in modern epochs is not without its penalties; in the unsound, in the over-tasked, in the over-sensitive, it has produced a state of feeling unknown to less enlightened but perhaps healthier epochs—the feeling of depression, the feeling of *ennui*. Depression and *ennui;* these are the characteristics stamped on how many of the representative works of modern times'.[3] Spontaneous feeling and tranquillity, those twin virtues of the Wordsworthian poetic ideal, came to be valued in reaction against this tendency to 'depression and *ennui*'.

The cross-currents of this critical debate about the poet and his social responsibilities, his role as public spokesman or private physician to the self-conscious tendencies of the age, compelled Tennyson to become more self-conscious about his own poetry. This new awareness is reflected in the ambivalences of 'The Hesperides' and 'The Lotos-Eaters', which express contradictory aesthetic and moral attitudes: in these poems serenity and spontaneity of feeling seem possible only at the cost of human sympathies. Another mythological poem in the 1832 volume, 'Oenone', again attempts to combine the expression of a state of feeling with a moral fable. Oenone, forsaken by her lover Paris, is another Mariana:

[1] Mill's *Autobiography*, 125.
[2] *The Poems of Matthew Arnold*, ed K. Allott, Longmans Annotated English Poets, 1965, 229.
[3] 'On the Modern Element in Literature', *Matthew Arnold: Poetry and Prose*, ed John Bryson, 1954, 279.

> *'O mother Ida, many-fountained Ida,*
> *Dear mother Ida, harken ere I die.*
> *The grasshopper is silent in the grass:*
> *The lizard, with his shadow on the stone,*
> *Sleeps like a shadow, and the scarletwinged*
> *Cicala in the noonday leapeth not*
> *Along the water-rounded granite-rock.*
> *The purple flowers droop: the golden bee*
> *Is lily-cradled: I alone awake.*
> *My eyes are full of tears, my heart of love,*
> *My heart is breaking, and my eyes are dim,*
> *And I am all aweary of my life.'*
>
> (PT, 386–87)

This poetry of feeling is interwoven with the story of the judgment of Paris, a moral allegory of the choice between the worldly power offered by Juno, the wisdom of Pallas and the sensual passion of Venus. Rejecting 'Self-reverence, self-knowledge, self-control', Paris is seduced by the promise of Helen's beauty, and so Oenone is betrayed and the destruction of Troy prophesied. This easy moral, however, is somewhat complicated by the poetic association between Venus and Oenone. 'Idalian Aphrodite ocean born' is a temptress who appeals to the senses, not to reason; after this description of her appearance, she has no need to use argument or persuasion:

> *Fresh as the foam, new-bathed in Paphian wells,*
> *With rosy slender fingers upward drew*
> *From her warm brow and bosom her dark hair*
> *Fragrant and thick, and on her head upbound*
> *In a purple band: below her lucid neck*
> *Shone ivorylike, and from the ground her foot*
> *Gleamed rosywhite, and o'er her rounded form*
> *Between the shadows of the vine-bunches*
> *Floated the glowing sunlights, as she moved.*
>
> (PT, 394)

Yet Oenone's complaint that she is equally as fair and as loving as Helen identifies her with the destructive sensuality of Venus:

> *Ah me, my mountain shepherd, that my arms*
> *Were wound about thee, and my hot lips prest*
> *Close, close to thine in that quick-falling dew*
> *Of fruitful kisses, thick as Autumn rains*
> *Flash in the pools of whirling Simois.*
>
>   (PT, 395)

Oenone is betrayed by false values, as the moral weighting of the poem works against its sensuous feeling. By the austere ideals of 'Self-reverence, self-knowledge, self-control', Oenone's life-weary melancholy and the luxuriant imagery in which it is couched represent a self-indulgent aestheticism. It is as though Tennyson has come to recognize and gain a measure of objective control over his own tendency to narcissism and excessive sensuousness. Nevertheless, the poem has it both ways; it invites us to feel with the forlorn Oenone amid the gorgeous splendours of the natural scenery, and at the same time to make a judgment ourselves, reversing that of Paris. In Oenone's lament for the felling of the trees it may not be too fanciful to hear Tennyson's reluctant parting from the poetry of pure feeling as he turned towards the sterner realities of the moral life:

> *They came, they cut away my tallest pines,*
> *My dark tall pines, that plumed the craggy ledge*
> *High over the blue gorge, or lower down*
> *Filling greengulphèd Ida, all between*
> *The snowy peak and snow-white cataract*
> *Fostered the callow eaglet*
> . . . .
> *Never, never more*
> *Shall lone Oenone see the morning mist*
> *Sweep through them; never see them overlaid*
> *With narrow moon-lit slips of silver cloud,*
> *Between the loud stream and the trembling stars,*

The poem is an augury of the kind of development which his Cambridge friend James Spedding described, looking back from the 1842 *Poems* to these earlier volumes: 'His genius was manifestly shaping a peculiar course for itself, and finding out its proper business; the moral soul was beginning more and more to assume its due predominance. . . . Considerable faults, however, still remained; a tendancy, for example, arising from the fulness of a mind which had not yet learned to master its resources freely, to overcrowd his composition with imagery . . . to which may be added an over-indulgence in the luxuries of the senses' (CH, 142–43).

'Oenone' illustrates well the subtlety with which Tennyson projected the conflicts of his inner consciousness upon mythological subjects. The moral conflict between spiritual and sensual values was to become one of the major themes of his poetry, but in 'Oenone' he is also intimate with his depths. The very ambivalence of the poem gives it dramatic tension, for Tennyson's characteristic use of the *persona* is as a means of suspending in symbolic form the tensions and divisions of his mind.

The other 1832 poems which resume the 'Mariana' theme are 'Mariana in the South', 'The Lady of Shalott', and 'The Palace of Art'. The first of these transports the lady to languish in the scenery of South-West France, where Tennyson conceived the poem while on holiday with Arthur Hallam. In these circumstances, it is not surprising that her earlier morbidity has gone, and, as Hallam observed, there is 'a less palpable transition of the poet into Mariana's feelings, than was the case in the former poem' (*Mem.*, I, 500). The feeling is less intense because Tennyson is more preoccupied with describing the landscape, displaying his technical virtuosity and powers of observation. It is altogether a slighter poem than its prototype, but the very conception of playing a variation on the theme shows the degree of self-consciousness with which Tennyson now reflected on his art.

'The Lady of Shalott' adds a new dimension of narrative to the Mariana theme, and the effect of movement and progression which this provides is a contrast with the static quality of the earlier poem. No longer does 'the feeling therein developed give importance to the action and situation': action is an important element in saving the Lady from morbid stagnation, imprisoned and isolated as she is in her island tower. Unlike Mariana, she has long been happy in her seclusion, and not inactive; her song 'that echoes cheerly' as she weaves 'A magic web with colours gay' reflects the moving and many-coloured world outside. But she has no direct contact with this external world; not only is she confined to the tower, she may not look upon the world except through her mirror. The central event of the poem is the moment when she rises to see Sir Launcelot riding by:

> *She left the web, she left the loom,*
> *She made three paces through the room,*
> *She saw the water-lily bloom,*
> *She saw the helmet and the plume,*
> *She looked down to Camelot.*
> *Out flew the web and floated wide;*
> *The mirror cracked from side to side;*
> *'The curse is come upon me,' cried*
> *The Lady of Shalott.*

(PT, 359)

Thereafter, in the last movement of the poem, the Lady slowly dies as her boat drifts down the river to Camelot.

Interpretation of the poem begins with Tennyson's own comment: 'The new-born love for something, for some one in the wide world from which she has been so long secluded, takes her out of the region of shadows into that of realities' (*Mem.*, I, 117). This is like the course of Tennyson's own development, from aesthetic isolation towards engagement with life, and it expresses the Romantic theme of the growth of consciousness; yet the operation of the mysterious curse, like that which fell upon the Ancient Mariner, suggests the destruction and loss of a primal innocence and spontaneous joy in life. A desire for the unattainable is awakened in the Lady and she remains in effect as lonely and isolated as before, except that now she knows her own apartness. Therefore it is difficult to interpret the poem either as a defence of aesthetic withdrawal or as a claim for moral commitment. This ambivalence is reflected in the poetic form itself, which offers a sense of forward movement through the narrative sequence at the same time as each stanza is a self-contained unit, sealed off by the reiteration of the rhyme 'Camelot—Shalott'. Tennyson's apparent difficulty with the ending of the poem, which he changed in the 1842 version while still leaving it oddly inconclusive, as well as his use of the imagery of the passing but cyclic seasons and of the river which flows by but is ever there, also combine the effect of linear progression with that of eternal repetition. Once again the poem demonstrates Tennyson's extraordinary skill in using the material of legend to make poetry out of his deepest self-conflict.

'The Palace of Art' is the most ambitious poem of the 1832 volume, and the most consciously realised version of the Mariana theme. It lacks the surface lucidity and coherence of pure symbolic form, such as 'The Lady of Shalott' and 'Mariana' itself possess; instead it is schematised as 'a sort of allegory'. So Tennyson called it in the dedicatory verses to R. C. Trench, which rather superfluously state the poem's subject to be 'A sinful soul possessed of many gifts. . . . That did love Beauty only' (PT, 399). Trench was one of the Cambridge 'Apostles', whose remark, 'Tennyson, we cannot live in Art' (*Mem.*, I, 118), occasioned the poem. Its basic image of the Soul dwelling alone in her pleasure-palace has several possible sources and analogues, amongst which is this passage from Shelley's 'Queen Mab':

> *This is a wondrous sight*
> *And mocks all human grandeur;*
> *But, were it virtue's only meed, to dwell*
> *In a celestial palace, all resigned*
> *To pleasurable impulses, immured*
> *Within the prison of itself, the will*
> *Of changeless Nature would be unfulfilled.*
> *Learn to make others happy.*[1]

The poem unfolds as the growth and development of the Soul; it begins in pure aesthetic delight with the description of the extravagantly ornate palace itself, then follow as a sequence of tapestries stanzas embodying different moods in symbolic landscapes, and after these a series of stanzas on myths and legends. Next come portraits of great artists, historical figures, and philosophers, as the Soul's capacities grow from feeling into knowledge, thought and the realm of ideas. As the Soul's horizons expand, and she develops an awareness of her own powers, so she becomes increasingly proud and complacent in her

---

[1] *Poetical Works*, ed Thomas Hutchinson (1960 edn), Oxford Standard Authors, 1905, 767.

intellectual aloofness. At this point, Tennyson allows her three years to thrive and prosper, before isolated consciousness turns into morbid introspection:

> *The abysmal deeps of Personality*
> *Plagued her with sore despair.*
>
> (PT, 415)

The palace of the mind is now filled with hideous fantasies:

> *But in dark corners of her palace stood*
> *Uncertain shapes; and unawares*
> *On white-eyed phantasms weeping tears of blood,*
> *And horrible nightmares,*
>
> *And hollow shades enclosing hearts of flame,*
> *And, with dim fretted foreheads all,*
> *On corpses three-months-old at noon she came,*
> *That stood against the wall.*
>
> *A spot of dull stagnation, without light*
> *Or power of movement, seemed my soul,*
> *'Mid downward-sloping motions infinite*
> *Making for one sure goal . . .*
>
> . . . .
> *And death and life she hated equally,*
> *And nothing saw, for her despair,*
> *But dreadful time, dreadful eternity,*
> *No comfort anywhere.*
>
> (PT, 416–17)

The psychological insight and poetic resources of this poem make it an impressive piece of self-realization. But again Tennyson has difficulty in finding an adequate resolution, and the concluding stanza is both limp and overtly ambivalent:

> *Yet pull not down my palace towers, that are*
> *So lightly, beautifully built:*
> *Perchance I may return with others there*
> *When I have purged my guilt.*
>
> (PT, 418)

The sense of guilt is self-induced, a symptom of the Soul's morbid condition rather than an impulse towards health. And significantly the Soul's decision to leave her palace and engage with the world beyond is prompted by no sudden access of moral responsibility or human sympathy, but by an instinct of self-preservation. As it concerns Tennyson's intimacy with his depths, the writing of the poem itself, by objectifying and evaluating the processes at work in his own mind, is the real act of purgation.

The ambivalence between engagement and withdrawal from life reflected in these 1832 poems was cruelly intensified and brought to its critical point by Arthur Hallam's sudden death in 1833. By one of those strange ironies of fate that attend the life of the Romantic artist, the loss of Hallam, his closest friend and mentor, precipitated the crisis which might have crushed Tennyson's precarious hopes for his poetic career, but which instead was to make a major poet of him. The disaster in fact came at a time when a series of recent family misfortunes, and the critical reception of the 1830 and 1832 volumes, were already exacerbating Tennyson's temperamental proneness to 'black-blooded' despondency, and it seemed to crystallize his profoundest inner conflicts. In the *Memoir*, Hallam Tennyson records that his father later told him of 'the cloud of this overwhelming sorrow' after the death of Arthur Hallam, which 'for a while blotted out all joy from his life, and made him long for death' (*Mem.*, I, 109). Yet, as *In Memoriam* shows, Tennyson literally wrote himself out of this despair. This progression through the heart of darkness to the light beyond is an essentially Romantic act of self-renewal, and it is the theme of several of the new poems published in 1842. It is also to be recognised in some of the revisions made to those 1832 poems which Tennyson reprinted in 1842; for instance, in the altered version of Pallas' speech from 'Oenone':

> *To push thee forward through a life of shocks,*
> *Dangers, and deeds, until endurance grow*
> *Sinewed with action, and the full-grown will,*
> *Circled through all experience, pure law,*
> *Commeasure perfect freedom.*

(PT, 394)

When the news of Hallam's death reached him, Tennyson was already at work on 'The Two Voices', which like 'Supposed Confessions' is in Matthew Arnold's phrase a 'dialogue of the mind with itself'.[1] The poem differs from its predecessor, however, in presenting a conflict of ideas, not simply a state of feeling, and therefore it has more sense of progression. The still small voice that insidiously counsels nihilism, despair and suicide, employs rationalist and scientific arguments to prove the insignificance and illusoriness of human values. The self tries to counter these arguments on their own intellectual ground, but finally resorts to an intuitive faith in a truth beyond the reach of reason, science or even words:

> *Moreover, something is or seems,*
> *That touches me with mystic gleams,*
> *Like glimpses of forgotten dreams—*
>
> *Of something felt, like something here;*
> *Of something done, I know not where;*
> *Such as no language may declare.*
>
> (PT, 539)

A resolution of this inner conflict is reached when the self turns for the first time to the world outside, and to the life going on around him. It is Sunday morning; he hears the church bells pealing, and sees the people on their way to church:

> *One walked between his wife and child,*
> *With measured footfall firm and mild,*
> *And now and then he gravely smiled.*
>
> *The prudent partner of his blood*
> *Leaned on him, faithful, gentle, good,*
> *Wearing the rose of womanhood.*
>
> *And in their double love secure,*
> *The little maiden walked demure,*
> *Pacing with downward eyelids pure.*
>
> (PT, 540)

---

[1] *Poems*, ed Allott, 591.

This picture of domestic piety, a harbinger of Victorian sentimentality, comes as an absurd anti-climax after the dark night of the soul. In one sense it is meant to be so, making its effect not as a revelation of transcendent truth but as an image of simple, mundane reality, dispelling the abstract speculations that cannot resolve themselves. The trouble is not merely that the particular values embodied in this image are unlikely to commend themselves to many modern readers, but that Tennyson attempts to combine the sense of ordinary life in the scene with a facile morality not grounded in the experience of the poem. Nevertheless the poetic intention is clear; as Christopher Ricks observes (PT, 540), the release from spiritual desolation which comes when the self blesses the family going to church is a parallel to the Ancient Mariner's liberation from the curse as he blesses the water-snakes. Though it is clumsily used in 'The Two Voices,' Tennyson has found the structure through which to express the movement of mind from a morbid sense of its own apartness to joy in knowing itself through the world around:

> *And forth into the fields I went,*
> *And Nature's living motion lent*
> *The pulse of hope to discontent.*
>
> (PT, 541)

Significantly, the poem ends with the same word that concludes Coleridge's 'Dejection': 'Rejoice!'

The need to go forward is also the theme of 'Ulysses' and 'Morte d' Arthur', both poems written in the shadow of Hallam's death. 'There is more about myself in *Ulysses,*' said Tennyson later, 'which was written under the sense of loss and that all had gone by, but that still life must be fought out to the end. It was more written with the feeling of his loss upon me than many poems in *In Memoriam*' (PT, 560). This lack of self-possession is reflected in the ambivalence of the poem, for Ulysses' last voyage is both a heroic endeavour and an escape from the burden of responsibilities, a quest for life and a desire for death:

> *The lights begin to twinkle from the rocks:*
> *The long day wanes: the slow moon climbs: the deep*
> *Moans round with many voices. Come, my friends,*
> *'Tis not too late to seek a newer world.*

> *Push off, and sitting well in order smite*
> *The sounding furrows; for my purpose holds*
> *To sail beyond the sunset, and the baths*
> *Of all the western stars, until I die.*
> *It may be that the gulfs will wash us down:*
> *It may be we shall touch the Happy Isles,*
> *And see the great Achilles, whom we knew.*
>
> (PT, 565)

It is difficult to know how critical we are meant to be of Ulysses'
wanderlust: the lines on Telemachus, 'He works his work, I mine',
express a deliberate contrast of values, yet there is no ironic manipulation of attitude towards the speaker, such as we are given in 'St Simeon
Stylites', a monologue more of the kind that Browning was to develop.
In 'Ulysses', Tennyson has once again found a myth of marvellous
appropriateness, capable of embodying in its single image an unresolved
moral conflict. Yet while the autonomy of myth frames and encloses the
experience, giving a sense of wholeness, the monologue form suggests
an action which will continue beyond the limits of the poem, but which
has not yet actually begun. This effect of a simultaneously closed and
open form is reproduced in the poem's central symbol of the arch:

> *I am a part of all that I have met;*
> *Yet all experience is an arch wherethrough*
> *Gleams that untravelled world, whose margin*
> *Fades for ever and for ever when I move.*
>
> (PT, 563)

Perpetually gleaming and fading, the receding end towards which he
moves makes the sense of progressive action an illusion.

   Like 'Ulysses', 'Morte d'Arthur' is an attempt to turn from the poetry
of feeling to the poetry of action, using heroic legend. The two situations are similar; in this poem, however, it is not the departing king
but the knight he leaves behind who must 'go forth companionless'.
Yet the moral theme is not fully translated into narrative; Sir Bedivere
twice fails to trust the dying king, but it is not explained why on the
third occasion he finds new faith and returns Excalibur to the lake.
Instead of an inner development in the action, the poem presents us

with a ritualized repetition. It functions as a sequence of symbolic pictures rather than as a progressive whole:

> *But the other swiftly strode from ridge to ridge,*
> *Clothed with his breath, and looking, as he walked,*
> *Larger than human on the frozen hills.*
> *He heard the deep behind him, and a cry*
> *Before. His own thought drove him, like a goad.*
> *Dry clashed his harness in the icy caves*
> *And barren chasms, and all to left and right*
> *The bare black cliff clanged round him, as he based*
> *His feet on juts of slippery crag that rang*
> *Sharp-smitten with the dint of armèd heels—*
> *And on a sudden, lo! the level lake,*
> *And the long glories of the winter moon.*
>
> (PT, 593)

This is a splendid picturesque embodiment of the theme, an analogue of the passage from spiritual darkness and despair towards the light of faith, but it is quite self-contained. The poem as a whole does not move towards a resolution; it presents an almost static situation, as Arthur gradually recedes into the distance and Sir Bedivere is left alone in the waste land. Again, as in 'Ulysses', the going forward does not take place in the poem itself: it is merely the need for action that the poem expresses.

Tennyson's use of epic in 'Morte d'Arthur' is itself ambivalent, for while it represents a world of heroic action he was also aware that his attraction to the past was scarcely in keeping with the theme of moving forward into life. He recognized this objection, at least after writing the poem, for the induction which he later added, like 'some prelude of disparagement', questions the value of its 'faint Homeric echoes' (PT, 583). At about the same time as this induction was added (1837–8) he wrote 'Locksley Hall', the monologue which returns to the theme of 'Ulysses' and 'Morte d'Arthur' ('I must mix myself with action, lest I wither by despair'), but gives it a contemporary setting. The action of this poem is psychological, a dialectic between pessimistic and optimistic views of society, as the hero's bitterness at the failure of love leads to an indictment of the false social values behind Amy's marriage, and a contrasting memory of his former idealistic vision of social progress. This movement is then repeated in terms of the future rather than the immediate past, rejection of society leading him to a fantasy of escape to some primitive paradise, which in turn is rejected for the higher claims of civilization and progress:

> *Not in vain the distance beacons. Forward, forward let us range,*
> *Let the great world spin for ever down the ringing grooves of change.*
>   (PT, 699)

Yet again, however, Tennyson has not succeeded in matching his images of progression with the form of the poem, which alternates between two conflicting attitudes without possessing an inner logic of development.

Tennyson's difficulty in resolving his poems of action, which is apparent in the weak endings of 'The Two Voices', 'The Lady of Shalott' and 'The Palace of Art', as well as in the lack of progression in 'Ulysses', 'Morte d'Arthur' and 'Locksley Hall', does not merely reflect an ambivalence of attitudes between engagement and withdrawal. It is related to his apocalyptic imagination, his sense of an ending which is also a new beginning. The aspiration of Ulysses 'to sail beyond the sunset' to the Happy Isles, Arthur's consolation of Sir Bedivere: 'The old order changeth, yielding place to new', and the futuristic visions of 'Locksley Hall', deny finality; they are images of perpetual renewal, like Shelley's apocalyptic vision in the chorus from 'Hellas':

> *The world's great age begins anew,*
> *The golden years return,*
> *The earth doth like a snake renew*
> *Her winter weeds outworn:*
> *Heaven smiles, and faiths and empires gleam,*
> *Like wrecks of a dissolving dream.*[1]

The fulfilment of Tennyson's Romantic impulse to self-realization is *In Memoriam*, in which the poetry of feeling expresses a growth of

[1] *Poetical Works*, ed Hutchinson, 477.

consciousness, an inner progression towards personal renewal which finds its resolution in apocalypse:

> *And one far-off divine event,*
> *To which the whole creation moves.*

(PT, 988)

So the Kraken arises from its depths:

> If a man is merely to be a bundle of sensations, he had better not exist at all. He should embark on his career in the spirit of self-less and adventurous heroism; should develop his true self by not shirking responsibility, by casting aside all maudlin and intro-spective morbidities, and by using his powers cheerfully in accordance with the obvious dictates of his moral consciousness, and so, as far as possible, in harmony with what he feels to be the Absolute Right.

(Mem., I, 317)

3: Tennyson and his Public 1827-1859

M. SHAW

Popular, Popular, Unpopular!
'You're no Poet'—the critics cried!
'Why?' said the Poet. 'You're unpopular!
Then they cried at the turn of the tide—
'You're no Poet!' 'Why?'—'You're popular!'
Pop-gun, Popular and Unpopular.

(PT, 1231)

TENNYSON WAS compelled to consider the question of popularity more seriously than any previous poet. His lifetime spanned a period of unprecedented growth in the reading public of Great Britain.[1] What this new mass audience was to read was of concern to politicians, educationists and writers alike. To 'educate the poor man before making him our master' was, as Tennyson said, 'one of the great social questions impending in England' (*Mem.*, I, 249). The issue was thoroughly debated in the periodical press of the period; it particularly coloured the literary reviews where the 'democratic' duties of authors

---

[1] The population of Great Britain increased from 12.5 million in 1811 to 33 million in 1891. The first official literacy figures were obtained in 1839-40: 67% of males and 51% of females were literate. 'Literate' often meant no more than the ability to sign a marriage register. R. D. Altick has calculated that in 1852, for instance, when the population was 20 million, the 'gross potential British reading public was between 5 and 6 million'. At the time of Tennyson's death 93.6% of the population were literate. This probably meant that the potential reading public was in the region of 13 million. See R. D. Altick, *The English Common Reader*, 1957, 170-2, and 'English Publishing and the Mass Audience in 1852' in *Studies in Bibliography*, VI, 1954, 3-24.

were consistently stressed. From the time of his earliest volumes to the height of his fame in 1864, Tennyson was never allowed to lose sight of the ideal of 'a poet of the people'. To a large extent he came to share this ideal and it rebounded on him when the reaction to the tastes and values of the people for whom he spoke—the Victorian middle-classes —set in. But even while he sought popularity he was disturbed and checked, possibly with beneficial effects on his poetry, by implications the idea of popularity carried for him. What these were may be glimpsed in a remark he made to William Allingham in 1866: 'Why am I popular? I don't write very vulgarly'.[1]

As Raymond Williams has pointed out,[2] the belief that what was popular was also likely to be vulgar gained peculiar strength during the early years of the nineteenth century. It was largely forgotten during the mid-Victorian period when the idea of social commitment in art dominated literary thinking but even then it retained its exponents and by the end of the century had re-emerged powerfully as an aspect of Aestheticism. For our purposes, its most important advocate was Arthur Hallam whose views on the subject influenced the young Tennyson and were probably responsible for the equivocal attitude towards popularity which characterized his maturity. Hallam maintained that popularity was no test of poetic worth but rather the reverse. Poets 'in the highest and truest sense' were those whose physical constitutions were such that 'susceptible to the slightest impulse from external nature, their fine organs trembled into emotion at colours, and sounds, and movements, unperceived or unregarded by duller temperaments'. These poets Hallam called Poets of Sensation, poets by nature who 'lived in a world of images' and whose 'whole Being was absorbed into the energy of sense'. Inferior to these were poets of reflection in whose minds the desire for beauty (the *sine qua non* of poetry) had not been the predominant motive in the act of creation. They were more likely to be popular because the grounds on which they made their appeal—'matters of daily experience'— were more readily and generally understood and appreciated. As types of the poet

---

[1] William Allingham, *Diary*, 1907, 132.
[2] 'The Romantic Artist' in *Culture and Society 1780–1950*, 1958.

of sensation, Hallam had Keats and Shelley principally in mind: 'How should they be popular, whose senses told them a richer and ampler tale than most men could understand and who constantly expressed, because they constantly felt, sentiments of exquisite pleasure and pain, which most men were not permitted to experience'.[1] Tennyson too was a poet of sensation and Hallam envisaged for him a similar unpopularity: 'He is a true and thorough poet', he wrote to Tennyson's mother in 1830, 'far too good to be popular' (*Mem.*, I, 51). Wordsworth was a type of the reflective poet; so too, on a lower level, was Robert Montgomery whom Hallam attacked at the beginning of his article. Montgomery's *Omnipresence of the Deity* went to eight editions in eight months when it was first published in 1828 and is worth quoting from here as an example of reflective poetry which Hallam despised and which he believed was of a type to have greater appeal to the generality of readers then 'art free and unalloyed':

> *And shall the soul, the fount of reason, die,*
> *When dust and darkness round its temple lie?*
> *Did God breathe in it no ethereal fire,*
> *Dimless and quenchless, though the breath expire?*
> . . . .
> *Ah, no! it cannot be that men were sent*
> *To live and languish on in discontent;*
> *That Soul was moulded to betrayful trust,*
> *To feel like God, and perish like the dust.*

Hallam made several interesting distinctions between poetry of sensation and poetry of reflection. The poet of sensation seeks to enrapture, the reflective poet to convince and instruct; the one is concerned primarily with beauty, the other with truth, and whereas the reflective poet favours descriptive and rhetorical writing as best suited to his purpose, the poet of sensation deals in the picturesque and impressionistic.

[1] 'On Some of the Characteristics of Modern Poetry, and on the Lyrical Poems of Alfred Tennyson' in *Englishman's Magazine*, I, August 1831, 616–628. Reprinted in *The Writings of Arthur Hallam*, ed T. H. Vail Motter, New York and London 1943, 187. See also CH, 34–49.

The implication of Hallam's argument is that high art is non-utilitarian, that it serves no moral or social purpose but only an aesthetic one. This seems out of keeping with what we have been told was the mission of the 'Apostles' 'to enlighten the world upon things intellectual and spiritual'.[1] Even the details disagree; 'Coleridge and Wordsworth were our special divinities', said Dean Merivale, yet Hallam considered Wordsworth's poetry predominantly reflective and therefore not of the highest species. But the truth was that the 'Apostles' were not of one mind on poetry; their writings reveal a variety of critical beliefs which, besides Hallam's aestheticism, included the 'emotionalism' of Sterling[2] and the highly moralistic views of R. C. Trench.[3]

In an exaggerated way, this range of critical opinion reflected the generally transitional and anarchic nature of contemporary English criticism.[4] Yet, however diverse in some respects, the literary journals which provided the main body of critical thought, were in majority agreement on two issues, that poetry should serve a moral purpose and that its appeal should be as general as possible. In 1830 and 1831 advice to Tennyson along these lines came from reviewers of widely differing political and philosophical views. W. J. Fox, a man of Radical and Utilitarian sympathies, wrote in his review of *Poems, Chiefly Lyrical*: 'A genuine poet has deep responsibilities to his country and the world, to the present and future generations, to earth and heaven . . . [Poets] can influence the sympathies of unnumbered hearts; they can

[1] Quoted by Harold Nicolson, *Tennyson*, 1925, 73.
[2] See, for example, Sterling's review of Tennyson's *Poems* in the *Quarterly Review*, LXX, Sept. 1842, 385–416 (CH, 103–25).
[3] See Tennyson's 'To — With the Following Poem' (PT, 399), which was addressed to Trench, and *Mem.*, I, 506. Trench's own poems were very moral.
[4] The range of critical theory and practice is illustrated in the following selection: J. H. Newman's treatise on Aristotle's *Poetics* (1829), Keble's *Lectures on Poetry 1832–1841*, Carlyle's 'Characteristics' (1831), the periodical reviews of Macaulay (for example, his review of Moore's *Life of Byron*, 1831) and of Leigh Hunt (for example, his 'A New Gallery of Pictures: Spenser', 1833).

disseminate principles; they can give these principles power over men's imagination . . . they can act with a force, the extent of which it is difficult to estimate, upon national feelings and character and consequently upon national happiness'.[1] The next year, the high Tory Christopher North jibed at the *Westminster Review* for liking Tennyson but the admonitory advice he gave Tennyson as 'a promising plant' assumed definitions of the purpose of poetry which were not at all dissimilar to Fox's: 'At present [Tennyson] has small powers over the common feelings and thoughts of man . . . what all the human race see and feel he seems to think cannot be poetical. . . .'[2] Unlike Hallam, both Fox and North assumed that the merit of a poem depended primarily on its philosophical content, on what it conveyed to the reader's understanding as true and wise about human experience. This was a view put most forcibly by Henry Taylor in the Preface to *Philip Van Artevelde* (1834), a long, historical closet-drama concerning a hero who possessed what Taylor thought of as the anti-Byronic qualities of 'courage, discretion, wit, An equal temper and an ample soul, Rock bound and fortified against assaults of transitory Passion'. Taylor won considerable success with *Philip*.[3] Tennyson himself admired it (*Mem.*, I, 141) and also took note of its Preface,[4] in which Taylor voiced a by now quite general critical reaction to 'the highly-coloured poetry which has been popular in these latter years'. Taylor's main targets were Byron and Shelley but he also referred to poetry after Byron in terms which suggest he may have had Tennyson in mind. This 'poetry of the day . . . consists in little more than a poetical diction, an arrangement of words implying a sensitive state of mind . . . which addresses itself to the sentient, not the percipient properties of the mind, and displays merely symbols or types of feelings, which might exist with equal force in a being the most barren of understanding'. Taylor's conviction was that 'no man can be a very great poet who is not also a great philosopher' and his wish was to impugn the idea that 'good sense stands in a species

[1] *Westminster Review*, XIV, Jan. 1831, 223–4 (CH, 32).
[2] *Blackwood's Edinburgh Magazine*, XXXI, May 1832, 725 (CH, 52).
[3] See Edmund Gosse, 'Philip James Bailey' in *Portraits and Sketches*, 1912, 64–67.
[4] *Tennyson and His Friends*, ed Hallam Tennyson, 1911, 401.

of antagonism to poetical genius instead of being one of its most essential constituents'.

The year after Taylor's Preface, John Stuart Mill reviewed Tennyson's poems in the *London Review*. We know that Tennyson read this review and that it was 'a great encouragement' to him (*Mem.*, I, 122). The review was in part a reply to North and Croker, two years after Croker had pilloried Tennyson. It was also a reply to Hallam's article; in terms so similar that there can be no doubt that he had read and admired what Hallam had written, Mill took up and developed certain arguments in the earlier review. These related to Hallam's belief in the specially constituted nature of the poet and to his relegation of philosophic poetry to an inferior position. Both had been part of Mill's critical position in his essay 'What Is Poetry?' of 1833 but he amended his views on philosophic poetry in his second essay of 1833, 'The Two Kinds of Poetry'. He had originally intended to incorporate this essay into a review of Tennyson but it was issued independently and 'a better review of Tennyson and with the same ideas too, in another way'[1] was written in 1835. Whatever its origins, it excellently summarized and drew together the critical ideas that surrounded Tennyson's early poems.

The central point of Mill's argument was 'that there are in the character of every true poet, two elements, for one of which he is indebted to nature, for the other to cultivation' (CH, 91). From nature, the poet derives 'fine senses . . . [a] peculiar kind of nervous susceptibility [which] constitutes the capacity for poetry'. Beyond this 'begins the province of culture. . . . Every great poet, every poet who has extensively or permanently influenced mankind, has been a great thinker;—has had a philosophy . . . has had his mind full of thoughts, derived not merely from passive sensibility but from trains of reflection, from observation, analysis, and generalisation'. Mill cited Shelley as an example of a poetic nature untempered by any systematic culture of the intellect whose poetry appealed only 'to persons of similar organization to the poet, but not likely to be sympathized in,

[1] Letter to W. J. Fox, 7th September 1833, *Earlier Letters of John Stuart Mill 1812-1848*, ed F. E. Mineka, *Collected Works*, XII, Toronto 1963, 177-8.

because not understood by any other persons; and scarcely conducing at all to the noblest end of poetry as an intellectual pursuit, that of acting upon the desires and characters of mankind through their emotions to raise them towards the perfection of their nature'. Mill considered Tennyson to be a poet by nature, possessing to an eminent degree the poetic temperament. He also saw evidence in the poems of intellectual culture and his advice to Tennyson was 'continual study and meditation' so that his intellect may be strengthened in order 'to render his poetic endowment the means of giving impressiveness to important truths. . . . He must cultivate, and with no half devotion, philosophy as well as poetry' (CH, 96).

What Mill did for Tennyson in this review was to reclaim the possibility of poetry of mixed energies. Where Hallam had split off the sensuous poet from the reflective, assigning to one a non-utilitarian élitism and to the other a popular inferiority of art, Mill conceived of the poet as a being in whom sensation and intellect, emotion and reason, and the love of beauty and of truth, were united. Of course, such a poet was morally effective, 'acting upon the desires and characters of mankind through their emotions, to raise them to the perfection of their nature'. How widespread the effectiveness depended on the type of poem, and on this point Mill revealed an attitude which almost brought him back to Hallam's position. 'Mariana', he said, would not be immediately popular; 'indeed if it were, its merit would be but of the humblest kind; for sentiments and imagery which can be received at once, and with equal ease, into every mind, must necessarily be trite'. 'The May Queen', on the other hand, 'is fitted for a more extensive popularity . . . Simple, genuine pathos, arising out of the situations and feelings common to mankind generally, is of all kinds of poetic beauty that which can be most universally appreciated; and the genius applied in it is, in consequence, apt to be overrated for it is also of all kinds that which can be most easily produced' (CH, 88).

The two most striking features of Tennyson's contributions to *Poems by Two Brothers* of 1827 were the literary quality of the poems and the predominance in them of a mood of morbid and guilty pessimism. Poets from Virgil to Moore and Byron were ransacked to provide epigraphs, themes, imagery and verse forms for a young poet obviously experimenting through imitation. As for the gloominess of the poems, no doubt life at Somersby was often depressing and there was always 'the black blood of the Tennysons' to contend with, but it was also fashionable to be tormented and violent in poetry at this time and most of the poems are sufficiently dramatized to suggest that Tennyson was consciously indulging a taste for Byronic excess in himself and his readers. Monkton Milnes recalled that when he went to Cambridge in 1828, it 'was there not only fashionable but almost indispensable for every youth to be Byronic',[1] and during Arthur Hallam's adolescence 'Byron was . . . far above the rest and almost exclusively his favourite'.[2]

That the Tennyson brothers were anxious to court favour with their public is further seen in the self-deprecating epigraph they chose (*'We know these efforts of ours are nothing worth.* Martial'), and the disarming advertisement, which virtually said that it was difficult to write poetry, that the authors were young and so would critics and readers please not be too severe in their judgments. Some poems, 'The Coach of Death' and 'The Bridal' amongst them, and the prodigious play *The Devil and the Lady*, were omitted as 'being too much out of the common for the public taste' (*Mem.*, I, 23). Tennyson's next volume was to show no such desire to ingratiate itself with an audience.

Although Tennyson said that *Poems, Chiefly Lyrical* of 1830 was composed 'before I had attained my nineteenth year' (*Mem.*, I, 96) (that is before October 1828 when Hallam entered Trinity College), this volume was prepared for the press during the first year of the Hallam–Tennyson friendship and its contents related closely to Hallam's ideas on poetry in the 1831 review. To begin with, the poems contained a very exalted notion of the poet's attributes and position. Admittedly, his purpose was 'to fling The wingèd shafts of truth', but the world where he was to do this was no common earth but 'a golden clime',

[1] 'Address to the Wordsworth Society', 1885, quoted James Pope-Hennessy, *Monkton Milnes: The Years of Promise*, 1949, 21.
[2] Introduction by Henry Hallam to A. H. Hallam, *Remains in Verse and Prose*, 1863, xiii.

'holy ground' set in an ideal time of 'the world's renewed youth'.[1] Nor did the poems themselves reveal any desire to please a general audience, particularly if we bear in mind the current taste for poetry like Montgomery's or Robert Pollok's[2] or, a little later, that of Tennyson's friends Alford and Trench.[3] Tennyson's new poems were less derivative than those of 1827 but their originality was wayward and capricious. They were, as J. F. A. Pyre has said, 'strangely and rashly anarchic in matters of form'; Tennyson was 'either remarkably careless or remarkably impatient of the ordinary restraints of metrical and stanzaic form which were the legacy of centuries . . . and which the most distinguished of his predecessors in the art of poetry had seldom neglected with impunity'.[4] There was much whimsy, even playfulness, in the style of the poems and the imagery was often self-conscious and arcane. Few of the poems were serious on an intellectual level; several had a mood of melancholy but with one or two possible exceptions, there was no exploration of ideas, little that could be called reflective or philosophic. The striking feature of the volume was what Hallam described as 'the picturesque delineation of objects . . .

[1] See 'The Poet', 'The Poet's Mind' and the unpublished poem 'To Poesy' (PT, 222, 224 and 168). Tennyson's mention of the world's youth as a propitious time for poetry echoes Hallam's cultural primitivism; see *Writings*, ed. Motter, 188–9.
[2] Robert Pollok's *Course of Time* was published in 1827 and keenly supported by Christopher North (*Blackwood's*, July 1827). It was a blank verse poem in ten books concerning the destiny of man and went to four editions by 1828.
[3] Henry Alford published *The School of the Heart* in 1835. It was 'heavily larded with instructive thoughts and pious sentiments' and was also praised by North (E. F. Shannon, *Tennyson and the Reviewers*, Cambridge, Mass., 1952, 51). R. C. Trench's *The Story of Justin the Martyr and Other Poems* was also published in 1835. These simple, reflective poems had quite a success in the religious world and reached a second edition in the same year (Shannon, 196 n. 66).
[4] J. F. A. Pyre, *The Formation of Tennyson's Style*, University of Wisconsin Studies 12, 1921, 26. Coleridge had commented similarly in *Table Talk*, 1835, II, 164–5. For Tennyson's comment see Charles Tennyson, *Alfred Tennyson*, 1949, 91.

fused . . . in a medium of strong emotion'. Poems where this picturesque element predominated ('Mariana', 'Recollections of Arabian
Nights') were the most successful.

The volume was surprisingly well received by the eight periodicals
that noticed it. Even North's grumblings were palliated by 'judicious
eulogy'. But it obviously didn't sell very well. Six hundred copies at
5s. each were issued; there was no second edition.

Tennyson was not particularly anxious to publish a further volume.
The initiative seems to have come from Hallam: 'I have persuaded him,
I think, to publish without further delay'.[1] But Tennyson wrote to
Moxon that he was in no hurry and would like to see all the proofs
twice: 'I should like the text to be as correct as possible . . . my MSS
(i.e. those I have by me) are far from being in proper order, and such a
measure would give me leisure to arrange and correct them'. At the
last minute, he wrote to Moxon to delete 'The Lover's Tale' from the
volume: 'it is too full of faults and though I think it might conduce towards making me popular, yet to my eye, it spoils the completeness of
the book, and is better away' (*Mem.*, I, 90). In view of this care for 'the
completeness of the book', it is surprising that Tennyson allowed the
ill-considered and incongruous trifle 'To Christopher North' (which
Hallam advised against including) to be published. But *Poems* of 1832
retained much of the poetic arrogance of *Poems, Chiefly Lyrical* and it
seems certain that as yet Tennyson was not very concerned to solicit
popular or critical success. In the first place, there was a continuance
from 1830 of the idea of the poet as a remote, exalted figure who

> *lifted high . . .*
> *Lets the great world flit from him, seeing all,*
> *Higher through secret splendours mounting still,*
> *Self-poised, nor fears to fall,*
> *Hearing apart the echoes of his fame.*[2]

Although, as Pyre points out, there was 'a clear advance towards

---

[1] Letter of March 1832 to R. C. Trench, quoted Shannon, *Tennyson and
the Reviewers*, 13.
[2] Prologue to 'A Dream of Fair Women', dropped from the poem after
1832 (PT, 440-1).

regularity in the metres of the 1832 volume' there were several of the
rather slight total of thirty poems which were complicated and perplexing in matters of rhythm and rhyme and many which had affecta-
tions of style such as, 'I sate alone: the goldensandalled morn Rosehued
the scornful hills: I sate alone With downdropt eyes' ('Oenone'
ll. 53–55). And in spite of the admonitions Tennyson had received from
some of his Cambridge friends on the need for 'poetry written in a
proper spirit' (*Mem.*, I, 68) there were no more than one or two poems
which showed any trace of their moralistic creed. In general, the
characteristics of *Poems* 1832 were those of the 1830 volume. The
sensuous, picturesque element predominated, poetry of statement and
reflection was eschewed and moral content was minimal. New to the
1832 volume, and important as a pointer to Tennyson's future development, was the use of narrative: 'The Lady of Shalott', 'The Miller's
Daughter' and 'A Dream of Fair Women' told a story, or stories, as no
poem of 1830 had done.

Sixteen of the *Poems* of 1832 were reissued in *Poems* of 1842. Those
kept back were irregular in form and complicated in metre; those that
were retained were revised, sometimes drastically (e.g. 'Oenone' and
'The Palace of Art'), and in every case the changes were towards
greater smoothness and regularity of form. These poems took their
place in volume I of *Poems* (1842) alongside twenty-five from the 1830
volume and six new ones. All the poems in volume II were new except
for 'St Agnes' Eve', which had appeared in *The Keepsake* for 1837, and
'The Sleeping Beauty' section of 'The Day Dream' which had appeared
in 1830. As Pyre has shown, practically every new poem of 1842 'was
in some standard and well-known metre and observed a definite stanzaic order of construction. The conventional form was usually modified
in some minute particular, but this modulation was always simple,
organic and consistently observed.' The new poems were also more intellectually and morally substantial than those of the earlier volumes. To
move from volume I to volume II of *Poems* (1842) is to move from
poetry of mood and fancy to poetry of ideas and themes in which
sensuous and picturesque imagery is contained and directed by the
demands of narrative form or the pressures of serious moral reflection.
In fact, by 1842 Tennyson had become a poet of culture as well as of

nature. His spokesman now was James Spedding whose review of *Poems* (1842) stood in the same relation to that volume as Hallam's had done to the earlier ones. Spedding had advised and encouraged Tennyson ever since their Cambridge days (*Mem.*, I, 139–145; 151; 198). Hallam Tennyson said that the review 'gives accurately the growth of his friend's mind' (*Mem.*, I, 190) and Tennyson himself regarded Spedding as 'just the man to do it, both as knowing me, and writing from clear conviction' (*Mem.*, I, 180). Spedding's conviction, with which we may assume Tennyson was by now largely in agreement, was that:

> All that is of true and lasting worth in poetry, must have its root in a sound view of human life and the condition of man in the world. Where this is not, the most consummate art can produce nothing which man will long care for—where it is, the rudest will never want an audience; for then nothing is trivial—the most ordinary incidents of daily life are invested with an interest as deep as the springs of emotion in the heart—as deep as pity, and love, and fear, and awe.[1]

By 1845, Tennyson himself was openly 'denouncing exotics and saying that a poem should reflect the time and place'.[2]

It is tempting to see this change as a result of critical pressures exerted on Tennyson during his youth. Since 1832 he had undoubtedly acquired 'a deeper and a fuller insight into the requirements of the age' (*Mem.*, I, 123). His critics and friends had told him what these requirements were but his response to these needs was by no means simply the result of 'a fear of again putting himself at the mercy of the reviewers'.[3] The reviewers could not have effected so profound a change as occurred in Tennyson's approach to his art during the 1830s without a strong predisposition in Tennyson himself to think along these lines. In fact, his poetic conformism was part of a general maturing process which began soon after he left Cambridge on the death of his father in 1831. This was a period of great emotional

[1] *Edinburgh Review*, LXXVII, April 1843, 382 (CH, 146).
[2] Wilfred Ward, *Aubrey De Vere*, 1904, 70–1.
[3] Shannon, *Tennyson and the Reviewers*, 59.

development and, as we shall see, of growth in social commitment. The Cambridge interlude over, Hallam's influence, if not his memory, waning, Tennyson quickly settled into a sincere and willing identification with 'the broad and common interests of the time and of universal humanity' (*Mem.*, I, 123). His youthful aspirations 'to be a *popular poet*' (*Mem.*, II, 79) were now resumed in the move towards reflective and narrative poetry. For although Tennyson never forgot Hallam's warnings about popularity, he now showed himself anxious to reconcile the 'highest and truest' with the popular in poetry in a way which Hallam had believed impossible for poets in a modern society. Tennyson's stylistic masters in this new commitment were Wordsworth, Burns and, above all, the classical poets, Theocritus and Virgil, familiarity with whom, as Pyre says, 'settles him the more firmly under the discipline of that *area mediocritas* which constitutes the classic message in art'.

Edward Fitzgerald, to whom the Cambridge period was an 'affectation', noted the change in Tennyson as early as 1833. Tennyson was, Fitzgerald said, 'purging and subliming . . . what he has already done: and repents that he published at all yet. It is fine to see how in each succeeding poem the smaller ornaments and fancies drop away, and leave the grand ideas single'. And in 1835, in reply to John Allen who had remarked on the absence of moral purpose in Tennyson's poems, Fitzgerald said, 'I think that you will see Tennyson acquire all that at present you miss: when he has *felt* life, he will not die fruitless of instruction to man, as he is'.[1] In fact, Tennyson had already '*felt* life' and was writing poems in which the new maturity was obvious and which anticipated several of the major concerns of his future writings. For instance, between 1831 and 1834 he wrote a group of political poems quite unlike anything he had written before. Hallam Tennyson says that at Cambridge Tennyson 'took a lively interest in politics' (*Mem.*, I, 41) but there is little evidence of this in the poems before 1831. Even the visit to Spain in 1830 apparently made no political impact on him. But in 1831 he seems to have suddenly woken up to what was happening in England and Europe. It would have been remarkable had he not

[1] *Letters and Literary Remains of Edward Fitzgerald*, 3 vol, ed W. A. Wright, 1889, I, 21 & 31.

because, as G. M. Young has said, anyone entering manhood at this time found the 'ground rocking under his feet as it had rocked in 1789. Paris had risen against the Bourbons; Bologna against the Pope; Poland against Russia; the Belgians against the Dutch. . . . At home forty years of Tory domination were ending in panic and dismay; Ireland, unappeased by Catholic emancipation, was smouldering with rebellion; from Kent to Dorset the skies were alight with burning ricks'.[1] The Polish insurrection of November 1830 was the first of these events to engage Tennyson's attention.[2] Russian rule in Poland and suppression of the revolt seemed to him an act of 'brute Power' by an 'o'ergrown Barbarian' and a type of oppression which he was long to fear, not least as it threatened England twenty years later in the person of Napoleon III. The rest[3] of his political poems of this period were concerned with the agitations over the passing of the Reform Bill. With an anger and immediacy new to his poetry, they expressed Tennyson's fear of rapid and violent change and his faith in 'seasonable changes fair, And innovation grade by grade'. As M. J. Donahue has pointed out, 'as a young man, at twenty-two or twenty-three, Tennyson had already taken up the conservatism of his maturity' and in the poems of this period he 'expressed many of his lasting political convictions'.[4]

But it is in the marriage poems of the 1830s that Tennyson most obviously assumed a maturity in which the problems of existence were no longer distilled into the inactivity of mood and enchanted reverie.

[1] *Victorian England: Portrait of an Age*, 1953, 1.
[2] See 'Sonnet written on hearing of the outbreak of the Polish insurrection' and 'Poland' and also lines 191–204 of 'Hail Briton!' (PT, 457–9 and 489). See also Arthur Hallam's 'Oh falsely they blaspheme us' (*Writings*, ed Motter, 104) which is something of a reply to Tennyson's 'Poland'. Tennyson told Allingham that 'when I was 22 I wrote a beautiful poem on Poland, hundreds of lines long, and the housemaid lit the fire with it' (*Diary*, 303).
[3] These include: 'You ask me, why, though ill at ease', 'The Goose', 'Mechanophilus', 'Love thou thy land', 'Of old sat Freedom on the heights' and the unpublished 'The wise, the pure . . .', 'Woe to the double-tongued', 'Hail Briton!', 'I loving Freedom for herself', and 'O Mother Britain'.
[4] 'Tennyson's *Hail Briton!* and *Tithon*', *PMLA*, LXIV, 1949, 397.

'The Miller's Daughter' (1832) began a series of narrative-reflective poems in which 'holy human love' was viewed in increasingly pessimistic terms in its context of class barriers and financial restrictions.[1] By the time of 'Locksley Hall' (1837–8) and 'Edwin Morris' (1839), the outlines of *Maud* (1855) and 'Aylmer's Field' (1863) had been mapped. In all, therefore, in 1835, when J. S. Mill offered his encouraging advice to Tennyson to develop his powers of 'observation, analysis, and generalization', it came as critical confirmation of tendencies already present in Tennyson's poetry. Mill's advocacy of poetry of dual properties—sensuous and philosophical—was anticipated in 'Ulysses', 'The Two Voices' and 'Morte d'Arthur'. And with pleasing coincidence, 'Dora', 'the story of a nobly simple country girl . . . told in the simplest possible language' (*Mem.*, I, 196), was being written at the same time as Mill was writing that 'simple genuine pathos, arising out of the situations and feelings common to mankind generally, is of all kinds of poetic beauty that which can be most universally appreciated' (CH, 88).

Finally, the poems themselves show how much more realistically and, in spite of their frequent humour, how seriously Tennyson now regarded his vocation. The poet was no longer the remote, exalted figure of 1830 but Will Waterproof or the speaker in 'Amphion' whose rueful conclusion is that:

> . . . *I must work through months of toil,*
> *And years of cultivation,*
> *Upon my proper patch of soil*
> *To grow my own plantation.*
> *I'll take the showers as they fall,*
> *I will not vex my bosom:*
> *Enough if at the end of all*
> *A little garden blossom.*
>
> (PT, 688)

---

[1] Principally 'The Gardener's Daughter', 'The Lord of Burleigh', 'Lady Clara Vere de Vere', 'Dora', 'The Flight' and the unpublished poems of 1836 and 1837 concerning Tennyson's disillusionment with Rosa Baring.

In many of the poems the problems of being 'a poet in the feverous days' were explored, either directly, as in 'The Epic', 'Edwin Morris' and 'The Golden Year', or obliquely, in 'Ulysses' and 'Tiresias' for example, through the exploration of subjects of central concern to the practice of poetry. Throughout all his deliberations Tennyson emerged as a poet anxious to define his role and justify his vocation in terms of social responsibility but not at the expense of poetic integrity and independence. From 'What Thor Said' (1832–3) to 'Will Waterproof' (1837) the resolve was 'to pap-meat-pamper not the times', 'nor cramp my heart, nor take Half-views of men and things'.

Up to 1842, Tennyson sold rather less than 1,000 volumes of poems and the £20 profit he and his brothers received from the 1827 volume was the only income from poetry he made during these early years. Almost certainly he lost money on the 1830 and 1832 volumes. After 1842, the position began to improve. Whereas *Poems* (1832) had sold only three hundred copies by 1835, the 1842 volumes, at 12s. for the two, sold five hundred in the first four months: 'according to Moxon's brother I have made a sensation' (*Mem.*, I, 212). A second edition was needed the next year, and by 1853 the eighth edition had been reached. Tennyson's sales at this time do not stand comparison with those of Martin Tupper's *Proverbial Philosophy* (1838), which by now was beginning to sell in the region of 5,000 copies annually, or even of Macaulay's *Lays of Ancient Rome* (1842), which was to sell 18,000 copies by 1850, but they are indicative of a sure and steady growth in Tennyson's appeal to a reading-public itself rapidly increasing at the time.

The reviewers of *Poems* (1842) were well aware of the changes taking place in the poetry-reading public as a result of the increased leisure, literacy and cultural aspirations of the middle-classes. Richard Monkton Milnes put the position very clearly. Poetry, he said, 'is now surely more respectable than it has ever been before in this country . . . every day [it] becomes more human, more true to the common heart of man'. The reason for this was the poet's new audience of 'the large and intelligent middle-class of this country' which had replaced aristocratic patrons and literary coteries as the most important readers and purchasers of poetry. This new influence, said Milnes, may be seen in the poetry of the period which was, in general, 'reflective or affectionate or pious . . . free from appeals to the baser passions and lower conditions of our nature' (CH, 137–38).

Milnes was not convinced that Tennyson was yet a fitting spokesman for this class and advised him in the future to 'be ever ready to sacrifice his fancy to the truth, his own world to the world of nature and of God . . . he must, in fact, reconcile his practical and his poetical existence, his dreams by night and his thoughts by day'.[1] Although their emphases differed, most of the reviewers required this 'reconciliation' (to use Milnes' word; Leigh Hunt called it a 'mixture') between what Francis Garden described in terms reminiscent of Mill as the 'natural', aesthetic tendency of the poet and his acquired 'cultural' duties and sympathies. The 'natural' was equated with the poet's inner world of personal feeling, imaginative intensity and heightened sensuous appreciation, and the 'cultural' with the 'real world' of common experience, of the 'daily thoughts, feelings and occupations similar to the rest of men'.[2] The reviewer in the *Spectator* observed the distinction but described it in different terms: 'the classical, presenting the most *general* view of things in the most natural manner: the *singular* which portrays some very limited reality and in whose portraiture the peculiar mind of the artist is prominent'.

The arguments harked back, quite consciously in most cases, to the criticisms of a decade earlier, usually with the intention, as in Spedding's case, of demonstrating how Tennyson had progressed from a 'wild and wanton' nonage to an appeal 'more to the heart and less to the ear and eye'. Francis Garden explicitly referred to Hallam's 'mistaken theory' which in his opinion had led Tennyson astray 'to revel amid visions of the beautiful, to surround himself with unreal images' to the exclusion of the 'fervant humanity' which was the hallmark of the great poets of the past.

According to Dean Bradley, immediately after 1842 there was an 'immense change' in Tennyson's reputation and 'his name was on everyone's lips, his poems discussed, criticized, interpreted' (*Mem.*, I,

[1] *Westminster Review*, XXXVIII, Oct. 1842, 390 & 372.
[2] *Christian Remembrancer*, VI, July 1842, 42–58 (CH, 102).

205). But Bradley referred to the university world at Oxford, and, in spite of the testimony of the old Radical Samuel Bamford, (*Mem.*, I, 283–5) there is not much evidence that Tennyson's reputation during the 1840s was at all widespread outside this sphere. For example, the *Penny Magazine*, a journal aimed at the lower middle-class and educated artisans, often included poems in its numbers but never one by Tennyson until 1845. In that year, when it had a weekly circulation of 40,000, it ran a series called 'The Year of the Poets' extending over eighteen issues and tracing the progress of the seasons by appropriate quotations with brief introductory comments. The magazine's taste was eclectic; Pope, Sidney, Jonson and Shelley shared a page in one issue, for instance. Tennyson was represented by one poem ('A spirit haunts the year's last hours') which was obviously included as the work of a contemporary minor poet no more, or even less, worthy of space than Joanna Baillie, Longfellow and Monkton Milnes. With this in mind, Aubrey de Vere's comment that Tennyson's 'larger fame made way so slowly' rings true; he continued, 'For many a year, we, his zealots were but zealots of a sect' (*Mem.*, I, 208) and considered that Tennyson's sectarian appeal lasted until at least the publication of *In Memoriam*. The views of those who did know and admire Tennyson's poems during the 1840s may be given in the words of Charles Kingsley's hero, Alton Locke, who found in the 1842 poems 'the embodiment of thoughts about the earth around me which I had concealed, because I fancied them peculiar to myself'. Of course this was Kingsley, not a typical 'working man' talking, and his middle-class, Broad-church sympathies were roused by what he called the 'specially democratic' tendency in Tennyson's poems which discovered in 'the trivial everyday sights and sounds of nature . . . in the hedgerow and the sandbank, as well as in the alp peak and the ocean waste . . . a world of true sublimity—a minute infinite—an ever fertile garden of poetic images, the roots of which are in the unfathomable and the eternal as truly as any phenomenon which astonishes and awes the eye'.[1] This kind of admiration, amounting at times to a hero-worship 'wild and uncritical . . . a sort of transcendental feeling which we call

[1] *Alton Locke* (1850) 1884, ch. IX, 104–5.

meteorosophia'[1] was common amongst the rising generation of poets and men of letters, some of whom—Swinburne, Meredith and James Thomson—were later to be Tennyson's severest critics. One whose devotion never waned was F. J. Palgrave; his 'hero-worship most utterly true and loyal' dated from his student days in the early 1840s and certainly influenced the *Golden Treasury* which in its turn moulded the poetical tastes of subsequent generations of Victorians.[2]

Of particular interest here are the comments of J. S. Mill on the new poems. The early poems he had thought the best since Coleridge but the new poems disappointed him. In a letter to Sterling he said that Tennyson had 'taken up . . . and miserably misunderstood' the theory that poetry should deal with the issues of its own age. 'Because mechanical things may generate grand results he thinks that there is grandeur in the naked statement of their most mechanical details'.[3] By 'mechanical details' Mill meant the topical references in 'Audley Court' and 'Walking to the Mail', 'and the *type* of what I object to is the three lines of introduction to "Godiva", which Mill, like Leigh Hunt,[4] believed Tennyson had included as a conciliatory or defiant gesture to topicality although incongruous to the spirit of the poems.

What J. W. Marston called a 'heterogeneous combination' of old and new was one of the main critical issues in the reception of *The Princess* in 1847. De Vere and Kingsley, both friends of Tennyson and possibly knowing his intention in the poem, tried to interpret its heterogeneity as 'a mirror of the nineteenth century, possessed of its own new art and science, its own new temptations and aspirations, and

---

[1] Richard Watson Dixon in a letter to Robert Bridges 1893, quoted James Sambrook, *A Poet Hidden*, 1962, 10.

[2] *A Golden Treasury* contained no Tennyson. This, Palgrave's biographer explained, was because of Tennyson's 'modesty in barring any lyrics from appearing . . . which had led Palgrave to exclude all living authors'. (G. F. Palgrave, *Francis Turner Palgrave*, 1899, 174. See *ibid.*, 37, 64 & 71 for comments on Tennyson's influence on *A Golden Treasury*).

[3] Letter to Sterling, Nov. 1842, *Earlier Letters*, ed Mineka, *Collected Works*, XIII 555-7.

[4] *Church of England Quarterly Review*, XLII, Sept. 1842 (CH, 132).

yet grounded on and continually striving to reproduce, the forms and experiences of all past time'.[1] But the general view was that 'lecture rooms and chivalric lists, modern pedantry and ancient romance, are antagonisms which no art can reconcile'.[2] Most critics, in fact, with Marston at their head, echoed Mill's complaint that although Tennyson was right to introduce problems and feelings from modern life into his poetry, his 'naked statement' of them was unsatisfactory; the familiar and topical required an idealized treatment to give it poetic credence. The implications throughout were that in *The Princess* Tennyson had attempted a reconciliation between his 'natural' tendency towards the picturesque and sensuous and an acquired 'cultural' concern with important issues of the day but that he had somehow failed in the task of amalgamation. As in 1842, there was a quite deliberate rehearsal by several critics of the arguments of fifteen years earlier. The terminology was changing but the notion that there were two kinds of poetic faculty, frequently mutually exclusive but co-existent in the greatest poets, was very persistent. Aubrey de Vere, whose review of *The Princess* in the *Edinburgh Review* earned Tennyson's gratitude (*Mem.*, I, 261), characterized the two kinds as 'vivid sympathy with reality on the one hand, or on the other, an ardent aspiration after the ideal . . . in the former interpreting the world to him[self], in the latter interpreting him to his fellow men . . . the one characterized by its plastic power and its function of embodying the abstractedly great and ideally beautiful; the other by its homebred sympathies, its affinities with natural history, character and manners'. Like Arthur Hallam, De Vere believed that the conditions of a civilization fostered one or other of the poetic types: 'if the age be a poetical one, the imagination will embody its sentiments, and illustrate its tendencies. If it be unpoetical . . . it will then create a world for itself—or revert to some historic period, the memorials of which it will invest with a radiance not their own'. A similar theme was taken up by the critic (possibly Lockhart) of the *Quarterly Review*. His argument was that how old a poet was determined the kind of poetry he wrote. In developing his case, the reviewer made explicit reference to Hallam's ideas on the two kinds of poetry and went

[1] Charles Kingsley, *Fraser's Magazine*, XLII, Sept. 1842, 250 (CH, 180).
[2] J. Westland Marston, *Athenaeum*, XXI, 1st Jan. 1848 (CH, 171).

on to suggest that poetry of sensation was youthful poetry, both in its authorship and in its appeal. The reviewer agreed with Hallam that such poetry was not generally appreciated and gave Shelley as an example of a poet of sensation whose admirers were 'almost confined to poets or students of poetry'. Tennyson, however, had progressed from this youthful and exclusive style to a more mature, reflective style which was gaining him more popularity than Shelley ever enjoyed amongst the many who 'wish but to find in any poem . . . a moral lesson or a tale of the heart in an ornate and compendious form'.

The Princess was commercially successful and remained so for many years. Two thousand copies at 5s. each were printed for the first edition and this was followed in three or four months by a second. There were seven editions by 1856 and seventeen by 1877, an indication that the poem, as well as the issues it raised, remained currently interesting. Of course Tennyson welcomed the popularity; it put an end to a relatively impoverished and miserable existence and enabled him to marry.

Shannon claims that the The Princess was considerably influenced by the reviewers of the 1842 Poems and that 'seldom has a poem owed so much to contemporary literary doctrines'. In a sense this was true in that Tennyson was by now a sincere adherent to the dominant literary philosophy of the time which Mill had so clearly propounded in his review of 1835—that there are two kinds of poetical power, the sensuous and the intellectual, and that the true poet unifies the two. But although The Princess was an attempt to put this creed into practice it was a highly original attempt and one which showed remarkable independence of the reviewers' advice. The woman-and-marriage question had long concerned Tennyson as one of the 'great social questions impending in England' (Mem., I, 249). He may have begun on The Princess as early as 1833 and he certainly talked the matter over with Emily Sellwood in 1839 (Mem., I, 248n). The Princess was therefore the culmination of years of thought on the subject and was no facile response to the critics' demand for poetry which mirrored the concerns of the age. The choice of subject showed a certain daring; the issue was topical, but only amongst a class of rather advanced thinkers, and Tennyson's handling of it—the even partial success of Ida's university and her grandeur and nobility in comparison with the men in the poem—was, for the times, almost revolutionary. As John Killham says, it was a 'serious attempt, artfully disguised, to change an outworn attitude to an important human problem'.[1]

Even the artful disguise was a refusal to conciliate the critics of his 1842 *Poems* who had disliked his legendary or historical poems. Sterling had disapproved of the Excalibur legend as 'not . . . very near to us' and Leigh Hunt had described 'the treatment of the modes and feelings of one generation in the style of another' as 'a thing fatal' (CH, 132), and had noticed Tennyson's 'involuntary exhibition of uneasiness' in relating the old to the new. Yet *The Princess* took shape in apparent disregard of these admonitions, its modern theme enshrined in a medieval setting and the link between the thematic present and the circumstantial past very consciously, even painfully, pointed out by the author. There was altogether a waywardness about *The Princess* that justified the critics' indignation. John Forster put it succinctly: 'he is worthy to be the poet of our time. Why does he not assume his mission? Why does he discredit it with trifling and with puerilities unworthy of him?'[2]

The alterations from the first to the third editions (the second edition having been published too soon after the first to allow for substantial revision) likewise indicated that Tennyson was not prepared to be craven in his response to criticism. Shannon has calculated that of the thirty-five passages in *The Princess* which were censured by critics, eight, or less than a quarter, were altered in the third edition. An examination of these revisions indicates that Tennyson altered when he thought the criticisms valid (over matters of obscurity, for instance) or when he realised that they pointed to some failure of the poem to convey what he had intended. A small instance of the latter can be seen in Tennyson's reply to Aubrey de Vere who had commented on the 'dying and the dead': 'Now I certainly did not mean to kill anyone, and therefore I put this new line into the old king's mouth, "I trust that there is no one hurt to death"' (*Mem.*, I, 261 and 282). A larger failure which concerned him more was Ida herself. Several critics, including

[1] *Tennyson and the Princess*, 1958, 3.
[2] *Examiner*, 8th Jan. 1848, 21.

De Vere, thought her 'a kind of monster' and this was certainly not
Tennyson's intention because he 'considered her as one of the noblest
among his women' (*Mem.*, I, 248). So he made alterations designed to
ennoble Ida and dignify the theme. One example was the insertion of
two lines before a passage which the *Quarterly Review* had condemned
as showing 'absence of refinement and failure of dignity and decorum'.
The offending lines, on the innkeeper, went thus:

> *For him, he reverenced his liege-lady there:*
> *He always made a point to post with mares;*
> *His daughter and his housemaid were the boys*
> *The land he understood for miles about*
> *Was till'd by women; all the swine were sows,*
> *And all the dogs—*

(PT, 757)

In the third edition, Tennyson prefaced these lines with, 'She once had
past that way; he heard her speak; She looked as grand as doomsday
and as grave'. Ida's dignity was increased and the innkeeper's vulgarity allowed to stand; Tennyson's own judgment and not the quibbles
of the reviewers, dictated the alterations.

The *Princess* did not prepare the Victorians for *In Memoriam*. The
Princess can be seen as a logical development of the style and forms of
many of the 1842 poems but only in a very few poems like 'The Deserted
House' and 'The Two Voices' had *In Memoriam* been anticipated. It
was, as the critic in the *Westminster Review* said, 'different . . . from
any work that could reasonably have been expected from him'. So,
in fact, when Tennyson finally decided to publish the 'elegies', having
found 'that I had written so many' (*Mem.*, I, 304), he was again risking
what reputation he had already earned by this new venture. The only
premonition of increased popularity came from personal friends like
Lushington and De Vere who warmly admired the individual lyrics
Tennyson read to them.

The publication of *In Memoriam* can further be seen as an act of
almost defiant independence of critical favour when it is remembered
that the poem's origins and shaping spirit belonged to the time when
Tennyson was most in critical disgrace and that in its intensely personal

preoccupations it was of the kind of poetry that had earned him this opprobrium. It was also a memorial to the man who, it had not been forgotten, had held the mistaken theories which led Tennyson astray. Very few of the reviewers of *In Memoriam* commented on the poem's subjectivity. Most acclaimed its 'popular' and universal qualities and were of a mind with George Henry Lewes who said, 'We shall be surprised if it does not become the solace and delight of every house where poetry is loved . . . All who have sorrowed will listen with delight'.[1] Coventry Patmore, however, felt the need to reconcile the poem's widespread moral and philosophical appeal with its obvious subjectivity. His explanation was that the subjectivity was so complete that it negated itself: 'the self-consciousness which, in most modern artists, has served only to intensify selfishness by offering a thousand fresh and plausible motives to its gratification, has arrived in the author of *In Memoriam* at a full conviction of the insignificance of self and of the sacred expediency of self-sacrifice'.[2]

More than any other of his poems, *In Memoriam* records Tennyson's concern about this very question of the relationship between the inner and outer worlds of the poet. In a sense, the debate between the two kinds of poetry governs the entire progress of a poem in which exceptional intensity of feeling is reflected and generalized on. More explicitly, the poem traces a movement, albeit a tentative one, from a use of poetry as mere personal release, 'a sad mechanic exercise, Like dull narcotics, numbing pain' (V), to a vision of the Muses in which:

> . . . *one would sing the death of war,*
> *And one would chant the history*
> *Of that great race, which is to be,*
> *And one the shaping of a star.*   (CIII)

Yet the main interest in the dialogue on poetry lies not in this simple development from self to the world but in the poet's self-conscious exploration of his own motivations. The exploration is presented dramatically; several reasons for the poetic activity are given—it soothes the mourner (V; LXXV), it would have pleased the dead man

---

[1] *Leader*, 22nd June 1850, 303–4.
[2] *North British Review* XIII, Aug. 1850, 551.

(VIII; XXXVIII) and builds a shrine for him (LVII) and above all it is a compulsive utterance of love and grief as spontaneous as a linnet's song (XXI; XXXVII; LXXVII)—and the total impression derived from these is of a reflective intelligence at work upon its own emotional and aesthetic resources and, by means of this 'thinking aloud', creating a rapport between itself and a potential audience. This exploration of self, of that special poetic self whose sensations Hallam had thought incomprehensible to all but a few, becomes the means by which the poetic experience is projected into the consciousness of others. The frequently diffident and apologetic tone the poet adopts, the deliberate underestimate of his powers, further establishes a sympathetic relationship between himself and his readers.

In others ways too, *In Memoriam* sought a popular audience. Tennyson had the wisdom of hindsight when he said to James Knowles in 1869, 'It is rather the cry of the whole human race than mine. In the poem altogether private grief swells out into thought of, and hope for, the whole world.'[1] Yet some such desire to 'speak to the hearts of all' (Hallam's words to describe the great popular writers of antiquity) was almost certainly present throughout its composition, even from the very beginning. Ironically, to mourn Arthur Hallam, Tennyson chose to write in the tradition of popular reflective and religious verse which had produced Robert Montgomery's *Omnipresence of the Deity* (for although *In Memoriam* is a much better poem than Montgomery's, it is not essentially different in kind) and, more important, a body of fine hymn-writing from Watts and the Wesleys to James Montgomery. Through the resemblances in imagery, diction and form which many of the lyrics in *In Memoriam* have to such well-known hymns as Wesley's 'Author of Faith, Eternal Word' and 'We Know, By Faith We Know', Tennyson exploited the familiar devotional responses of his readers. How conscious this exploitation was is difficult to assess. There was an edition of Wesleys' *Hymns* at Somersby and Tennyson may well have remembered it at the time of Hallam's death as a model for poetry which would provide 'a means of raising or quickening the spirit of devotion; of confirming his faith, of enlivening his hope; and of kindling

---

[1] 'Aspects of Tennyson', *Nineteenth Century*, XXXIII, Jan. 1893, 182.

and increasing his love to God and man'. In terms almost equally relevant to *In Memoriam*, Wesley went on to describe the hymns as containing 'nothing turgid or bombast, on the one hand, or low and creeping on the other . . . there are no cant expressions; no words without meaning . . . there are both the purity, the strength and the elegance of the English language; and, at the same time, the utmost simplicity and plainness, suited to every capacity'. Tennyson acknowledged the Wesleys' achievement when he said, 'A good hymn is the most difficult thing in the world to write. In a good hymn you have to be common-place and poetical' (*Mem.*, II, 401). 'Common-place and poetical'— he could have been describing *In Memoriam* in which, more perhaps than in any other of his poems, the search for a union of 'high imagination and intense popular feeling' (*Mem.*, I, 123) was satisfied.

By 1852 Tennyson was an established figure: he was Poet Laureate and *In Memoriam* had sold 25,000 copies since its publication. Yet far from being a complacent time in his life, this year saw him shaken by a social and political distress which brought him into conflict with his official position. The immediate issue was the *coup d'état* by Louis Napoleon in 1852 and the threat of French invasion during the months afterwards. Tennyson's political poems of this period[1] were primarily a call to arms to defend Britain's ancient freedoms against 'this French God, the child of Hell'. The poems also anticipated the attacks in *Maud* on complacent commercialism and social injustice:

> *I feel the thousand cankers of our state,*
> *I fain would shake their triple-folded ease,*
> *The hogs who can believe in nothing great,*
> *Sneering bedridden in the down of Peace,*
> *Over their scrips and shares, their meats and wine,*
> *With stony smirks at all things human and divine!*

('Suggested by Reading an Article in a Newspaper': PT, 1005–6)

As Poet Laureate, however, Tennyson was in a rather delicate position

---

[1] 'The Penny-Wise', 'Rifle Clubs', 'Britons, Guard Your Own', 'For the Penny-Wise', 'The Third of February, 1852', 'Hands All Round', 'Suggested by Reading an Article in a Newspaper' (See PT, 994–1007).

at this time. In the first place, Britain's official relations with Napoleon III were cordial, although popular feeling, particularly amongst Liberals and Radicals, was hostile. Secondly, an attack on Britain's 'commercial mire', though perhaps all very well from Carlyle, who had reopened the Condition of England question with his *Latter-day Pamphlets* of 1850, and with whom Tennyson was by now quite intimate [*Mem.*, I, 267 and 340], was not the expected thing from a newly-appointed Laureate writing only a few months after the opening of the Great Exhibition. Therefore these emotional and outspoken poems were published anonymously or under the names Merlin and Taliessin in periodicals. 'The Ode on the Death of the Duke of Wellington', Tennyson's first official Laureate publication, was an interesting compromise between his personal convictions and his official position. Napoleon III was condemned by inference: the noble Duke was 'clearest of ambitious crime', and his 'eighty winters freeze with one rebuke, All great self-seekers trampling on the right'. The virulent social criticism of the Merlin and Taliessin poems was modified into a decorous reminder to statesmen of their duty to 'save mankind/Till public wrong be crumbled into dust,/And drill the raw world for the march of mind,/Till crowds at length be sane and crowns be just' (166–9). Looked at closely, the poem was not very specific about the Duke at all; his leadership in war, for instance, was little mentioned. Instead the Duke was used as a point of reference for all Tennyson's most dearly held beliefs on liberty, patriotism, constitutional monarchy and gradual social reform. The Ode summarized the political thought of twenty years.[1]

Paul Baum calls the poem 'Laureate work'[2] but the critics of the time did not think so and were loud in their disappointment at its lack of martial splendour and heroic solemnity. What had pleased in *In Memoriam*—tenderness of memory and the idealization of the commonplace—did not suit here. *The Times* said there was 'less of grandeur than of beauty' and that rather than a requiem for a great soldier it was a summons 'to weep because a brother has gone from us' (Nov. 15th 1852). Lewes, in the *Leader*, called it 'an intrinsically poor performance

---

[1] See E. F. Shannon, 'Tennyson's Ode on the Death of Wellington', *Studies in Bibliography*, XXII, 1960, 149–77.
[2] *Tennyson Sixty Years After*, 1963, 247.

. . . The substance of the Ode is made up of common-place reflections; the form wants the redeeming splendour of imagery befitting a great event'. Amongst the general public the poem was only moderately successful considering the fame of both its subject and its author. A. H. Clough said he was one of its few admirers, but more than Clough thought must have at least bought the poem. Moxon ordered 10,000 copies for the first edition (published 16th November 1852) at 1/- each and although in January 1853 Tennyson was complaining to his wife that 'only about 6,000' had been sold, this was sufficient for Moxon to produce a second edition in late February, or early March, 1853. But if Tennyson was very gloomy at the poem's reception, characteristically overlooking what favourable comments there were, he again did not allow this to influence his revisions of the poem at the expense of his poetic integrity.

Maud was the most violent and the most controversial poem that Tennyson wrote. It was also the major poem of his first full-length volume as Poet Laureate. Again, it took his critics by suprise; they were eager for a new volume but were not prepared by *In Memoriam* or the Ode for what followed in *Maud*. There seems to be little doubt that *Maud* was influenced by the work of the Spasmodic poets. Tennyson had admired P. J. Bailey's *Festus* as early as 1846,[1] and also thought well of Alexander Smith and Sidney Dobell (*Mem.*, I, 264 and 468; II, 73) whose *Life-Drama* and *Balder* were published in 1852 and 1853 respectively. Tennyson had begun work on the Arthurian legend by this time but he laid this aside for *Maud*, the composition of which occupied him during the last six months of 1854. The Spasmodic controversy had come to its climax during the first six months of that year with W. E. Aytoun's advance 'review' of *Firmilian* in May and the publication of *Firmilian* itself, by 'T. Percy Jones', in July. Almost immediately the critical climate began to change from widespread adulation to general condemnation.[2] Tennyson cannot have been ignorant of *Firmilian* which received great acclaim as 'the most perfect as it is the most elaborate and

[1] *Mem.*, I, 234 and Charles Tennyson, *Alfred Tennyson*, 1949, 215.
[2] M. A. Weinstein, *William Edmondstoune Aytoun and the Spasmodic Controversy*, New York and London 1968, 153.

the most legitimate parody that has ever been written',[1] and he must have been aware even during the middle months of 1854, that it was becoming too late to write a Spasmodic poem. The tide was turning against passionately introspective Byronic heroes and extravagant imagery and the call once again was for restraint, intelligibility, good sense and what the *North British Review* called 'the real in poetry'. P. J. Bailey's *Festus* (1839) which served as a model for the later Spasmodics, had been written in reaction to these qualities which, during the 1830s, were epitomized by *Philip Van Artevelde*. Now the balance was being redressed again and once more Tennyson was caught out of phase.

In his famous 'review' of *Firmilian*, Aytoun, the arch-foe of the Spasmodics, had listed four characteristic vices in their poetry: no clear plot, profanity, prurience and lack of intelligibility. The reviewers had no difficulty in finding these vices in *Maud* and classed the poem with the other 'maniacal howls' of the period. Aytoun described it as 'unhappy, unwholesome, and disagreeable'[2] and Coventry Patmore (who was nevertheless quite sympathetic towards it) saw it as pitched in 'the key of extraordinarily high poetic sensibility . . . with almost total irresponsibility on the part of the poet'.[3] Though there were favourable comments, the majority of the reviewers subjected Tennyson to some of the most scathing abuse of his career.[4] The most controversial issue was the war-mongering ending of the poem, not so much from an abhorrence of war but because, as Goldwin Smith put it, 'to wage "war with a thousand battles and shaking a hundred thrones" in order to cure a hypochondriac and get rid of chicory in coffee, is a bathos'.[5]

In spite of the critical abuse, *Maud, and Other Poems* sold very well. Perhaps 'The Brook', which was included in the volume and was acclaimed by the reviewers (of its type 'incomparable . . . we wish that

1 *The Times*, 27th February 1856, 4.
2 *Blackwood's Magazine*, LXXVIII, Sept. 1855, 315.
3 *Edinburgh Review*, CII, Oct. 1855, 512–3.
4 See E. F. Shannon, 'The Critical Reception of Tennyson's *Maud*', *PMLA*, LXVIII, 1953, 397–417.
5 *Saturday Review*, 3 Nov. 1855, quoted Shannon, 'The Critical Reception of *Maud*', 404. See also CH, 187.

he might ever do nothing but that', said Patmore), contributed to the success but it alone could not have sold the 8,000 copies in three months that Moxon boasted of in October 1855. Tennyson bought Farringford with the proceeds. He was, of course, very hurt by the critical reception of *Maud* but he ought not to have been surprised in view of the controversy which raged over the Spasmodics before and during the writing of the poem. For a man so notoriously sensitive to criticism, the wonder is that he embarked on such a venture which, by his remarks on the poem (*Mem.*, I, 296 and 402), he surely knew would be classed with *A Life-Drama* and *Balder*. It may have been simply that he wished to share in the Spasmodics' popularity and underestimated the reaction to their style of poetry. But Tennyson's imitation of other poets was always motivated by more subtle and compelling reasons than the wish to be fashionable and the likelihood is that Spasmodic poems suggested to him new ways in which his lyrical and satiric gifts could be combined within a protective dramatic framework. G. H. Lewes, in *The Leader*, was right when he said that *Maud* 'does not develop any positively new gift in Tennyson, it shows his gifts in new combination'. In fact, *Maud* was a complete *résumé* of what had gone before; every feature of it had been anticipated, individually, in previous poems. It was a brilliant attempt to combine in one poem what he had been taught to believe were warring elements within his poetic nature. The monodramatic form, using as sole speaker a man in or near a state of madness, permitted a range and flexibility of expression entirely to Tennyson's purpose here.

The critics could not accept the excuse of madness for the excesses of the poem. The old cry was raised again that Tennyson had 'somehow or other been led astray by poetic theories' (Aytoun) but criticism was now interestingly divided on what constituted the falsity in Tennyson's art. Aytoun was one of the most vehement of those who disliked the heightened emotional effects, believing they resulted in poetry that was either 'exceedingly silly' ('Go not, happy day') or 'a screed of bombast'. Other critics liked the love sections but thought the political and social satire ill-conceived and ill-done. 'The fever of politics should not have been caught by the Laureate even under the disguise of a monomaniac,' said Patmore and went on to regret that Tennyson had got hold of the 'oddest' notion that 'a poet must belong to his age'. The echo of Hallam's theories is even stronger in Patmore's comments on those sections of *Maud*—'I have led her home' was an example—which he particularly liked: 'This kind of poetry, which is almost a modern invention, and of which Mr Tennyson is probably the greatest master, asks to be read, as it was written, in a mood in which reflection voluntarily abandons for a time its mental leadership; and thought follows, instead of guiding, the current of emotion.'

The years 1859 to 1864, which G. M. Young has described as the dawning of the late Victorian age,[1] were the high tide of Tennyson's reputation. During these years he became the most popular living poet this country had known. He silenced the criticisms which had dogged his youth and the criticism of reaction was as yet scarcely to be heard. *The Idylls of the King* (1859)[2] sold 10,000 copies in the first week, *Enoch Arden* sold more than 40,000 copies in 1864, the year of its publication, and earned Tennyson over £5,000. Many reviewers were prompted to comment on Tennyson's popularity, 'at once great, growing and select', as Gladstone said, and to debate whether such popularity was 'an argument against the permanence of his fame', or 'proves the existence of genius'. On the whole there were few misgivings about Tennyson's popularity and the conclusion was rather that, as the *Quarterly* said, 'the English people are to be congratulated on their choice'. With the *Idylls* Tennyson hit the taste of both his public and his critics and it was, as Alfred Austin said, 'settled once and for all that he is a great poet'. *The Times,* which previously had been very severe on Tennyson's poems, was now prepared to rank him with Milton as 'a great and original genius'.

Criticism in 1859 was most exercised over the choice of the Arthurian legends for the new poems. As Kathleen Tillotson has pointed out,[3] Tennyson pioneered the subject for the nineteenth century and even as late as 1859 it was still an unfamiliar myth to many people. Although the *North British Review* said that 'of late years there has been a great development of the feeling in favour of this subject', it and other

[1] *Victorian England: Portrait of an Age*, 1953, 102.
[2] Comprised of *Enid, Vivien, Elaine* and *Guinevere.*
[3] 'Tennyson's Serial Poem', *Mid-Victorian Studies*, 1965, 82.

journals felt it necessary to preface their criticism of Tennyson's poems with information on Arthur and the literature concerning him. When the *Saturday Review* described the material as 'a forgotten cycle of fables which never attained the dignity or substance of a popular mythology', it was voicing a quite widespread reaction to the Round Table legends. Yet only a few critics thought the subject unsuitable. The *Westminster Review* admired the adaptation of old material to modern needs but thought Tennyson could have done even better with a modern subject: the Arthurian legends 'do not touch us so nearly as they should do because they bear about them an air of distance'. Ludlow, in *Macmillan's Magazine*, thought the subject élitist, 'far removed from the great mass of readers', and the *Saturday Review* reminded Tennyson that he had successfully reproduced modern life in *Maud* and the domestic Idyls and regretted that he had not done so again here. But most reviewers assumed that Tennyson's choice had not been based merely on antiquarian interests but was laudably concerned to shed 'fire from the fountains of the past to glorify the present'. Arthur, said Gladstone, was the supreme national and Christian hero, 'human in the largest and deepest sense; and therefore though highly national [his story] is universal'. The *British Quarterly Review* said that 'the meadow of Camelot represents the field of the world's battle' and that the characterization 'touches us with a sense of the social truths that are of all time'. In general, the critics accepted Tennyson's own view that in the *Idylls* he had 'restored the idealism, and infused into the legends a spirit of modern thought and an ethical significance' (*Mem.*, II, 122).

Yet is it worth remembering that the *Idylls* of 1859, more obviously then than now when they are usually read within the larger moral framework of the completed sequence, were daringly concerned with adultery and seduction, and treated of immorality more than *Maud* had done. Yet only a few readers were offended on this score and the generally respectful tone of the reviewing was in marked contrast to the reception of *Maud*. The difference was that the *Idylls* observed a poetic decorum where *Maud* had not. The emotional intensity and vehement social satire of the earlier poem was transposed in the *Idylls* into the quieter key of romance narrative told in a style of measured, even austere, elegance. The sensuous and violent elements in Tennyson's conception were largely subsumed into the 'ethical significance' of the stories and, as never before, his imagery and characterization could be seen as functional towards a moral end.

With the *Idylls*, and even more with *Enoch Arden*, it was widely agreed that Tennyson had at last successfully mediated between the two kinds of poetry. The reviewer of *Enoch Arden* in the *Quarterly*, praising Tennyson's 'self-culture', summarized the whole debate: 'the imaginative writers of the present time, if they are to rise to high literary rank, must have knowledge as well as genius. . . . Success is achieved, not by natural powers alone, but also by deep study and thought. Those works which in our own day have a living meaning and interest for us were not brought forth as mothers bring forth beautiful children, but were self-conscious efforts, the equal products of passion and reflection'. Walter Bagehot, in the *National Review*, saw the issue in terms of Tennyson's increasing desire to reach a popular audience: his early poetry was 'written, almost professedly, for young people—especially young men—of rather heated imaginations' but 'Everybody admires Tennyson now [1859]' because he 'has sided with the world' (CH, 216–17). But as far as the *Idylls* were concerned, one or two reviewers still considered that Tennyson had not yet reached a really popular level and urged him to write poetry which would 'go straight home to the hearts of the great mass of his countrymen, by broad pictures of human pathos, and clear exhibitions of lofty purpose'. This was J. M. Ludlow's comment in *Macmillan's Magazine* which may well have influenced Tennyson's choice of subject in *Enoch Arden*. Ludlow's whole review turned very much on the question of how far Tennyson was capable of becoming 'a poet of the people'. Ludlow himself had known an audience of poor women in Soho amused by 'Amphion' and had heard a group of working men declaim *Maud*, but the *Idylls* were a different matter and reinforced the view that the colouring in Tennyson's poetry 'is too luscious for the dwellers amid grey smoke and fog; his thought is too subtle even for cultivated minds, let alone the rude; his style is too peculiar for the unlettered'. But when *Enoch Arden* was published it seemed, at least to the critic in *Chambers' Journal*, a paper similar to the *Penny Magazine* in price (1½d) and popular appeal, that Ludlow's strictures had been answered: 'A child may understand it; and the wisest man that ever wore grey hairs need not be ashamed to own the power of its tenderness'. Ludlow was in a minority in caring about the Unknown Public.[1] Most critics, truly representative of middle-class reading tastes, considered the style of the *Idylls* one of 'perfect naturalness and ease' and contrasted this with the mannerisms and exaggerations of earlier poems, particularly *Maud*. Robert Bridges blamed Tennyson for educating the poetry-reading audience 'to be specially observant of blemishes and . . . to regard finish not only as indispensible, but as the one satisfying positive quality'.[2] But such an audience existed before Tennyson became its spokesman and until 1859 he had always surprised or shocked it in matters of style. Certainly neither *In Memoriam* nor *Maud* are 'finished' and unblemished in the sense Bridges meant.

Many of Tennyson's friends and early admirers welcomed the *Idylls* as 'maturer and better than any poetry he has written hitherto'.[3] 'How fine the *Idylls* are!' said Dickens, 'Lord! What a blessed thing it is to read a man who can write.'[4] This was in a letter to Forster, who was himself so moved by the 'touching words' of the poems that he wept.[5] And of course there was praise from Macaulay, Prince Albert, the proprietor of *The Times*, and Thackeray who wrote of 'the splendour of happiness' the *Idylls* had given him (*Mem.*, I, 444–455). But to others, particularly of the younger generation, the *Idylls* marked 'the point at which some disciples were sensible of a partial refrigeration of their zeal'.[6]

---

[1] This was the name given by Wilkie Collins in 1858 (*Household Words* XVIII, 217–22) to the three million or so (that is 50%) of the reading public who read nothing but penny-novel journals. Collins's phrase caught on; twenty-five years later, for instance, the *Nineteenth Century* (XIII, 1883, 279–96) contained an article 'Concerning the Unknown Public' in which the writer recorded that Collins's 'lost literary tribes' now numbered five million. Tennyson never really penetrated into this audience, even towards the end of the century when cheap editions were plentiful.

[2] 'Richard Watson Dixon', *Three Friends*, 1932, p. 139.

[3] A. H. Clough, *Correspondence*, 2 vol., ed F. L. Mulhauser, 1957, II, 539.

[4] *Letters of Charles Dickens*, 2 vol., ed M. Dickens and G. Hogarth, 1880, II, 98.

[5] Walter White, *Journals*, 1898, 149.

[6] Leslie Stephen, *Studies of a Biographer*, 1907, II 192.

Maud had been widely condemned, but its experimental, iconoclastic nature had at least left open the question of 'Where next?' But it seemed to some that with the *Idylls*, which were, one journal triumphantly said, 'a tacit admission that in *Maude* [sic] he had taken a false step', Tennyson settled down, became respectable and predictable. 'After *In Memoriam* and *Maud*', said Sidney Colvin, 'these Arthurian idylls had been to many a grievous disappointment. In spite of their sustained and subtle filagree finish of execution and many exquisite passages, we felt they were but tame drawing-room versions of the great Arthur legends, versions into which the taint of the Victorian age and of Victorian ethics had passed with paralysing effect'.[1]

James Smetham recorded as early as 1864 that 'the rabies for Tennyson has passed with the public'[2] but, as we have seen, the sales of *Enoch Arden* do not support this as far as the general public was concerned. Yet there was a growing disaffection in the literary world, different in kind from the old criticisms of Tennyson and prophetic of the later revulsion against his Victorianism. Arnold's and Bagehot's comments of 1862 and 1864[3] on Tennyson's elaborate and ornate style were the first public statements of this new discontent. Others, however, like Swinburne and Meredith, both boyhood worshippers at the shrine, were now complaining privately of the sanctimony of the *Idylls*[4] and *Enoch Arden*'s appeal 'to the depraved Sentimentalism of our drawing-rooms'.[5] James Thomson 'B.V.', for instance, writing on Blake in 1865, depreciated Tennyson as 'an exquisite carver of luxuries on ivory' with 'scanty revenues of thought. . . . Nothing gives one a keener insight into the want of robustness in the educated England of the age than the fact that nine-

[1] Sidney Colvin, *Memories and Notes*, 1921, 66.
[2] Quoted Amy Cruse, *The Victorians and Their Books*, 1935, 199.
[3] Matthew Arnold, 'Last Words on Translating Homer' (1862), *Complete Prose Works*, ed R. H. Super, New York 1960, I, 204–7. Walter Bagehot, 'Wordsworth, Tennyson and Browning', *National Review*, NS I, Nov. 1864, 27–66 (See also CH, 282–93).
[4] Letter to Lord Houghton, March 1864, *Letters of A. C. Swinburne*, ed Gosse and Wise, 2 vol., 1918, I, 21.
[5] Letter to Augustus Jessop, Dec. 1864, *Letters of George Meredith*, ed. C. L. Cline, 3 vol., 1970, I, 297.

tenths of our best-known literary men look upon him as a profound philosopher'.[1]

By the 1870s, the reaction was really under way. In 1869 Afred Austin had quoted Carlyle's 'the completeness of a limited mind'[2] with reference to Tennyson, Swinburne in *Under the Microscope* (1872) was demonstrating that Tennyson had 'lowered the note and deformed the outline of the Arthurian story' by a prurient and narrow-minded morality, and a year later W. J. Courthope was complaining of Tennyson's 'tendency to treat language, which ought to be the living vehicle of thought, as the mere inanimate material of style'[3]—and so it went on. These complaints have a modern ring and anticipate the critical tendency of this century to see the natural genius of Tennyson as warped and limited by cultural pressures. But such a view oversimplifies Tennyson's response to his age and does less than justice to the originality and complexity of his poetry. As we have seen, there was nothing forced in Tennyson's interest in the social and political issues featured in his poems. Indeed the problem, particularly in *The Princess* and *Maud,* was rather to contain his social impulses within a proper 'poetic' setting. Social commitment was, in fact, as 'natural' to him as the tendency to write picturesque imagery. Furthermore, his treatment of contemporary issues was frequently highly original and often even daring. In this respect, the Tennyson of the Cambridge period never quite disappeared but remained to qualify his future popular aspirations and to strengthen his resistence to the less sensitive and intelligent critical demands made on him. At the very least, Hallam's critical influence served to remind him that reflective verse can easily become platitudinous and that popularity is a commodity to be purchased warily.

Finally, it must be granted that the critical climate in which Tennyson wrote was not as stifling as has often been supposed. Much modern criticism has focused on the two voices in Tennyson's poetry, assuming that the inner voice of sensuous intensity was the forbidden fruit of his

[1] Quoted by H. S. Salt, *The Life of James Thomson* (*'B.V.'*), 1889, 289.
[2] *Temple Bar*, XXVI, May 1869, revised as 'Mr Tennyson' in *The Poetry of the Period*, 1870. See CH, 297.
[3] 'The State of English Poetry', *Quarterly Review*, CXXXV, July 1873, 18.

labours, to be snatched at in moments of dream or vision or under the guise of historical parable. But in general, the critics of his time sanctioned and encouraged the two voices in their consistent appeal for poetry which combined the natural and cultivated talents of a poet. Although their insistence on this duality may have promoted in Tennyson a false sense of the tension and division between the aesthetic and reflective elements in his nature, it nevertheless challenged his versatility and allowed him immense scope for the development of his complex poetic personality.

4: *Tennyson's Religious Faith and Doubt*

JOHN D. JUMP

THE INTERESTING question about Tennyson's religious faith and doubt is not what reasons he gives for his doubt and for his faith but how he communicates these states of mind in his poetry. His arguments contribute little to theology, but the poems in which he voices his spiritual insights, aspirations and fears contain much of his finest writing.

Conspicuously the most agitated of his juvenile poems is that which appeared in his volume of 1830 under the cumbrous title, 'Supposed Confessions of a Second-Rate Sensitive Mind Not in Unity with Itself'. He dropped the last five words when he republished the poem in 1884, but even after curtailment the title protests too much. Robert Browning feels no need to announce a 'Supposed Soliloquy of the Spanish Cloister' and T. S. Eliot feels no need to announce 'The Supposed Love Song of J. Alfred Prufrock'. It is not their business to cast doubt on their own fictions. Nor do they see fit to affix disparaging labels to their characters. They know that the only poetic way of establishing the second-rate nature of a monologist's mind is by making the reader aware of an other-than-second-rate mind as finally responsible for the form taken by the monologist's words.

In the poem itself, Tennyson does nothing to prevent us from identifying the monologist with the author. The 'Confessions' come from a man who has sought truth by doubting all that can be doubted:

> *Shall we not look into the laws*
> *Of life and death, and things that seem,*
> *And things that be, and analyse*
> *Our double nature, and compare*
> *All creeds till we have found the one,*
> *If one there be?*

(PT, 202)

These have been his methods, and this his aim. Now, far from having found a truth upon which he can repose, he acknowledges in himself a frightened longing for the Christian faith which he imbibed in childhood but has repudiated:

> *How sweet to have a common faith!*
> *To hold a common scorn of death!*
> *And at a burial to hear*
> *The creaking cords which wound and eat*
> *Into my human heart, whene'er*
> *Earth goes to earth, with grief, not fear,*
> *With hopeful grief, were passing sweet!*

(PT, 198)

The hope to which he alludes in this last line, the hope of the immortality of the soul, was to remain a lifelong preoccupation with Tennyson.

'Supposed Confessions' is one of the more successful of the 1830 poems. Though a patent fraud as a dramatic monologue, it compels respect as an intimate and moving piece of self-revelation. At the same time, neither the emotional disturbance which it records nor the exclamations which punctuate and conclude it quite rescue it from monotony.

In his next important religious poem, 'The Two Voices', started in 1833 but not published until 1842, Tennyson reduced the risk of monotony by employing more than one speaker. The narrator tells how he was tempted to despair and suicide by an insidious, sceptical voice. He reports its speeches of temptation at length, as also his own replies. Then, in the last few dozen lines, the second voice of the title encourages him to hope and to rejoice.

His dialogue with the sceptical voice seems to shift from one particular topic to another without deliberate plan. Nevertheless, there is a general progression. At first the narrator upholds the dignity of man, who is 'so wonderfully made' (l. 6); the race has dominion over the earth, and each of its members is unique. He then speaks of the achievements possible to the race and to its individual members. Finally he speculates on man's place in the metaphysical scheme, his condition before birth, and the condition that will be his after death.

The sceptical voice never flatly contradicts him. Instead, it takes what he has said and extends or elaborates it in such a way as to sap the assurance it gives him. Thus, when the narrator claims that man has dominion over the earth, the voice observes that in a boundless universe he must have many superiors; when the narrator assumes the uniqueness of his own individuality, the voice reduces him to tears by asking ironically who will feel the removal of this unique being; and, when he admires the progress achieved by human endeavour, the voice asks what possible significance progress along an infinite scale can have.

The second voice, too, develops what the narrator already has in mind. Despite the sceptical spirit's sneer at 'the Sabbath morn' (l. 402), the sight of the three members of a churchgoing family illustrates and confirms the narrator's statement that it is 'More life, and fuller, that I want' (l. 399). He blesses them as they pass, and the second voice at once assures him of 'A hidden hope' (l. 441) and enables him

> *To feel, although no tongue can prove,*
> *That every cloud, that spreads above*
> *And veileth love, itself is love.*

(PT, 541)

The two voices, starting from what the narrator says and thinks but moving in opposite directions from each other, evidently represent alternative possibilities within himself. Similar possibilities exist in the speaker of 'Supposed Confessions', but by projecting them into separate voices Tennyson has given the later poem a variety, a clarity, and even an incisiveness lacking in the earlier one.

The attitudes which prevail are characteristic of him. The lines just quoted illustrate that intuitive and confessedly unverifiable sense of the divine love to which he is to give fuller expression in *In Memoriam*. Earlier in the poem he has taken up the question, already briefly raised in 'Supposed Confessions', of the immortality of the soul. All living things appear to face extinction at death. If man is no exception, how does he come to suppose that he is? The narrator speaks:

> *Why, if man rot in dreamless ease,*
> *Should that plain fact, as taught by these,*
> *Not make him sure that he shall cease?*

Who forged that other influence,
That heat of inward evidence,
By which he doubts against the sense?

He owns the fatal gift of eyes,
That read his spirit blindly wise,
Not simple as a thing that dies.

Here sits he shaping wings to fly:
His heart forebodes a mystery:
He names the name Eternity.

That type of Perfect in his mind
In Nature can he nowhere find.
He sows himself on every wind.

He seems to hear a Heavenly Friend,
And through thick veils to apprehend
A labour working to an end.

(PT, 534)

The verse of 'The Two Voices' develops a characteristic range of cadences. Whereas the thought of 'Supposed Confessions' proves its urgency in syntactical structures which sweep across the precise limits of the irregularly rhyming tetrameter lines, that of 'The Two Voices' discreetly accommodates itself to the rhyming tetrameter triplets, most of them complete in themselves, which Tennyson now adopts. Again and again, the third line of a triplet is crucial. It may be illustrative, for example, or climactic, or aphoristic. However used, it is likely to be followed by a brief pause, after which the thought collects itself for a further limited advance. All three speakers proceed in this slow, deliberative, brooding rhythm. Tennyson's record of anxious and tentative exploration has found a form that suits it well.

For a long time, critics followed Hallam Tennyson, the poet's son and biographer, in believing that 'The Two Voices' was begun while Tennyson was shattered by grief at the death of the much loved and admired Arthur Hallam. But news of Hallam's death, which had occurred in Vienna on 15 September 1833, reached his friend only on 1 October, and Christopher Ricks has shown that a draft of the poem was in existence by 22 June 1833 (PT, 522). So Hallam's death cannot have prompted 'The Two Voices'. Nevertheless, some time elapsed before Tennyson finished the poem, and we need not doubt that the bereavement deeply influenced it in the form it eventually took. According to the poet, an almost immediate outcome of his 'sense of loss and that all had gone by, but that still life must be fought out to the end,'[1] was 'Ulysses', written on 20 October 1833. *In Memoriam*, however, gives richer and fuller expression both to the loneliness and desolation which he experienced on learning of his friend's death and to the hope which eventually he wrung from a state bordering on despair. *In Memoriam* must unquestionably occupy the chief place in any consideration of Tennyson's religious writings. At the same time, we have a reminder from Tennyson himself that

this is a poem, *not* an actual biography. It is founded on our friendship, on the engagement of Arthur Hallam to my sister, on his sudden death at Vienna, just before the time fixed for their marriage, and on his burial at Clevedon Church. The poem concludes with the marriage of my youngest sister Cecilia. It was meant to be a kind of *Divina Commedia*, ending with happiness. The sections were written at many different places, and as the phases of our intercourse came to my memory and suggested them. I did not write them with any view of weaving them into a whole, or for publication, until I found that I had written so many. The different moods of sorrow as in a drama are dramatically given, and my conviction that fear, doubts, and suffering will find answer and relief only through Faith in a God of Love. 'I' is not always the author speaking of himself, but the voice of the human race speaking thro' him. After the Death of A. H. H., the divisions of the poem are made by First Xmas Eve (Section xxviii), Second Xmas (lxxviii), Third Xmas Eve (civ and cv etc.).

(*Mem.*, I, 304)

As early as the year of Hallam's death, Tennyson started to write the lyrics which eventually became the sections of *In Memoriam*; by 1842, he had composed about one half of them; and in 1850 he published the long philosophical poem into which he had shaped them. He made very

[1] James Knowles, 'Aspects of Tennyson, II', *Nineteenth Century*, XXXIII, January 1893, 182 (See also CH, 172).

few changes in later editions. For the published version he arranged the sections, written in fact over a period of seventeen years, to suggest an emotional and spiritual development completed in three years. As he explained, the three Christmases define this fictional span. They also serve, like the other anniversaries that he notes, to mark stages in the development which the poem records: for example, the first Christmas Eve falls 'sadly' (xxx), the second 'calmly' (lxxviii), and the third 'strangely' (cv).

On another occasion, Tennyson pointed out that the sections form nine natural groups or divisions.[1] The initial, unnumbered lyric, 'Strong Son of God, immortal Love', falls outside these. A hymn to the divine love which we embrace by faith alone and not in consequence of any rational proof, it seems to be less a prologue than a summing-up. An appended date, 1849, confirms that this is so.

The lyrics which open the poem proper describe the first overwhelming onset of grief. Approaching the 'Dark house' (vii) which had once been Hallam's, the poet relives his eager expectation on former visits of grasping his friend's hand. A repetition of the word 'hand' introduces the desolating recognition that it 'can be clasped no more', and the sleepless poet sees himself as now creeping to the door in the darkness 'like a guilty thing'. The bare simplicity of 'He is not here' poignantly conveys his sense of bereavement; at the same time, by echoing Luke xxiv. 6, the phrase points forward to later developments. Then, in the distance, the daily cacophonous 'noise of life begins again',

> *And ghastly through the drizzling rain*
> *On the bald street breaks the blank day.*

The words 'bald', 'breaks', and 'blank', each contributing an essential element to the meaning and each accentuated and linked with the others by alliteration, come at points where the metrical pattern leads the reader to expect slack, or unstressed, syllables. As a result, this last line drags and halts, and the baldness and blankness seem to invade the entire prospect.

Section ix starts the second series. In this, the poet follows in imagination the ship that is bringing home Hallam's body and then speaks of the

[1] Knowles, 182.

burial in England. A lyric in which he hauntingly repeats and plays upon the word 'calm' assures us that the only calm now available to him is 'a calm despair':

> *Calm and deep peace in this wide air,*
> *These leaves that redden to the fall;*
> *And in my heart, if calm at all,*
> *If any calm, a calm despair.*

(xi)

Even this calm is precarious, however. But for his concern for the safety of the vessel, he would rejoice at a stormy night:

> *The wild unrest that lives in woe*
> *Would dote and pore on yonder cloud*
>
> *That rises upward always higher,*
> *And onward drags a labouring breast,*
> *And topples round the dreary west,*
> *A looming bastion fringed with fire.*

(xv)

In the next group, xx-xxvii, he looks back upon the 'four sweet years' (xxii) of friendship he and Hallam had known. He concludes with a declaration which he effectively preserves from facility by twice retarding it with adverbial clauses acknowledging his pain and grief:

> *I hold it true, whate'er befall;*
> *I feel it, when I sorrow most;*
> *'Tis better to have loved and lost*
> *Than never to have loved at all.*

(xxvii)

The first Christmas awakens thoughts of personal immortality, thoughts which can be set against the agonizing sense of loss. Such thoughts develop throughout the fourth division of the poem, xxviii-xlix. The pain of separation persists, however, for

> *thou and I have shaken hands,*
> *Till growing winters lay me low;*
> *My paths are in the fields I know,*
> *And thine in undiscovered lands.*

(xl)

In any case, the poet deprecates any attempt to read his verses as a serious contribution to theology. The sorrow that inspires him seeks merely to subordinate each 'slender shade of doubt' to love:

> *Nor dare she trust a larger lay,*
> *But rather loosens from the lip*
> *Short swallow-flights of song, that dip*
> *Their wings in tears, and skim away.*

(xlviii)

The fifth group opens with a plea to the spirit of Hallam, 'Be near me when my light is low' (l). This lyric expresses with the utmost poignancy a condition of nervous collapse, of agonized subjection to doubts and terrors. Its first stanza moves slowly, with irregular, tortured halts, the emphasized verbs ('creeps', 'prick', 'tingle') forcing the reader fully to know and to feel the state of body and mind described:

> *Be near me when my light is low,*
> *When the blood creeps, and the nerves prick*
> *And tingle; and the heart is sick,*
> *And all the wheels of Being slow.*

(l)

In the following section, the poet asks whether we do really wish the dead to be near us and to perceive our 'inner vileness' (li). Though he decides that the question wrongs the dead, the problem of evil continues to engage him. He 'can but trust' (liv) in the final triumph of good. Wishing to believe in survival after death and in the enduring spiritual value of human achievement, he feels unable to do so without his friend's support: 'O for thy voice to soothe and bless!' (lvi).

A continuing dependence upon Hallam's spirit dominates the next series of lyrics, lix-lxxi, and persists through the seventh group, lxxii-xcviii, to the end of the poem. The anniversary of Hallam's death is blamed as a

> *Day, marked as with some hideous crime,*
> *When the dark hand struck down through time,*
> *And cancelled nature's best.*

(lxxii)

But from section lxxxiii onwards springtime imagery tends to displace autumn and winter imagery in the references to nature. What broods over the second Christmas is not the acute distress of twelve months earlier but a 'quiet sense of something lost':

> *Who showed a token of distress?*
> *No single tear, no mark of pain:*
> *O sorrow, then can sorrow wane?*
> *O grief, can grief be changed to less?*
>
> *O last regret, regret can die!*
> *No—mixt with all this mystic frame,*
> *Her deep relations are the same,*
> *But with long use her tears are dry.*

(lxxviii)

Though the poet is still capable of anger at the thought that death has

> *put our lives so far apart*
> *We cannot hear each other speak,*

(lxxxii)

he detects in himself the 'low beginnings of content' (lxxxiv).

Towards the end of this long seventh division, a number of lyrics appeal to the spirit of Hallam to revisit his friend. A delicate and exact evocation of early spring, one of those poetic renderings of natural phenomena in which Tennyson excels, introduces the second of these:

> *When rosy plumelets tuft the larch,*
> *And rarely pipes the mounted thrush;*
> *Or underneath the barren bush*
> *Flits by the sea-blue bird of March;*
>
> *Come, wear the form by which I know*
> *Thy spirit in time among thy peers;*
> *The hope of unaccomplished years*
> *Be large and lucid round thy brow.*

(xci)

The sequence culminates in section xcv when the solitary poet, re-reading the letters written to him by Hallam, undergoes a fleeting mystical experience such as Tennyson himself described in his statement, 'I've often had a strange feeling of being bound and wrapped in the Great Soul'.[1] This forms the climax and turning-point of the entire poem.

In more prosaic senses, too, fresh starts characterize this part of *In Memoriam*. The main theme of the eighth of the natural groups Tennyson defined is the poet's departure from the home where he had spent his childhood and where he had later known Hallam. The ninth and last of these groups, civ-cxxxi, opens with the third Christmas, spent on 'new unhallowed ground' (civ), and before long the New Year hymn is proclaiming, 'Ring out the old, ring in the new' (cvi).

In the remainder of the poem, fond and admiring recollections of Hallam lead to confident assertions of faith. One of the most beautifully formed of these is an allegorical lyric of a gravity and elegance that bring George Herbert to mind:

> *Love is and was my Lord and King,*
> *And in his presence I attend*
> *To hear the tidings of my friend,*
> *Which every hour his couriers bring.*
>
> *Love is and was my King and Lord,*
> *And will be, though as yet I keep*
> *Within his court on earth, and sleep*
> *Encompassed by his faithful guard,*
>
> *And hear at times a sentinel*
> *Who moves about from place to place,*
> *And whispers to the worlds of space,*
> *In the deep night, that all is well.*

(cxxvi)

As an epilogue to the whole, Tennyson appends a section joyfully celebrating the marriage of one of his sisters and concluding with a prediction of 'the crowning race' of the future,

> *Whereof the man, that with me trod*
> *This planet, was a noble type*

[1] Knowles, 186.

> *Appearing ere the times were ripe,*
> *That friend of mine who lives in God,*

> *That God, which ever lives and loves,*
> *One God, one law, one element,*
> *And one far-off divine event,*
> *To which the whole creation moves.*

(II. 137–144)

In Memoriam, then, is in the first instance a personal poem; it express-es the desolation of a man whose friend has died with his great promise unfulfilled, and it evokes for us the love which bound, and binds, the two of them. But the poet's experiences naturally lead him to questions about death and survival after death and the existence of a loving God. As a result, *In Memoriam* is both a personal and a philosophical poem.

The poet's concern with the problem of evil becomes explicit in section liv, where he starts by trusting

> *that somehow good*
> *Will be the final goal of ill.*

The confession of uncertainty in 'somehow' contrasts pathetically with the vast categories of 'ill' to be transcended:

> *pangs of nature, sins of will,*
> *Defects of doubt, and taints of blood;*

and with the unyielding insistence of the negatives (here in roman) which emphasize the speaker's hope

> That *nothing walks with aimless feet;*
> That *not* one *life shall be destroyed,*
> . . . .
> That *not* a *worm is cloven in vain;*
> That *not* a *moth with vain desire*
> *Is shrivelled in a fruitless fire.*

He has to confess his ignorance and to repeat that he 'can but trust'. But what, after all, is he? The final image conveys his inarticulate feebleness:

> *An infant crying in the night:*
> *An infant crying for the light:*
> *And with no language but a cry.*

In the next section, he takes up his wish that 'not one life shall be destroyed' and asks whether our hope of eternal life does not spring from what is most nearly divine in us. But, if God himself inspired this hope and expectation, how can it be that Nature, which seems so careful of each species, should seem so careless of the individual? This initial questioning leads to a single complex sentence which extends from the second stanza to the end of the fifth and last stanza of the lyric:

> *So careful of the type she seems,*
> *So careless of the single life;*
>
> *That I, considering everywhere*
> *Her secret meaning in her deeds,*
> *And finding that of fifty seeds*
> *She often brings but one to bear,*
>
> *I falter where I firmly trod,*
> *And falling with my weight of cares*
> *Upon the great world's altar-stairs*
> *That slope through darkness up to God,*
>
> *I stretch lame hands of faith, and grope,*
> *And gather dust and chaff, and call*
> *To what I feel is Lord of all,*
> *And faintly trust the larger hope.*

Though the subject of the sentence emerges in the third of the lines quoted, the main clause is kept in suspense while adjectival phrases evoke the poet's anxious and gloomy ponderings. Completed in the first line of the penultimate stanza, it is followed by a second main clause which is likewise held back until the beginning of the last stanza. These delays create a syntactical and rhythmical equivalent of the frustrations which justify the main verbs, '*falter* where I firmly trod' and '*stretch* lame hands of faith'; and the kinaesthetic suggestions of these verbs are developed in the rapid sequence of main verbs in the last four lines, '*stretch*', '*grope*', '*gather* dust and chaff', and '*call*'. After so much thwarted exertion, there is a melancholy inevitability about the adverb 'faintly' which modifies the final main verb, '*trust* the larger hope'. The poet 'can but trust', and 'faintly', that 'somehow' the good will prevail.

In section lvi, however, his doubts become more radical still. He has assumed that Nature, though neglectful of the individual, takes care of the species. But is this the case?

> '*So careful of the type?*' *but no.*
> *From scarpèd cliff and quarried stone*
> *She cries, 'A thousand types are gone:*
> *I care for nothing, all shall go.*'
>
> '*Thou makest thine appeal to me:*
> *I bring to life, I bring to death:*
> *The spirit does but mean the breath:*
> *I know no more.*'

The geological record shows how many species have perished. Shrinking from Nature's strictly materialistic interpretation of the facts—'The spirit does but mean the breath'—the poet delivers a desperate protest on behalf of the spiritual aspirations and intuitions of humanity. But his protest is corroded by doubt. Perhaps man is 'fair' only in appearance. Certainly, the sky to which he addresses his worship is 'wintry', his prayers are 'fruitless', and a ruthless and predatory Nature contradicts his trust in the divine love. Moreover, the whole protest takes the form of a rhetorical question that fails to ring with confidence. 'And he,' asks the poet, 'shall he,'

> *Man, her last work, who seemed so fair,*
> *Such splendid purpose in his eyes,*
> *Who rolled the psalm to wintry skies,*
> *Who built him fanes of fruitless prayer,*
>
> *Who trusted God was love indeed*
> *And love Creation's final law—*
> *Though Nature, red in tooth and claw*
> *With ravine, shrieked against his creed—*
>
> *Who loved, who suffered countless ills,*
> *Who battled for the True, the Just,*

> *Be blown about the desert dust,*
> *Or sealed within the iron hills?*

If human endeavour is to amount merely to this, man's whole career is absurd. The poet cries out for the help of his dead friend. Fuller knowledge is beyond his reach, 'behind the veil':

> *No more? A monster then, a dream,*
> *A discord. Dragons of the prime,*
> *That tare each other in their slime,*
> *Were mellow music matched with him.*
>
> *O life as futile, then, as frail!*
> *O for thy voice to soothe and bless!*
> *What hope of answer, or redress?*
> *Behind the veil, behind the veil.*

Sir Charles Lyell's *Principles of Geology* (1830–33) seems to have suggested some of the scientific ideas used in sections lv and lvi. From the evidence of the rocks, Lyell infers that the biological species were simultaneously created and have been subject to gradual elimination in the struggle for existence. 'It is not only the individual that perishes, but whole species' (PT, 911). The time-scale Lyell requires is much longer than that envisaged in the Old Testament, and many orthodox Christians took offence at his implicit rejection of the Mosaic cosmogony. Tennyson may well have had Lyell's grim conclusions in mind when speaking of Nature's carelessness of the single life, when withdrawing his initial reference to her carefulness of the type, when describing her as 'red in tooth and claw', and when alluding to the evidence 'sealed within the iron hills'. These ideas serve to project his nightmare vision of man as the merely ephemeral product of physical forces.

But this is not his last word on the subject. Towards the end of *In Memoriam*, he draws again upon ideas suggested by advances in geology. This time, he feels able to regard them optimistically, and even to see them as compatible with belief in a benign deity. The change conforms with the general change in the poem from the profound dejection voiced in many of the earlier sections to the hope and confidence which inspire many of the later ones.

Tennyson's reading of Robert Chambers's *Vestiges of the Natural History of Creation* (1844) may also have helped on at least one occasion. Whereas Lyell was a scientist of distinction, Chambers was merely a popularizer, and a somewhat inaccurate one at that. He was to irritate T. H. Huxley, for example, by his ignorance and his unscientific thinking. These disabilities did not prevent his book from having a tremendous success, and Tennyson is known to have ordered a copy of it in the year of its publication. Chambers puts forward an evolutionary theory of the origin of species. He believes that God is bringing creation gradually into existence and that the ascertainable laws which regulate this process testify to the divine plan.

We have it on Hallam Tennyson's word that his father's friends had read the sections of *In Memoriam* dealing with evolution some years before the appearance of Chambers' book (*Mem.*, I, 223n.). But it seems possible that the unnumbered section printed as an epilogue to the poem followed Tennyson's introduction to Chambers' doctrines. At all events, there are similarities between the conclusion of Tennyson's lyric and certain passages in *Vestiges of Creation*. Though not decisive, these similarities permit us to entertain the notion that Tennyson may have owed something to Chambers in at least this one section of *In Memoriam*.

It ends with a complex, forty-four-line sentence in which Tennyson brings together the matters which have principally concerned him throughout the poem. The sentence culminates in the prediction of a 'crowning race'

> *Of those that, eye to eye, shall look*
> *On knowledge; under whose command*
> *Is Earth and Earth's, and in their hand*
> *Is Nature like an open book;*
>
> *No longer half-akin to brute,*
> *For all we thought and loved and did,*
> *And hoped, and suffered, is but seed*
> *Of what in them is flower and fruit;*
>
> *Whereof the man, that with me trod*
> *This planet, was a noble type*

Appearing ere the times were ripe,
That friend of mine who lives in God,

That God, which ever lives and loves,
One God, one law, one element,
And one far-off divine event,
To which the whole creation moves.

(II. 129–144)

These lines formulate several important articles of the creed that Tennyson has now come to accept. He believes that the evolutionary process will give rise to 'a higher race' (cxviii); that Hallam in his own being anticipated this development; and that the emergence of 'that great race, which is to be' (ciii), will bring nearer to fulfilment the providential plan of the loving God in whom Hallam now dwells.

This employment of phrases from earlier sections to illustrate a commentary on the last of them indicates that the ideas we have been reviewing emerge well before the end of the poem. But in only one of the numbered lyrics, cxviii, is there the slightest ground for suspecting an indebtedness to Chambers. On balance, we may reasonably assume that Tennyson was anticipating *Vestiges of Creation* both there and elsewhere in the numbered lyrics. When he ordered a copy of the book in 1844 he did after all say that 'it seems to contain many speculations with which I have been familiar for years, and on which I have written more than one poem' (*Mem.*, I, 223).

Section cxxiii might seem to have been one of the lyrics he had in mind, and the temptation to linger over it is strong. But this compelling vision of geological change as a vast insubstantial pageant, while possibly owing something to Lyell, does not really look forward to Chambers. What does look forward to him is section cxviii, perhaps Tennyson's finest exposition of an optimistic evolutionism.

It starts with an exhortation to us to contemplate the whole progress of time, to believe that human values are of more than merely temporary validity, and to trust that the dead enjoy eternal life for 'ever nobler ends'. A colourless 'They say' introduces the long sentence which then runs from the second to the seventh and last stanza:

> *They say,*
> *The solid earth whereon we tread*
>
> *In tracts of fluent heat began,*
> *And grew to seeming-random forms,*
> *The seeming prey of cyclic storms,*
> *Till at the last arose the man;*
>
> *Who throve and branched from clime to clime,*
> *The herald of a higher race,*
> *And of himself in higher place,*
> *If so he type this work of time*
>
> *Within himself, from more to more;*
> *Or, crowned with attributes of woe*
> *Like glories, move his course, and show*
> *That life is not as idle ore,*
>
> *But iron dug from central gloom,*
> *And heated hot with burning fears,*
> *And dipt in baths of hissing tears,*
> *And battered with the shocks of doom*
>
> *To shape and use.*

From its quiet beginning, the sentence mounts in dramatic intensity as it proceeds. The poet first sees the earth, like the other planets and the stars, as originating in the condensation of inter-stellar gas. To this, the nebular hypothesis, he adds the catastrophism of Baron Cuvier, according to which the fossil record of the pre-history of the earth pointed to a series of cataclysms—'cyclic storms'—after each of which fresh species prevailed. By the time the sentence gets to 'man', we have lost sight of its quiet beginning and are closely engaged in watching humanity thrive and branch and show its power to ameliorate itself and to announce 'a higher race'. More compelling still is the description, in the last full stanza quoted, of the effort and agony such progress may require; the sensory properties of the verbs, 'dug', 'heated', 'dipt', and 'battered', especially their kinaesthetic and tactile properties, make the operation almost painfully present to us.

In the last stanza the poet resumes his exhortation. He urges his fellows to rise above sensuality, cruelty, and greed:

> *Arise and fly*
> *The reeling Faun, the sensual feast;*
> *Move upward, working out the beast,*
> *And let the ape and tiger die.*

Though there is no direct reference to a divine plan, belief in God could appropriately complement the hope embodied in this lyric. Eighteenth-century theologians such as William Paley had attempted to demonstrate the existence of God by reasoning from natural phenomena. Tennyson, however, was something of a Coleridgian and a good deal of a modern in that he based his belief in God not upon external evidences but upon inner experience. This is his theme in section cxxiv:

> *I found Him not in world or sun,*
> *Or eagle's wing, or insect's eye;*
> *Nor through the questions men may try,*
> *The petty cobwebs we have spun:*
>
> *If e'er when faith had fallen asleep,*
> *I heard a voice 'believe no more'*
> *And heard an ever-breaking shore*
> *That tumbled in the Godless deep;*
>
> *A warmth within the breast would melt*
> *The freezing reason's colder part,*
> *And like a man in wrath the heart*
> *Stood up and answered 'I have felt'.*

But at once he reflects that his heart cannot maintain this assurance as of 'a man in wrath'. Without denying what he has experienced, he reformulates it in movingly humble terms:

> *No, like a child in doubt and fear:*
> *But that blind clamour made me wise;*
> *Then was I as a child that cries,*
> *And, crying, knows his father near;*
>
> *And what I am beheld again*
> *What is, and no man understands;*

> *And out of darkness came the hands*
> *That reach through nature, moulding men.*

This 'child that cries' has come far from the 'infant crying in the night' of section liv. For Tennyson, belief in a loving God necessarily entailed belief in eternal life. 'If you allow a God,' he said, 'and God allows this strong instinct and universal yearning for another life, surely that is in a measure a presumption of its truth. We cannot give up the mighty hopes that make us men' (*Mem.*, I, 321). This thought finds expression as early as in section xxxiv of *In Memoriam:*

> *My own dim life should teach me this,*
> *That life shall live for evermore,*
> *Else earth is darkness at the core,*
> *And dust and ashes all that is;*
> . . . .
> *What then were God to such as I?*

Confirmation comes in section xcv, which records a mystical experience of a sort Tennyson knew at intervals throughout his life.

A kind of waking trance I have frequently had, quite up from boyhood, when I have been all alone. This has generally come upon me thro' repeating my own name two or three times to myself silently, till all at once, as it were out of the intensity of the consciousness of individuality, the individuality itself seemed to dissolve and fade away into boundless being, and this not a confused state, but the clearest of the clearest, the surest of the surest, the weirdest of the weirdest, utterly beyond words, where death was an almost laughable impossibility, the loss of personality (if so it were) seeming no extinction but the only true life.   (*Mem.*, I, 320)

The setting of section xcv is a summer night in the garden of the old home which the poet is soon to leave. The tapers burn stilly in the calm, warm air; bats and moths circle around. The distant brook and the 'fluttering' tea urn on the table provide the only sounds until the poet and his companions begin to sing

> *old songs that pealed*
> *From knoll to knoll, where, couched at ease,*
> *The white kine glimmered, and the trees*
> *Laid their dark arms about the field.*

One by one his companions withdraw, and eventually the poet is literally, as he has long been metaphorically, 'all alone':

> *A hunger seized my heart; I read*
> *Of that glad year which once had been,*
> *In those fallen leaves which kept their green,*
> *The noble letters of the dead:*
>
> *And strangely on the silence broke*
> *The silent-speaking words, and strange*
> *Was love's dumb cry defying change*
> *To test his worth; and strangely spoke*
>
> *The faith, the vigour, bold to dwell*
> *On doubts that drive the coward back,*
> *And keen through wordy snares to track*
> *Suggestion to her inmost cell.*

The dead man lives still in his letters. Reading them, the poet has an intimate sense of Hallam's presence:

> *So word by word, and line by line,*
> *The dead man touched me from the past,*
> *And all at once it seemed at last*
> *The living soul was flashed on mine,*
>
> *And mine in this was wound, and whirled*
> *About empyreal heights of thought,*
> *And came on that which is, and caught*
> *The deep pulsations of the world,*
>
> *Æonian music measuring out*
> *The steps of Time—the shocks of Chance—*
> *The blows of Death. At length my trance*
> *Was cancelled, stricken through with doubt.*

Tennyson originally wrote '*His* living soul' and 'mine in *his*' (italics added). This meant that the mystical union was with Hallam alone. When he changed the words in 1872 he opened up the possibility that he had experienced a brief union with the Deity. At the same time, he did not exclude contact with his friend, since Hallam's soul had already become an inseparable part of the divine spirit. In describing this experience of union, Tennyson resorts to imagery similar to that used in some of the geological passages—section cxviii, for example—and so achieves the grandeur his record requires. But 'human kind/Cannot bear very much reality' (T. S. Eliot, 'Burnt Norton', i). The trance ends, 'stricken through with doubt', and the poet despairs of communicating what he has known:

> *Vague words! but ah, how hard to frame*
> *In matter-moulded forms of speech,*
> *Or even for intellect to reach*
> *Through memory that which I became:*
>
> *Till now the doubtful dusk revealed*
> *The knolls once more where, couched at ease,*
> *The white kine glimmered, and the trees*
> *Laid their dark arms about the field:*
>
> *And sucked from out the distant gloom*
> *A breeze began to tremble o'er*
> *The large leaves of the sycamore,*
> *And fluctuate all the still perfume,*
>
> *And gathering freshlier overhead,*
> *Rocked the full-foliaged elms, and swung*
> *The heavy-folded rose, and flung*
> *The lilies to and fro, and said*
>
> *'The dawn, the dawn,' and died away;*
> *And East and West, without a breath,*
> *Mixt their dim lights, like life and death,*
> *To broaden into boundless day.*

The delicate picture of the landscape in the 'doubtful dusk' of early morning echoes that of the same landscape in the 'dusk' of the previous evening. As before, the trees hold the field in a comforting embrace, and the white cattle gleam faintly in the darkness. Tennyson renders the morning breeze with all his usual skill. Quickly swelling, it trembles over the 'large leaves of the sycamore', rocks the 'full-foliaged elms', swings the 'heavy-folded rose', and flings the 'lilies to and fro'. Having announced the day, it abruptly dies. In the dusk of dawn which so resembles that of evening, the 'East and West' of sunrise and sunset mix 'their dim lights, like life and death', to suggest to the poet the 'boundless day' of everlasting life after death.

There is nothing specifically Christian about the religious faith expressed in the lyrics so far quoted. The poet's inner experience has led him to accept a form of theism that includes a belief in the immortality of the soul. This falls far short of the full Christian faith, but very seldom does the poet affirm anything more. One of the very few places where he does go further is in the opening stanzas of the unnumbered lyric which serves as a prologue to *In Memoriam*:

> *Strong Son of God, immortal Love,*
> *Whom we, that have not seen thy face,*
> *By faith, and faith alone, embrace,*
> *Believing where we cannot prove;*

> *Thine are these orbs of light and shade;*
> *Thou madest Life in man and brute;*
> *Thou madest Death; and lo, thy foot*
> *Is on the skull which thou hast made.*

> *Thou wilt not leave us in the dust:*
> *Thou madest man, he knows not why,*
> *He thinks he was not made to die;*
> *And thou hast made him: thou art just.*

> *Thou seemest human and divine,*
> *The highest, holiest manhood, thou:*
> *Our wills are ours, we know not how;*
> *Our wills are ours, to make them thine.*

Even here, however, we may legitimately wonder whether Tennyson was availing himself of the traditional comprehensiveness of the Anglican Church, of which he was a member, and referring to the divinity of Christ in a merely metaphorical sense. Certainly, the measured assertiveness of these lines, though impressive enough in its way, seems to go beyond anything that would be justified by the poem they introduce.

As we have seen, many widely different phases of the poet's faith and doubt find expression in the lyrics that make up *In Memoriam*. This fact will surprise no one who recalls that Tennyson began to write them when he was only twenty-four and printed the complete poem before he was forty-one. But the religious position reached by the end of the poem was, broadly speaking, to remain his position for the rest of his life.[1]

Naturally, there were some shifts of emphasis. In writing 'The Holy Grail' (1869), he was much concerned to show that moments of mystical vision are not for everyone and that most persons will more usefully devote themselves to the practical work of the world. Indeed, he makes the neglect of this work by men engaged in the pursuit of mystical experience one of the causes of the decline of the order of the Round Table. Explaining why he did not himself go upon the Holy Quest, Arthur says:

> *the King must guard*
> *That which he rules, and is but as the hind*
> *To whom a space of land is given to plow.*
> *Who may not wander from the allotted field*
> *Before his work be done; but, being done,*
> *Let visions of the night or of the day*
> *Come, as they will; and many a time they come,*
> *Until this earth he walks on seems not earth,*
> *This light that strikes his eyeball is not light,*

[1] A number of recent writers on *In Memoriam* must have influenced my discussion of the poem, despite the fact that I have made no direct borrowings from them. Some of the best of their work is reprinted in John Dixon Hunt's *Tennyson: 'In Memoriam'*, Casebook Series (1970). Of the books published since the appearance of Hunt's anthology, one of the most useful is Alan Sinfield's *The Language of Tennyson's 'In Memoriam'*, Language and Style Series, IX, Oxford 1971.

> *This air that smites his forehead is not air*
> *But vision—yea, his very hand and foot—*
> *In moments when he feels he cannot die,*
> *And knows himself no vision to himself,*
> *Nor the high God a vision, nor that One*
> *Who rose again.*
>
> (PT, 1687)

This vision that comes to a receptive Arthur resembles that which comes to the solitary poet of *In Memoriam* while reading the letters of his dead friend. It resembles equally the experience described towards the end of 'The Ancient Sage' (1885), which Tennyson judged to be one of his best later poems and admitted to be 'very personal' (*Mem.*, II, 319):

> *more than once when I*
> *Sat all alone, revolving in myself*
> *The word that is the symbol of myself,*
> *The mortal limit of the Self was loosed,*
> *And past into the Nameless, as a cloud*
> *Melts into Heaven. I touched my limbs, the limbs*
> *Were strange not mine—and yet no shade of doubt,*
> *But utter clearness, and through loss of Self*
> *The gain of such large life as matched with ours*
> *Were Sun to spark—unshadowable in words,*
> *Themselves but shadows of a shadow-world.*
>
> (PT, 1356)

In all three verse accounts of this trance-like state, Tennyson allows himself to relax, almost to relinquish, his customarily firm syntax. While it is assuredly possible to trace a regular grammatical structure in each of the crucial sentences, we do not in fact follow them grammatically in the course of a normal reading. Instead, the separate ¦phrases come to seem a series of attempts, none subordinated to any other, to convey the reality of an inexplicable experience. Perhaps even 'series' implies too much in that it contradicts the evident simultaneity of the impressions the phrases record.

Such experiences seemed to Tennyson to expose the inadequacy of the philosophical materialism which attracted many of his more scientifically-minded contemporaries during his later years. Convinced of the reality of spirit, he could have faith in a loving God and in human survival. Men needed this faith. If it were to be destroyed in them, nothing could prevent them from lapsing into bestiality and chaos.

In several of his later poems he asserts these views with sombre emphasis. 'Despair' (1881), for example, is the dramatic monologue of a man who has just been rescued from drowning. He and his wife having, as Tennyson explains in a prefatory note, 'lost faith in a God, and hope of a life to come, and being utterly miserable in this', have concluded a suicide pact. Only the wife has perished. The husband asks:

> *Why should we bear with an hour of torture,*
> *a moment of pain,*
> *If every man die for ever, if all his griefs*
> *are in vain,*
> *And the homeless planet at length will be*
> *wheeled through the silence of space,*
> *Motherless evermore of an ever-vanishing race,*
> *When the worm shall have writhed its last,*
> *and its last brother-worm will have fled*
> *From the dead fossil skull that is left in*
> *the rocks of an earth that is dead?*
>
> (PT, 1302)

'What matters anything in this world without full faith in the Immortality of the Soul and of Love?' (*Mem.*, II, 343). This is Tennyson's own note on 'Vastness' (1885), another insistent and hortatory rendering of his views. A series of rhetorical questions leads up to its last line:

> *Spring and Summer and Autumn and Winter, and*
> *all these old revolutions of earth;*
> *All new-old revolutions of Empire—change of*
> *the tide—what is all of it worth?*
>
> *What the philosophies, all the sciences, poesy,*
> *varying voices of prayer?*

> *All that is noblest, all that is basest, all*
> *that is filthy with all that is fair?*
>
> *What is it all, if we all of us end but in*
> *being our own corpse-coffins at last,*
> *Swallowed in Vastness, lost in Silence, drowned*
> *in the deeps of a meaningless Past?*
>
> *What but a murmur of gnats in the gloom, or a*
> *moment's anger of bees in their hive?—*

An expression of lonely yearning and earnest trust interrupts and silences this vehement and gloomy denunciation:

> *Peace, let it be! for I loved him, and love him*
> *for ever: the dead are not dead but alive.*

(PT, 1348)

Written more than half a century after Hallam's death, this carries us back in a flash to the personal centre of *In Memoriam.*

Nothing could make a reader more acutely aware of the assertively polemical tone of 'Vastness', and for that matter of 'Despair'. There would be no point in unduly belittling either the later or the earlier work of Tennyson. But *In Memoriam*, in its hope and its despondency, its doubt and its faith, possesses an inwardness and a desperate sincerity, recorded with the most delicate artistry, that make it unquestionably its author's major achievement as a religious poet.

5: Tennyson and the Dramatic Monologue: A Study of 'Maud'

PHILIP DREW

TENNYSON'S MONOLOGUES are of two kinds—the simple and the violent. The best that critics have done for them is to suggest that some of the simple ones are not as insipid as they look. For reasons which I shall give I do not think that this is a very convincing line: instead I shall try to show that the violent ones are not all out of Tennyson's control. In particular I shall consider the argument that *Maud* is firmly enough organized to contain its explosive mixture of powerful emotions and passionate political rhetoric.

The easiest way to understand Tennyson's handling of the monologue is to read quickly through the volume *Ballads and Other Poems* (1880). The poems are almost all formally dramatic monologues, but it is clear that Tennyson has no interest in their form. 'The First Quarrel', (PT, 1254), for example, is simply an anecdote told in the first person, offered because of its pathetic quality. 'Rizpah' (PT, 1245) is the same, but with more passion than pathos. 'In the Children's Hospital' (PT, 1261) is of a similar kind: there is a half-hearted attempt to point the difference between the good old ways and the callousness of the new order, but in general the poem relies on the intrinsic appeal of the anecdote and the free use of the word 'little'. The narrator is used to enrich the sentiment by adding an extra set of feelings and sufferings. Again in 'The Sisters' (PT, 1291) the point of the poem lies in the unfolding of a bitterly ironic situation of a kind often exploited by Hardy. The poem is very like one of *Life's Little Ironies* narrated by a participant, who can contribute no more than a sense of helplessness. In short, the present situation of the speaker in each of these monologues is of no immediate interest: he is simply a narrative convenience.

The same is true of many of Tennyson's dialect poems, of which 'Owd Röa' (1889: PT, 1379) may stand as a fair example, and of the historical monologues such as 'Sir John Oldcastle' and 'Columbus' (PT, 1285 and 1264). The first realizes the historical situation with some competence but offers no additional light on Oldcastle: once again he is no more than a completely endorsed narrator. 'Columbus' is rather more interesting. Most of the poem is a straightforward narration of past events, but the last two paragraphs and the three-line coda, which refer immediately to the circumstances of the monologue, suggest a possible way in which the form can be used to do more than tell a story. A word should perhaps be said about 'Romney's Remorse' (PT, 1417), which in style and subject demands comparison with 'Andrea del Sarto', a comparison by no means entirely in Browning's favour, for Tennyson finds in the figure of the painter on his deathbed a genuinely dramatic embodiment of the debate between the claims of life and those of art. With this exception the fairest verdict on all these later poems is that the best of them are not unlike the less successful of Browning's *Dramatic Idyls* of about the same period. Those who know the *Idyls* will recognize that this is faint praise indeed.

There are however a few early poems for which rather larger claims have been made, notably 'St Simeon Stylites' and 'Ulysses' (PT, 542 and 560). It has been suggested in particular that 'Ulysses' is a work of some dramatic complexity and that instead of regarding the poem as a straightforward projection of the historical imagination we should take it as representing an attitude of mind which Tennyson repudiates and which the reader is expected to recognize as defective from the monologue itself.[1] The case is persuasively set out, but it is of course open to say of any account in the first person that it does not necessarily carry with it the writer's endorsement of the speaker's position. The mere

---

[1] See E. J. Chiasson, 'Tennyson's *Ulysses*—A Re-interpretation,' *UTQ* XXIII, 1954, 402–409. Chaisson says, 'Tennyson is writing here . . . a dramatic portrayal of a type of human being who held a set of ideas which Tennyson regarded as destructive of the whole fabric of his society.' For a full account of the argument see John Pettigrew, 'Tennyson's *Ulysses*—A Reconciliation of Opposites,' *VP* I, 1963, 27–45.

fact that we can regard Ulysses' statement of his motives with scepticism because we have only his word for them and he may be dishonest or deluded therefore does nothing to show that they should indeed be so regarded. It is true that Ulysses speaks as a pagan and Tennyson was a Christian: to that extent Ulysses' values cannot be identified with Tennyson's. It is true also that the poem has an elegiac tone which makes it hard to read as a simple assertion of a set of heroic ideals. Even so we need not necessarily conclude that Tennyson is offering us anything more complex than words of strenuous aspiration in the mouth of a man in old age. In brief, if we find shortcomings in Ulysses they are not so judged by virtue of standards implied by the poem but by virtue of some external standards which we believe to have been present in Tennyson's mind and which we infer he expected his readers to apply to the poem. This inference is not necessary, and it does not seem to me to be even probable.

'St Simeon Stylites' is another poem which tempts the reader to hunt for ironic reversals, but which in the end seems to rest more easily if it is accepted that Tennyson is presenting a character in a historical situation without indicating to the reader a position from which this character is to be critically viewed. The parallel with the early poem 'St Lawrence' (PT, 298) is especially revealing. There is an obvious confusion in Simeon's mind between salvation and sanctity and it is clear that his mind is not yet purged of worldly things. The details of his penance still obsess him and, of course, the dominant question of whether he will in fact achieve sainthood. All this would be perfectly compatible with the sort of monologue where the reader is expected to recognize and repudiate the unbalanced mind, or the self-deceiver, or the disingenuous arguer, or the self-centred man falsely laying claim to modesty, and this especially since Simeon is in fact staking his life on earth and his hopes of heaven on the achievement of a particular kind of purity and disinterestedness. The last twenty-six lines, in which he has the vision of the angel and the crown, would then have to be taken as an episode in delirium or a particularly vivid instance of self-deception. But the manner of writing of these lines, especially the last five, is not sufficiently distorted to support this way of taking them. Simeon says, 'Let me not be fooled, sweet saints: I trust/That I am whole . . .', which indicates that his mind is not entirely occupied by delusion. If one concedes that the poem is an imaginative reconstruction of the mixed motives which led men to a life of extreme asceticism and of the unsettled state of mind in which they faced death, one must add also that Tennyson makes no attempt to order the complexity of his material by means of the resources which the dramatic monologue offers and which we later find used for this purpose by Browning.

In Browning's hands the dramatic monologue normally consists of a narrative spoken by a single character and amplified by his comments on his own story and the circumstances in which he is speaking. The reader builds up a quasi-dramatic context for the poem, and is eventually in a position to assess the intelligence and sincerity of the narrator and the value of the views he expresses. There is thus always an element of irony, actual or potential, in the dramatic monologue, since it depends on the unconscious provision by the speaker of the evidence by which he is to be judged.

If it is accepted that a crucial part of the response to a dramatic monologue is the understanding of the speaker's limitations, Tennyson is to be credited with hardly any monologues that can be called dramatic. His concern is with the telling of a story, not with the progressive revelation by the narrator of his own character nor with any developing interaction between the speaker and his situation. Nevertheless he shows a continued interest in first person narrative with at least sufficient fictional colouring to forestall the assumption that the poet himself is speaking. 'Locksley Hall' is an obvious example. The framework of a story is quickly sketched in to establish the narrator as a person distinct from the poet, but the main interest lies in the speaker's opinions considered out of their dramatic context. The poem offers a series of reflections on modern life: the speaker shifts abruptly from one passionately stated position to its contrary, expressed with equal power. These transitions would be perfectly comprehensible if they corresponded to a change in the hero worked, for example, by the passage of time, but in the poem there is no pause, simply a succession of incompatible attitudes.

In Memoriam marks a crucial difference here. It is a commonplace that the speaker, inevitably identified with Tennyson himself, depicts his grief and his doubt and his resolution of his doubt in a series of lyrics each set a little later in time than the one before. In fact the period covered by the poem is a span of several years; long enough, that is, for the speaker not only to overcome his sorrow but to be changed by the passage of time. As Tennyson puts it in the Epilogue, 'For I myself with these have grown/To something greater than before'. *In Memoriam*, that is, may be regarded as a series of dramatic lyrics, consecutive and each with its own distinct occasion. The shifting time-centre accounts for the changes in mood and opinion, and takes the place of a connected argument or dramatic plot. Tennyson is fully in command of the technique and consciously adopted the form for his next major poem, *Maud* (PT, 1037). 'This poem of *Maud or the Madness* is a little *Hamlet*, the history of a morbid, poetic soul, under the blighting influence of a recklessly speculative age. He is the heir of madness, an egoist with the makings of a cynic, raised to a pure and holy love which elevates his whole nature, passing from the height of triumph to the lowest depth of misery, driven into madness by the loss of her whom he has loved, and, when he has at length passed through the fiery furnace, and has recovered his reason, giving himself up to work for the good of mankind through the unselfishness born of a great passion. The peculiarity of this poem is that different phases of passion in one person take the place of different characters' (*Mem.*, I, 396).

If we accept Tennyson's account of the pattern of the poem it is clear that it has the following rhythm: (1) Hysteria, (2) Rapture, (3) Mania, and (4) Sanity. I shall argue that (4) can be seen as a true deliverance from (1), dramatically and thematically. The chief objection which I shall examine is that while the language and opinions of (1) and (3), with their febrile over-emphasis, can be justified easily enough on the grounds that they are not Tennyson's own language or opinions but those of a fictitious character, who is himself represented as not completely sane, a similar, though less radical, unbalance of thought and diction persists even in those parts of the poem where the narrator is represented as seeing clearly.

A consideration of the opening of the poem will illustrate the nature of the objection. The first section of Part One is notorious for its fierce denunciations of the adulteration of food and drugs and the defrauding of burial societies. Taken out of their context they border on the ludicrous: in the poem they form a sensational but not inappropriate part of the speaker's general condemnation of the 'lust of gain, in the spirit of Cain'. Tennyson carefully indicates the dramatic justification for the violence of tone of the opening sections of the poem. Each section has its own time-centre: each of the opening sections therefore represents the hero at an unregenerate moment before Maud has enabled him to break free from his misanthropy. What is interesting about these sections of the poem is that while the hero's language is intemperate and his deductions from what he sees in Britain lead him to a fatalism which will be shown to be erroneous, nevertheless the flaws that he sees are in fact there. We may make allowances for his tone and repudiate his conclusions, but it is essential to see that his indictment of the commercial ethic is not just a symptom of his madness. The society in which the action takes place is an integral part of the dramatic situation.

The hero's father has been driven mad and has presumably killed himself:

> *for a vast speculation had failed,*
> *And ever he muttered and maddened, and ever wanned with despair,*
> *And out he walked when the wind like a broken worldling wailed,*
> *And the flying gold of the ruined woodlands drove through the air.*
> *(Maud, 1. I, iii; 9–12)[1]*

These lines are perhaps the best example of the kind of control that Tennyson is exerting at this point in the poem. They are immediately effective and immediately suspect. Yet on closer reading it is clear that the alliteration and the pathetic fallacy and the over-energetic vocabulary are not heedlessly employed, but fairly characterize a state of bitterness bordering on insanity. Even the apparent extravagance of involving the entire landscape in a commercial calamity will be justified by the line of argument in section IV.

Before that, however, Maud makes her first appearance. The hero does not see her clearly or respond to her rationally. Section III illus-

---

[1] References to *Maud* are given as follows: part number (where not obvious); section number; stanza number; line number from PT.

trates Tennyson's extraordinary skill in finding metrical equivalents
for a state of mind. The single proliferating sentence is simultaneously
inordinate and rigidly subdued to the form of the sonnet:

> *Cold and clear-cut face, why come you so cruelly meek,*
> *Breaking a slumber in which all spleenful folly was drowned,*
> *Pale with the golden beam of an eyelash dead on the cheek,*
> *Passionless, pale, cold face, star-sweet on a gloom profound:*
> *Womanlike, taking revenge too deep for a transient wrong*
> *Done but in thought to your beauty, and ever as pale as before*
> *Growing and fading and growing upon me without a sound,*
> *Luminous, gemlike, ghostlike, deathlike, half the night long*
> *Growing and fading and growing, till I could bear it no more,*
> *But arose, and all by myself in my own dark garden ground,*
> *Listening now to the tide in its broad-flung shipwrecking roar,*
> *Now to the scream of a maddened beach dragged down by the wave,*
> *Walked in a wintry wind by a ghastly glimmer, and found*
> *The shining daffodil dead, and Orion low in his grave.*
>
> (1. III; 88–101)

Her part in the poem is already clearly indicated. She is to be the
means of freeing the hero from the bitter disillusionment which has
led him to say:

> *Sooner or later I too may passively take the print*
> *Of the golden age—why not? I have neither hope nor trust;*
> *May make my heart as a millstone, set my face as a flint,*
> *Cheat and be cheated, and die: who knows? we are ashes and dust.*
>
> (1. I. viii; 29–32)

His conclusion 'I will bury myself in myself' reverberates ironically
through the rest of the poem.

But Maud's tonic effect is not an immediate one. There is a most
revealing passage in section IV where in the space of three lines the
hero brings together all his main concerns in the poem:

> *O child, you wrong your beauty, believe it, in being so proud;*
> *Your father has wealth well-gotten, and I am nameless and poor.*
> *I keep but a man and a maid, ever ready to slander and steal.*
>
> (1. IV. iii-iv; 118–120)

It is in this section that the hero's hysteria is most clearly defined and his personal situation most directly related to the commercialism which is ruining Britain. This in turn conforms to the laws of Nature red in tooth and claw:

> *For nature is one with rapine, a harm no preacher can heal;*
> *The Mayfly is torn by the swallow, the sparrow speared by the shrike,*
> *And the whole little wood where I sit is a world of plunder and prey.*
>
> (I. IV. iv; 123–125)

If Nature is in fact one with rapine the hero is exposed to all the terrifying fears against which Tennyson fought in *In Memoriam*. He must accept that 'we men are a little breed,' that man is not Nature's last word, that 'the drift of the Maker is dark,' that 'our planet is one, the suns are many' and is finally driven to the conclusion which Tennyson had personally in the earlier poem been able to resist, that 'we are puppets.' Since neither the scientist nor the poet can offer an ideal of a life worth living everything impels man to a comfortable indifferentism, stoic or epicurean, in which he rejects responsibility in favour of 'a passionless peace'. 'I will bury myself in myself.'

The beginning of section V shows the care with which Tennyson looked to the larger design of his poem:

> *A voice by the cedar tree*
> *In the meadow under the Hall!*
> *She is singing an air that is known to me,*
> *A passionate ballad gallant and gay,*
> *A martial song like a trumpet's call!*
> *Singing alone in the morning of life,*
> *In the happy morning of life and of May,*
> *Singing of men that in battle array,*
> *Ready in heart and ready in hand,*
> *March with banner and bugle and fife*
> *To the death, for their native land.*
> . . . .
> *Singing of Death, and of Honour that cannot die,*
> *Till I well could weep for a time so sordid and mean,*
> *And myself so languid and base.*
>
> (I. V. i–ii; 162–172, 177–179)

The 'martial song,' casually mentioned, is not carelessly introduced. It helps to thaw the hero from his depression and looks forward to the means by which Britain is to shake off the sloth and selfishness of peace.

The narrative line is sketched in without much detail—the hero falls in love with Maud but they are kept apart by her family's insistence that she should make a wealthy marriage. This is not, as it might seem, merely a conventional device borrowed from the novel. It is important that the hero should be presented throughout the poem as one who has suffered personally from the values of 'the golden age', not just as a man vainly outraged by the way the world is. Similarly the financial rapacity of Maud's relations at once ruins the hero's life and symbolizes the dominant impulse in British society.

The unbalanced tone of the first four sections can be reasonably accounted for on grounds of dramatic verisimilitude, that is to say, the lack of balance is the hero's lack of balance, but what of the rest of part one? Here we find the hero wavering between trust and suspicion but finally wakened into new life and hope by his love for Maud. Presumably his 'morbid-hate and horror' have been allayed, yet there is still a disturbing violence of language. In X. i (330–351) and the last nine lines of X. ii (357–365) or in XIII. i. 11–13 (454–456) the viciousness is turned against the representatives of the mercantile ethic which is corrupting Britain. These passages thus find some justification since it is the commercialization of marriage which is threatening and is eventually to ruin the hero's happiness. Again in XIV. ii (497–510) we are in a world of over-expression, yet in XIV. iii (511–515) this is detected and reprobated by the hero himself: similarly XIV. iv (516–526) is noted as unbalanced in XV (527–536). The purpose of these observations is to establish that, up to this point at any rate, the passages of rancorous over-statement need not be taken as evidence of lack of control on Tennyson's part but may fairly be ascribed to a deliberate attempt to depict the still not wholly balanced response of the imaginary hero.

XVI is not so easy to dispose of in this way however; the exaggerated expression of contempt for the brother is protracted into an exaggerated expression of love for Maud, without sufficient, or indeed any, indication that the excess is a symptom of the hero's continuing instability and is recognized as such by the poet:

> *This lump of earth has left his estate*
> *The lighter by the loss of his weight;*
> *And so that he find what he went to seek,*
> *And fulsome Pleasure clog him, and drown*
> *His heart in the gross mud-honey of town,*
> *He may stay for a year who has gone for a week:*
> *But this is the day when I must speak,*
> *And I see my Oread coming down,*
> *O this is the day!*
> *O beautiful creature, what am I*
> *That I dare to look her way;*
> *Think that I may hold dominion sweet,*
> *Lord of the pulse that is lord of her breast,*
> *And dream of her beauty with tender dread,*
> *From the delicate Arab arch of her feet*
> *To the grace that, bright and light as the crest*
> *Of a peacock, sits on her shining head . . .*
>
> (XVI. i; 537–553)

In XVII ('Go not, happy day') the indulgence in rhapsodic exclamation is even more marked and even more disconcerting. The infantile repetitions, the choppy rhythm and the obvious rhymes do not suggest the sanity of true love but a feverish excitement. At this point I may perhaps repeat that our concern here is not simply with the power of the emotions expressed but also with the extent to which the hero's ability to master his emotions is reflected in his ability to master the expression of them. To some degree this must be a matter of individual taste. For example, in XVIII ii (605–610)—

> *None like her, none.*
> *Just now the dry-tongued laurels' pattering talk*
> *Seemed her light foot along the garden walk,*
> *And shook my heart to think she comes once more;*
> *But even then I heard her close the door,*
> *The gates of Heaven are closed, and she is gone,*

the first five lines to me seem admirably precise and vivid, while the last line offers an unnecessary and unacceptable hyperbole. It is worth noting that XVIII iv (627–638) once more touches on the theme of free will and determinism by presenting the stars as symbols of human insignificance: the care with which this is done shows that on one level at least Tennyson is working with notable understanding and command of the patterning of his material. The source of continuing uneasiness is, as I have suggested, to be traced not to the plan of the poem but to its detailing.

The narrow margin between success and failure is clearly illustrated by the stanza which closes section XVIII:

> *Is that enchanted moan only the swell*
> *Of the long waves that roll in yonder bay?*
> *And hark the clock within, the silver knell*
> *Of twelve sweet hours that past in bridal white,*
> *And died to live, long as my pulses play;*
> *But now by this my love has closed her sight*
> *And given false death her hand, and stolen away*
> *To dreamful wastes where footless fancies dwell*
> *Among the fragments of the golden day.*
> *May nothing there her maiden grace affright!*
> *Dear heart, I feel with thee the drowsy spell.*
> *My bride to be, my evermore delight,*
> *My own heart's heart, my ownest own, farewell;*
> *It is but for a little space I go:*
> *And ye meanwhile far over moor and fell*
> *Beat to the noiseless music of the night!*
> *Has our whole earth gone nearer to the glow*
> *Of your soft splendours that you look so bright?*
> *I have climbed nearer out of lonely Hell.*
> *Beat, happy stars, timing with things below,*
> *Beat with my heart more blest than heart can tell,*
> *Blest, but for some dark undercurrent woe*
> *That seems to draw—but it shall not be so:*
> *Let all be well, be well.*

(660–683)

The first two lines, with their Arnoldian cadence, are unexceptionable. but then the lyrical cry begins to sound forced. 'The silver knell,' the 'sweet hours,' the 'dreamful wastes' and the 'footless fancies' and the 'golden day' take us to a world of literary convention where rapture is to be expressed either in genteel cliches such as 'maiden grace' and 'drowsy spell' or in gushing outbursts such as 'My bride to be, my evermore delight,/My own heart's heart, my ownest own, farewell.' Then by means of a deft reference to the stars the section closes on a note of foreboding. Their 'soft splendours' drive from the hero's mind their function as symbols of man's 'nothingness'. With an ironic assurance he dismisses as groundless his deeper misgivings. Here the immediate situation reflects the larger patterning of the poem. But the uncertainty of tone in the middle of the section is not required by dramatic verisimilitude: possibly it arises because Tennyson is trying to express an intense emotion entirely unqualified by the dramatic situation.[1] There is of course a corresponding uneasiness when Tennyson offers us passages of narration without any leavening of emotion:

> *A grand political dinner*
> *To the men of many acres,*
> *A gathering of the Tory,*
> *A dinner and then a dance*
> *For the maids and marriage-makers,*
> *And every eye but mine will glance*
> *At Maud in all her glory.*
>
> *For I am not invited,*
> *But, with the Sultan's pardon,*
> *I am all as well delighted,*
> *For I know her own rose-garden,*
> *And mean to linger in it*
> *Till the dancing will be over.*
>
>   (XXI iii, iv; 817–829)

The poem requires a most delicate balance not only between narration and expression, but also between the hero's new-found sanity and his

---

[1] This theory is given some support when we learn that I XVII ('Go not, happy day'), which is in many ways the most embarrassing section of the poem, was in fact written for another occasion and placed in *Maud* later. Its awkwardness can be ascribed in part to its lack of dramatic connection.

rapturous love for Maud, a balance which is faultlessly struck in section XXII ('Come into the garden, Maud'). To explain why people laugh when they hear this line would be to explain why they are blind to the things that make *Maud* a good poem. Presumably the memory of Balfe's lilting melody transports the whole poem into the realms of Victorian song, which is well known to be ridiculous *per se*. This may account for popular reaction, but it is not adequate as an explanation of educated critical response. A careful reader can hardly fail to observe that in this section the poem is operating with complete success on all levels. The hero's immediate state of tremulous expectation is completely expressed in the movement of the verse; the setting provides a justification for the flood of natural imagery and reference: the hero's delight in the flowers and the trees indicates how effectively Maud has thawed his earlier frigid responses. All these show how thoroughly Tennyson realizes and presents the interaction between the hero's emotional excitement and his actual physical situation at the moment of speaking:

> *I said to the lily, 'There is but one*
> *With whom she has heart to be gay.*
> *When will the dancers leave her alone?*
> *She is weary of dance and play.'*
> *Now half to the setting moon are gone,*
> *And half to the rising day;*
> *Low on the sand and loud on the stone*
> *The last wheel echoes away.*

(XXII iv; 868–875)

The imagery, as John Killham has shown,[1] is intricately patterned without any sense of strain, and beneath the dancing rhythm and the effortless weaving of simple rhyme-words there is an ominous beat which tells the reader that all is not well:

> *There has fallen a splendid tear*
> *From the passion-flower at the gate.*
> *She is coming, my dove, my dear;*

[1] 'Tennyson's *Maud*—The Function of the Imagery,' in *Critical Essays on the Poetry of Tennyson* ed J. Killham, 1960, 219–35. Chiasson's essay (see footnote p. 116) is also in this collection.

> *She is coming, my life, my fate;*
> *The red rose cries, 'She is near, she is near;'*
> *And the white rose weeps, 'She is late;'*
> *The larkspur listens, 'I hear, I hear;'*
> *And the lily whispers, 'I wait.'*
>
> *She is coming, my own, my sweet;*
> *Were it ever so airy a tread,*
> *My heart would hear her and beat,*
> *Were it earth in an earthy bed;*
> *My dust would hear her and beat,*
> *Had I lain for a century dead;*
> *Would start and tremble under her feet*
> *And blossom in purple and red.*

(XXII x, xi; 908–923)

So Part One of the poem ends. The function of the second part is to explain what has happened, to convey the changes in the hero's situation and to trace his gradual descent into madness. At first the narrative burden is heaviest:

> *For she, sweet soul, had hardly spoken a word,*
> *When her brother ran in his rage to the gate,*
> *He came with the babe-faced lord;*
> *Heaped on her terms of disgrace,*
> *And while she wept, and I strove to be cool,*
> *He fiercely gave me the lie,*
> *Till I with as fierce an anger spoke,*
> *And he struck me, madman, over the face,*
> *Struck me before the languid fool,*
> *Who was gaping and grinning by:*
> *Struck for himself an evil stroke;*
> *Wrought for his house an irredeemable woe;*
> *For front to front in an hour we stood,*
> *And a million horrible bellowing echoes broke*
> *From the red-ribbed hollow behind the wood,*
> *And thundered up to Heaven the Christless code,*
> *That must have life for a blow.*

(2, I i; 11–27)

The language, especially in lines 21–22, has deliberate echoes of Greek tragedy.[1] Maud's part is left mysterious:

> *Then glided out of the joyous wood*
> *The ghastly Wraith of one that I know;*
> *And there rang on a sudden a passionate cry,*
> *A cry for a brother's blood:*
> *It will ring in my heart and my ears, till I die, till I die.*

(I i; 31–35)

Had she tried to stop the duel? Why is the hero so sure that her cry was 'for a brother's blood'? And does this mean 'because her brother was wounded' or 'that the shedding of her brother's blood should be revenged'? This ambiguity diminishes her importance for the hero at this point, and also retrospectively, making it more difficult to believe that she ever had enough substance or vitality to work the earlier changes in him.

One of the most conspicuous features of Tennyson's technique for representing loss of sanity in Part Two is the abruptness of the transitions between sections. This makes it difficult to discuss this section of the poem in general terms: part of the point of it is to convey madness as a rapid succession of states of mind with no obvious connection. Even those which are not completely successful as self-contained lyrics further the impression of disintegration. For example, Section II concludes with a stanza which seems clearly intended to be the good and unselfish centre of the poem, showing the nobler side of the hero even in madness, but it is in fact rather hollow, partly because of the impossible line 'However this may be,' and partly because the hero keeps obtruding his own concerns into his prayer for Maud. Section III, which was not added until 1856, is a necessary climax in the poem. The hero has learned for the first time of Maud's death. The phrase 'poor stupid heart of stone' does a lot of work. As well as recalling I VI viii (267–8) it looks forward to section IV. This section ('O that 'twere possible') was the first part of the poem to be written and expresses most

---

[1] Recalling earlier suggestions of doom in I XIII iii; 484–6 and I XIX iv; 714–16.

powerfully the hero's utter dejection and retreat, with the correlative
implied that withdrawal from the society of men is itself a form of madness:

> *I loathe the squares and streets,*
> *And the faces that one meets,*
> *Hearts with no love for me:*
> *Always I long to creep*
> *Into some still cavern deep,*
> *There to weep, and weep, and weep*
> *My whole soul out to thee.*
>
>   (IV xiii; 232–238)

Section V represents a further stage in the progression of the hero's
madness. Tennyson is here, more obviously than elsewhere in the poem,
trying to represent mimetically an imagined character in an imaginary
situation. The hero is meant to be mad yet, like Hamlet, able to comment
shrewdly on his world. What then is the status of an observation such
as 'The churchmen fain would kill their church,/As the churches have
killed their Christ'? Is it an obvious lie which shows the hero to be mad?
Or is it true? In which case why is it put into the mouth of a madman?
To ask this is to call in question Tennyson's entire conception in the
poem. On the one hand it can be argued that the idea of using a personal
dilemma as a vehicle for expounding a national dilemma is perfectly
legitimate, and that a melodramatic violent personal situation is the
appropriate correlative of a national situation which is apparently one
of peaceful commercial prosperity but is in reality one of deadly selfish
competition and exploitation: on the other that the national situation is
so involved and delicate as to call for a notably balanced and rational
observer, and that by choosing a man half out of his mind Tennyson
forfeits any claim to be offering fair comment on the world around him.
One thing that seems reasonably clear is that Tennyson is very far from
repudiating all that his hero says in his madness. Consider stanza vi, for
example:

> *Prophet, curse me the blabbing lip,*
> *And curse me the British vermin, the rat;*
> *I know not whether he came in the Hanover ship,*

> *But I know that he lies and listens mute*
> *In an ancient mansion's crannies and holes:*
> *Arsenic, arsenic, sure, would do it,*
> *Except that now we poison our babes, poor souls!*
> *It is all used up for that.*
>
> (295–302)

While this cannot be taken at face value, since it is intemperate in expression and clearly designed to suggest the disturbed logic of madness, it would be equally mistaken to suggest a simple reversal of meanings, since the passage takes up matters of genuine popular concern and ideas which Tennyson himself uses elsewhere. The first step then towards a thorough critique of the poem is to understand how the choice of a protagonist who is not completely sane enables Tennyson to write in this permanently ambiguous way, on the one hand disclaiming personal responsibility for the intemperance of the language, on the other allowing it to be supposed that the hero is but mad north-north-west and like Blake, for example, sees a corruption working in society to which men of normal vision are blind.[1] The next step is to determine how far this handy-dandy with madness and sanity is compatible with the form of the monodrama, which requires a felt change in the situation of the speaker between one section and the next: if this change is, as I have suggested, to be in terms of salvation from or reversion to insanity it is necessarily obscured if Tennyson also wishes to make his madman saner than other men. It seems that we have either to say that Tennyson jettisons the dramatic framework for the sake of emphasizing the method in the madness, or that we have here a further example of Tennyson's habit of overstating his case and that he is, in effect, saying 'This poor devil is mad—so mad that he thinks he is dead—yet even a raving lunatic can see that there is something dreadfully amiss in the state of Britain', without realizing how far this compromises the entire structure of his poem. To resolve this problem we must consider the final sections.

2 V x (326–333) presents a crucial step in the poem's argument. The hero reasons as follows: 'Remorse for "the red life spilt for a private blow" is something whose terrible nature I have myself experienced. I know that private vengeance is unforgivable and can therefore say

[1] Cf. 2 II viii; 106–18.

confidently that there is a vital distinction between "lawless and lawful war." If this is so, it follows that "whatever the Quaker holds" there is a kind of just war, so that for instance "to be struck by the public foe,/ Then to strike him and lay him low" far from being a sin would be "a public merit".' There are obvious flaws in this argument from the evil of private vengeance to the merit of public vengeance, but the sentiment that emerges—that there is such a thing as a righteous war—is not only emphatically stated in accents of the utmost sincerity by the hero but is also authenticated, however illogically, because it is offered as something which he has learned from all the passions of his earlier experiences in the poem, from his hysteria, his rapture and his anguish. In poetic terms the insight has been earned.

'My mood is changed' (3 VI i; 4)[1] strikes at once the note of the new life. The mention of the shining daffodil and Orion's grave, and the return of the season, take the reader's mind back to Maud's first appearance and her power to free the hero from torpor and unbalanced depression. The same work is done even more powerfully by the form of sections VI i and ii. They are both single-sentence sonnets with complicated rhyme-schemes, *tours de force* of the same nature as section III in Part One. This deliberate recollection of Maud's earlier ability to bring sanity from madness has the effect of giving the most emphatic endorsement possible in terms of the poem to the hero's decision to find 'a hope for the world in the coming wars'.[2]

This choice of war as the instrument by which the hero is to be regenerated and Britain is to be saved from the perils of prosperity has proved from the first a stumbling-block to Tennyson's readers.[3] It seems to me to be pointless to try to ignore the final section as an unimportant aberration, and it would be equally wrong to pretend that Tennyson allows a tactful vagueness to cloud his meaning here. The

---

[1] For Part Three Tennyson did not use a fresh sequence of section numbers: thus 3 VI immediately follows 2 V.

[2] Notice that even the agency of this second redemption has been prefigured: it is a martial song which Maud sings in 1 V and which is remembered by the hero in 1 X iv and again in his madness at 2 IV vi.

[3] PT, 1092, quotes an illuminating passage from *Tait's Edinburgh Magazine* for September 1855.

section is unambiguous and emphatic. Far from moderating his language the speaker expresses himself with extreme force and takes the strongest line of argument available to him. In effect he challenges those who prefer a life of peace to justify the values of peace: at the same time he threatens to destroy any general defence of a peaceful life as universally good by insistently confronting it with the actual deficiencies of a peaceful Britain. VI ii and VI iv show the force of this technique. The key lines of the climax of the poem are:

> *yet it lightened my despair*
> *When I thought that a war would arise in defence of the right,*
> *That an iron tyranny now should bend or cease,*
> *The glory of manhood stand on his ancient height,*
> *Nor Britain's one sole God be the millionaire:*
> *No more shall commerce be all in all . . .* (18–23)

Instead the hero will, he trusts,

> *wake to the higher aims*
> *Of a land that has lost for a little her lust of gold,*
> *And love of a peace that was full of wrongs and shames,*
> *Horrible, hateful, monstrous, not to be told.* (38–41)

This single line with its four fierce strokes might serve as a test-case for the whole of *Maud*. Unless the reader grants that the hero has established his right to such abnormal vehemence of language, this way of describing the state of Britain in the 1850s must be repudiated and, as a consequence, the whole idea of the hero's restoration to sanity called in question. This in turn entails a rejection of the entire poem as a coherent structure. Tennyson is, so to speak, gambling everything and is content with nothing less than complete victory. He insists that the reader shall accept not only the 'easy' image for the coming war at the end of VI ii:

> *And the cobweb woven across the cannon's throat*
> *Shall shake its threaded tears in the wind no more,* (27–28)

but also the far more difficult conclusion of VI iv:

> *For the peace, that I deemed no peace, is over and done,*
> *And now by the side of the Black and the Baltic deep,*

> And deathful-grinning mouths of the fortress, flames
> The blood-red blossom of war with a heart of fire.   (50–53)

The imagery is deliberately designed to recall the red rose which has earlier (e.g. 1 XVII, 1 XXII) been associated, if not identified, with Maud herself: to reject it is to reject the poem as a whole.

The obvious possibility that we are still in the presence of madness, dramatically presented, which we are meant to recognize and reprobate, will hardly survive in the face of the last six lines of the poem. The language is measured, which fits a solemn dedication of purpose, and the major themes of the poem are touched on in turn with a note of finality. The war is the Briton's chance to show that he has a heart, not merely a lust for gold. The hero, cleaving to a cause that he feels 'to be pure and true' can at last win free from the dangers of torpor and madness.[1] He must do this, of course, by finding a purpose outside himself, feeling 'with [his] native land' and being 'one with [his] kind.' Only in this way is he able to reconcile himself to the loss of free will and personal power and thus 'embrace . . . the doom assigned'.

The last movement is not, clearly, an accidental one: it is implicit in the whole design of the monodrama. It will clarify the argument to recapitulate at this point the various progressions which Tennyson manages in parallel. The hero moves gradually from intense and morbid depression through awakening love to rapture: then more suddenly into madness and painfully back to sanity. In more general terms he proceeds from a conviction of helplessness ('We are puppets') to a conviction of power ('We have hearts in a cause, we are noble still'). It is not surprising that this is accompanied by a hope that the nation will find salvation by moving from sloth to militancy, from the lethargy of peace to the energy of war, from a selfish obsession with material prosperity to a sense of national purpose. It is perhaps more remarkable that the change from a feeling of constraint to a feeling of purpose should be represented as a change from disengagement to commitment, from competitive comm-

---

[1] Cf. 'It is time, O passionate heart and morbid eye,/That old hysterical mock-disease should die.' (3 VI iii; 32–33) It seems probable to me that this 'mock-disease' is the 'dreary phantom' referred to in line 36 rather than the ghost of Maud, as Ricks suggests.

erce and individualist economics to cooperative action for the common good. The hero is looking forward to an idealist conception of the State (such as was later to become familiar in Britain from the work of Bradley and Bosanquet, for example) as the instrument by which individual wills are subdued into a general purpose and acquire a genuine freedom by losing personal identity in a larger cause. 'Freedom' of course must not be defined in terms of individualism, which leads to *laisser faire* in corporate life and isolation in personal life, but in terms of joint action, the provision of a social context within which individual action is significant.[1]

The critical application of this general account of the poem is in correcting a common misreading of Part Three. It is often taken as a jingoist glorification of war for its own sake, and therefore as a totally unacceptable conclusion, especially if it is intended to convey the hero's newly recovered sanity. But to restate the ending in a much more attractive way we do not even need to use more sympathetic terms, simply more fashionable ones—'The hero learns that freedom involves commitment, and concern, and an acceptance of violence to destroy the cash-based class-conscious regime which is hostile to love and the good of humanity'. If it is accepted that Tennyson is expecting the reader to agree with a statement of this kind at the end of *Maud* it is plain that the poem embodies a view of human activity which cannot simply be dismissed on the grounds that the sentiments themselves are patently wrongheaded. When the hero asks at the beginning of the poem, 'Shall I weep if a Poland fall? shall I shriek if a Hungary fail?' (I IV iii; 147) his question is rhetorical and implies the answer 'No'; by the end of the poem he sees that the question must be taken as a serious inquiry into personal and national responsibility and answered 'Yes'. We do not need to remember what Poland and Hungary have come to stand for in our time to realize that the hero's new resolution is very different from a simple desire to put the Tsar in his place. The planet Mars, glowing 'like a ruddy shield on the Lion's breast' shows that to fight these wars is indeed Britain's destiny. Now instead of railing against his fate the hero finds comfort in the acknowledgement that he is part of a large plan.

[1] Cf. 'Ode on the Death of the Duke of Wellington' (1852), lines 198–217.

I have stated the movement of the poem in general terms in order to show that charges of slackness of construction are not easy to substantiate: in particular Maud herself and her effect on the hero are related with notable care to the wider themes of the poem. Nor should I accept T. S. Eliot's diagnosis of 'a fundamental error of form'.[1] It must be conceded that we have no sense of a felt actual progressive change in the character of the hero, as we feel that Sludge and Blougram are actually changed in the course of their monologues by what they are discovering about themselves. The monodrama simply presents us with the hero in a new attitude for each episode, like the figures in early animated cartoons, the movement having taken place between frames. The more conscious we are of this careful intercalary manipulation of poses by Tennyson, the more questions we are bound to ask about the hero's free agency.

But this does not necessarily invalidate my claim that one of the particular triumphs of Tennyson's art in the poem is the subtle interplay of and discriminations between different definitions of freedom. The crucial lesson which the hero has to learn is that 'freedom' is not simply a synonym for 'individual self-assertion', that there are forces outside the individual that shape his destiny, and that some ways of acknowledging this fact lead to despair and madness while others lead to resolution and sanity. The changes between one section and another are convincingly enough accounted for in dramatic terms. For example the hero's initial desperation is accounted for by the manner of his father's death, his subsequent lightening of spirit is caused by Maud's arrival, his doubts by the opposition of Maud's family, his anger by the arranged marriage, his hopes by the gradual discovery of Maud's love for him. The catastrophe, the news of Maud's death, his vision and the news of the wars similarly provide adequate causal mechanisms for the rest of the poem—that is to say, they are sufficient to prevent us from saying simply that it is Tennyson who pulls out a suitably varied stop for each section. This careful linking of events, taken together with an insistent use of premonitory signs and the frequent references to the stars as agents of destiny, confirms that the hero is not accidentally but delibera-

[1] *In Memoriam* in *Essays Ancient and Modern*, 1936.

tely presented as learning by painful experience that human life is en-
meshed in a web of circumstance and that wisdom lies in embracing the
doom assigned, which in the poem's last line is not distinguished from
'the purpose of God'. The monodrama, then, provided that the shifts of
mood between one section and the next are given an acceptable dramatic explanation, is as a form perfectly compatible with Tennyson's over-
riding argument.

If then *Maud* is finally to be judged as a failure, the failure need not
be ascribed to an intellectual deficiency nor to an incompatibility
between the argument and the action, nor to an incongruity between
either of these and the form chosen. The principal source of uneasiness
is a want of correspondence between the argument of the poem and the
diction adopted. This also calls in question the free agency of the hero,
but does so in a way which does nothing to reinforce the meaning of the
poem.

The point can be most readily illustrated by saying that the language
seems deliberately designed to recall that of the Old Testament. When
the speaker offers his observations about the human condition in the
gnomic utterance of Proverbs or denounces the corruption of the popu-
lace in the inspired invective of the major prophets it is hard not to feel
that he is simply Tennyson's mouthpiece.

Those who allege a failure of control of diction in *Maud* are thus in a
position to assert also a failure of dramatic consistency and to argue that
in *Maud* we have not a work of fiction but a work of autobiography. An
impressive amount of evidence can be amassed to corroborate this position, though it seems to me that strictly speaking the most that it shows
is that the sentiments attributed to the speaker are not such as Tennyson
would himself have repudiated. His unhappy love for Rosa Baring, his
continuing grief for Hallam, his private opinions as shown in his letters
—all these have been exhaustively investigated and scrupulously set out,[1]
but they are of no coercive force.

Of a different order, and distinctly stronger, is the argument derived
from other poems of Tennyson's—we can find in 'The Two Voices' the

---

[1] Notably by R. W. Rader, *Tennyson's 'Maud': The Biographical Genesis*,
Berkeley and Los Angeles, 1963.

justification of a righteous war; in poems such as 'Riflemen Form!',
'Jack Tar', 'The Penny-Wise', 'The Third of February 1852', and
'Suggested by Reading an Article in a Newspaper', the habitual note of
militant aggression when international politics are the theme; in 'Rifle
Clubs!!!' his detestation of 'Peace of sloth or avarice born'; in 'Sea
Dreams' his bitterness about the world of finance; in 'Edwin Morris',
'Edward Gray', and 'Aylmer's Field' his scorn for the marriage arranged
or forbidden for social reasons; in 'Come hither', 'The Dead Prophet',
and 'To—, After Reading A Life and Letters' his dread of malicious
gossip. The argument is, of course, not conclusive, but it is persuasive.
It is hard not to accept the view that the passions which erupt so fiercely
in *Maud* are Tennyson's private obsessions breaking through the thin
pretence at a dramatic disguise.

The reason why this is a damaging criticism is not that there is something illicit in mingling the confessional and the dramatic but that this
mingling compromises, if not completely betrays, the operation of the
monodrama. Tennyson exercises an extraordinarily tight control of
argument and action and metrical pattern, but he requires the reader, as
Gladstone observed,[1] 'to comprehend rightly the relation between
particular passages in the poem and its general scope'. Let me repeat
also that the monodrama works by enabling readers to classify successive sections, as, for example, honest or dishonest, balanced or unbalanced, by discriminating between the emotions which dominate
them. But if the reader is to be able to place the different phases of the
hero's passions with any accuracy he must be able to rely on variations
in diction as being significant and not arbitrary. If the diction is not
sufficiently precise to allow this kind of discrimination it is impossible to
read the poem as a monodrama with any confidence. There is a telling
contrast in 'James Lee's Wife', where Browning eschews strong variations of idiom so that small variations, as for example in sections VI and
VIII, can be detected and made part of our reading of the poem.
Tennyson offers no such precise indications: instead he surges at a new
emotion.

An illustration may make the point clearer. I have tried to show that

---

[1] *Gleanings of Past Years*, 1879, II, 146n.

the hero's enthusiasm for a righteous war in Part Three is not incompatible with Tennyson's own account of the poem in which at the end the hero 'has recovered his reason' and 'sane, but shattered' gives himself up to work 'for the good of mankind'. But the sentiments he is expressing at the end of the poem are not on the face of it different from those he expresses in the very first section (1 I vi, xii-xiii; 21-24, 47-52). One can argue, of course, that in Part One the hero is debating with himself whether peace would be better than war or not: at this point it is still an open question to him, which in the end he decides wrongly— 'I will bury myself in myself'. Similarly it is possible to point to stanza xiii as conditional and in the third person, whereas the resolution at the end of the poem is an actual decision made by the hero himself. But to claim these arguments as convincing one would have to point to a precision of diction which the poem does not offer.

If, then, *Maud* cannot be held to operate as a completely successful monodrama it is perhaps best understood as a semi-objectified autobiographical fantasy—more like *In Memoriam* than 'James Lee's Wife'. Tennyson, on this view, is giving up the potentialities of the monodrama in exchange for other, bolder effects. Perhaps the most interesting parallels are with two later poems not usually considered of first importance—'Despair' (1881) and 'Locksley Hall Sixty Years After' (1886), which are, technically at least, dramatic monologues, and may suggest something of Tennyson's intentions in *Maud*.

The speaker in 'Despair' (PT, 1299) is certainly placed in a powerful enough situation. He and his wife have tried to drown themselves: his wife has succeeded but he has been rescued by a Calvinist minister. This situation is not exploited in any way. It is hard not to conclude that the speaker, as in the monologues which I discussed earlier, is simply there to add an extra layer of anguish, as his dead wife certainly is: a peculiarly distressing personal grief is used as the medium for expounding a general distress. Alternatively, and more charitably, we may say that the intensity of the situation is given as an index of the intensity of the speaker's despair. He has renounced religion, 'the drear night-fold of your fatalist creed' (21), and tells the minister of a God of wrath, 'You flung us back on ourselves, and the human heart, and the Age' (40). Nor does he find any comfort in the world offered by scientific theory, a world of 'brainless Nature' in which men are 'poor orphans of nothing' and the earth is their 'dead brute mother'. Thus he can say that now in 'the new dark ages . . . of the popular press' 'the Sun and the Moon of our science are both of them turned into blood' (88, 91) and Hope has vanished from the earth: 'We had past from a cheerless night to the glare of a drearier day' (28). This dilemma of the impossible choice between Hell-fire determinism and agnostic vacuity is presented by Tennyson as an intolerable one, so intolerable that death is the only solution—'I am frighted at life not death' (14). There is a casual reference to the 'world of arrogant opulence' (78) but the real force of social denunciation comes in lines 30–32, where the speaker laments that God the Father is now no more than

The guess of a worm in the dust and the shadow of its desire—
Of a worm as it writhes in a world of the weak trodden down by the strong,
Of a dying worm in a world, all massacre, murder, and wrong.

The technique of 'Locksley Hall Sixty Years After' (PT, 1359) is similar, the speaker's situation being sketched in equally briefly. The poem is formally a sequel to 'Locksley Hall': the two poems constitute in effect the two sections of a monodrama. The great interval between them leads naturally to reflections on the passage of time, which in turn lead the speaker to meditate on the changes he has seen. The bulk of the poem is his attempt to decide whether in these changes there is any evidence of progress, if indeed the concept of progress has any meaning at all. Once again the immediate dramatic situation is swept aside, and is not used, as Browning for example almost invariably used it, to qualify the views expressed. Instead the monologue is a series of general observations, full of large terms with capital letters, on the deplorable way the world is going downhill. The speaker is a man of eighty, talking to his grandson, and can thus plausibly suggest that he is no longer responsible for the way things are—it is the young who keep talking about Progress. The personality of the speaker is built up with some skill:

Fires that shook me once, but now to silent ashes fallen away.
Cold upon the dead volcano sleeps the gleam of dying day.   (41–42)

Yet these very touches serve to remind the reader that Tennyson himself was an old man looking back at the vast upheavals of the century. The poem begins with another statement of the dilemma that tortured Tennyson from the time of Hallam's death, that of giving some permanence to human values in an age in which it was increasingly difficult to believe in personal immortality:

> *Truth for truth, and good for good! The Good, the True, the Pure, the Just—*
> *Take the charm 'For ever' from them, and they crumble into dust.*   (71–72)

But if this is true what are we to make of the claims that the nineteenth century is an era of Progress and human advancement, since we are unable to decide in what terms human advancement is to be defined? Certainly to the man who looks about him the signs of progress are not universally evident—'When was age so crammed with menace? madness? written, spoken lies?'

In particular the speaker directs his scorn against the false doctrines of egalitarianism ('Envy wears the mask of Love') and ridicules the notion that great affairs of state should be left to the mercy of a popular vote:

> *Those three hundred millions under one Imperial sceptre now,*
> *Shall we hold them? shall we loose them? take the suffrage of the plow.*
> (117–118)

The responsibility is placed on the shoulders of political demagogues:

> *You that woo the Voices—tell them 'old experience is a fool,'*
> *Teach your flattered kings that only those who cannot read can rule.*
>
> *Pluck the mighty from their seat, but set no meek ones in their place;*
> *Pillory Wisdom in your markets, pelt your offal at her face.*
>
> *Tumble Nature heel o'er head, and, yelling with the yelling street,*
> *Set the feet above the brain and swear the brain is in the feet.*
>
> *Bring the old dark ages back without the faith, without the hope,*
> *Break the State, the Church, the Throne, and roll their ruins down the slope.*
> (131–138)

When the tirade is broken off it is in terms which once more take the reader's attention not to the fictitious circumstances of the speaker but to the figure of the elderly poet himself—'Heated am I? you—you wonder—well, it scarce becomes mine age—' (151). The same pattern is repeated, with the same effect, later in the poem:

> *Poor old Heraldry, poor old History, poor old Poetry, passing hence,*
> *In the common deluge drowning old political common-sense!*
>
> *Poor old voice of eighty crying after voices that have fled!*
> *All I loved are vanished voices, all my steps are on the dead.*
>
> *All the world is ghost to me, and as the phantom disappears,*
> *Forward far and far from here is all the hope of eighty years.* (249–254)

There follows a row of asterisks. In the concluding thirty lines the
speaker attends more closely to his immediate situation: the effect of
the asterisks is to separate the dramatic from the reflective passages and
thus to make it almost impossible to avoid identifying Tennyson with
his speaker when he despairs of the age in general terms.

The difficulty here, as in *Maud*, is that the speaker stands in much
the same relation, that is an external one, as Tennyson himself does to the
public issues under discussion. When Browning wishes to consider the
question of popular government, he does so from the inside by creating
the character of Prince Hohenstiel-Schwangau who, being in the seat
of power, presents the exercise of power as a series of personal decisions.
Tennyson's characters, however, are usually, like their creator, unhappy
victims of the way things are and can only express their fury and their
helplessness in a kind of baffled bewilderment. If then we look to the
poet to offer a clear and objective explanation of the workings of his
world we shall be disappointed by Tennyson. What he offers instead is
perhaps most clearly illustrated by a couplet which has received more
than its fair share of derision:

> *'Forward' rang the voices then, and of the many mine was one.*
> *Let us hush this cry of 'Forward' till ten thousand years have gone.*
> (77–78)

This is usually taken as the voice of an aged reactionary rejecting the
liberal ideals of his youth: in fact the speaker is represented as questioning with the salutary scepticism of age, not the progressive ideas of his
time, but the entire basis of the definition of human progress. How do we
know, he asks, that we are in fact better than our ancestors?[1] Possibly

[1] Cf. 'The Dawn' (1892) (PT, 1452), which stands in a particularly close
relationship to 'Locksley Hall Sixty Years After', lines 77–108.

after ten thousand years a positive advance will be discernible, but only a rash man would declare that the nineteenth century demonstrably represented a higher stage in human development than the 'vanished races',

> *Evolution ever climbing after some ideal good,*
> *And reversion ever dragging Evolution in the mud.* (199–200)

In conclusion let me refer once more to John Killham's valuable essay. In order to avoid discussing the difficult ideological questions raised by *Maud* he says, 'Theme and story are secondary, and . . . the reader should concentrate on poems and poetry'.[1] I cannot accept the implication that there is a sense in which we can study the 'poetry' while not studying what Tennyson is writing about, nor, as is plain, do I think that Tennyson has anything to fear from a close scrutiny of the theme and the story, especially if we extend our consideration beyond the specific rights and wrongs of the Crimean War to the general case which Tennyson is examining, that of how man should live with his fellow-men.

This is a question which Tennyson explores in poem after poem with a thoroughness and independence which make nonsense of statements such as John Lucas's that Tennyson 'increasingly settled for this "mask of conformity" ', 'had little interest in politics', 'has no political ideas', and 'can do no more than mouth the available clichés about the ringing grooves of change'.[2] It would be hard to find four less accurate statements about Tennyson. Even an early poem like 'The Lotos-Eaters' has its revealing comment to make on the social issues of the day. The speaker is far from repudiating Lotos-land: if anything he is questioning the values that require modern man to go on climbing the climbing wave. Since it is put in the mouth of a fictitious speaker the case for withdrawing permanently from the struggle can be fully articulated. The speaker of 'Locksley Hall' is equally tempted by the seductions of the 'summer isles of Eden lying in dark-purple spheres of sea'. 'There methinks would be enjoyment more than in this march of mind,/In the steamship, in the

---

[1] Killham, 225.

[2] In John Lucas (ed), *Literature and Politics in the Nineteenth Century,* 1971, pp. 12, 13, 16.

railway, in the thoughts that shake mankind.' But he reproaches himself, 'Fool, again the dream, the fancy! but I *know* my words are wild'
and shoulders once again the burden appropriate to 'the heir of all the
ages'. But the haunting question of the value of human activity is not
to be stilled by a brave resolution. It is a continual theme in *In Memoriam*
and, as I have said, lies behind the whole plan of *Maud*. As the century
wore on Tennyson worried at the idea in poems such as 'Locksley Hall
Sixty Years After' and 'The Ancient Sage'. Indeed it is tempting to
regard all the poems which I have mentioned in this paragraph as themselves composing a massive monodrama on the subject of the proper
duties of man in so far as these can be established without reference to
the church and in so far as we have to take account of what scientists
tell us about the nature of the human race.

Other poems could clearly be given a place,[1] but these seem to me to
constitute the most interesting and the most important set. I do not
suggest that the later poems supersede the earlier ones. Each offers a
possible political attitude expressed with extreme force without com-
mitting Tennyson personally. The dramatic form enables him to put
before his readers the critical case in the argument as a fully worked-out
hypothesis. Thus at the end of *Maud* he can put a hard question, because
the hero does not embrace cooperative action at its easy VSO level, but
welcomes the really difficult case—war. If Tennyson had been writing
directly about his own situation he would have had to say, 'It is better to
work for the good than to rail at the ill': his fictitious persona can say, 'It
is better to *fight* etc'. The crucial question which lies at the root of all
discussion of the state is thus posed—are we prepared to welcome the
service of the nation-state as the only way in which its citizens can
become truly free even if the consequences are the use of force to settle
international arguments and the espousing by these citizens of their
country's quarrels as their own? In short, is patriotism freedom? If
not, what is?

With the help of the monodrama and the dramatic monologue
Tennyson was able to put before his public a series of investigations of
the first importance, continually testing the received attitudes which he

[1] 'Ulysses', for example, and even 'St Simeon Stylites', suggest possible
ways of engaging or not engaging with one's society.

expressed so emphatically and so memorably in his public poems. Both are proper activities for a poet. The unusual thing is to find a poet who has sufficient breadth of mind to do both.

For example, the poem which immediately follows 'Locksley Hall Sixty Years After' is 'On the Jubilee of Queen Victoria'. The contrast is almost absolute:

> *Fifty years of ever-broadening Commerce!*
> *Fifty years of ever-brightening Science!*
> *Fifty years of ever-widening Empire!*

In the last stanza doubts are raised only to be stifled:

> *Are there thunders moaning in the distance?*
> *Are there spectres moving in the darkness?*
> *Trust the Hand of Light will lead her people,*
> *Till the thunders pass, the spectres vanish,*
> *And the Light is Victor, and the darkness*
> *Dawns into the Jubilee of the Ages.*

In 'Locksley Hall Sixty Years After' the best that can be offered is

> *Hope the best, but hold the Present fatal daughter of the Past,*
> *Shape your heart to front the hour, but dream not that the hour will last,*
>
> (105–106)

and

> *Follow Light, and do the Right—for man can half-control his doom.*
>
> (277)

Are we to take it that one of these poems represents the private or 'real' Tennyson and the other the public or 'hypocritical' Tennyson? Or that both are equally dramatic monologues, each carefully in character? The second seems to me nearer the truth if it is accepted that Tennyson normally chooses as the persona of his monologues and monodramas a character who allows him to express an extreme version of some of his own views. Since he was on many issues a man of divided mind this offered him a reasonably wide choice of stances. Even in *Maud*, which comes closest to preserving the 'classic' relationship of poet to speaker, the dramatic cannot be pointed to as clearly distinguished from the confessional.

In a sense, therefore, the title of this chapter is disingenuous, since it could be plausibly argued that Tennyson wrote no dramatic monologues which fully deserve the name. I do not think that this is a powerful objection: what is interesting is Tennyson's persistent setting up of a dramatic façade which he then no longer bothers to maintain consistently because his method does not require it and because the façade is so very like what is behind it. His most interesting experiment is, of course, *Maud*, where he tries to represent a character with a wide range of emotions. To account for the variations in his hero's state of mind he fabricates a much more fully worked-out dramatic framework, but even there, especially when the lines are long, the advantages of obliquity grow faint and the temptation to most direct frontal denunciation with Tennyson's own damaging rhetorical weapons grows stronger.

The result is not a pure or a deeply satisfying poem but a worrying uneasy poem. The burden of my discussion of it is that it becomes even more worrying if we take it not as a series of lyrics, some successful, some not, but as a serious contribution to the argument about the condition of England in the nineteenth century and after, and as part of a continuing debate about the nature of human freedom. The questions that vex Tennyson here and in the other poems I have mentioned are still unanswered.

6: *Tennyson and Victorian Social Values*

JOHN KILLHAM

THE NINETEENTH CENTURY has been aptly called 'an age of multanimity', one which managed to keep an uneasy balance or equipoise between practices and ideals which were quite opposed to one another. So to speak of Victorian social attitudes as if they could be simply enumerated as fixities is quite misleading. Not only did controversies flourish on almost every question: decisions were taken with small idea of the consequences. But these consequences could be very great. For instance the prosperous period between 1851 and 1867, the Great Exhibition and the Second Reform Act, differed markedly from the periods before and after, when economic conditions were depressed. Though outwardly prosperous and calm, it was nevertheless a time of intellectual ferment which may be measured by the importance of the achievement of Darwin in 1859.

No one needs reminding that the class into which one was born in the nineteenth century made infinitely more difference than nowadays, and in no respect more than in the kind and amount of work one had to do, or whether one had any to do at all. Work, responsible or exacting, was the central human consequence of the industrial revolution, and its demands made their presence felt in the art of the nineteenth century, draining it, if not of beauty, of joy. The task confronting thinkers, writers, painters, churchmen and others, was to interpret the social effects of labour and its products, whether in personal relationships like love, family life and class, or in the wider fields of politics and religion. The 'multanimity' and the 'equipoise' reflect the compromises which allowed the final transition between cultural epochs to take place relatively peacefully. It would be legitimate, I believe, to suggest that some of Tennyson's most admired early poems, 'The Lady of Shalott',

'The Lotos-Eaters', 'Ulysses', 'The Palace of Art' (PT, 354, 429, 560 and 400), can be best understood as examples of the effect upon one of markedly aesthetic temperament of the sense of the new burdens of responsibility. Symbolically, even on occasion allegorically, they represent the pull of opposed inclinations and that ironically-guarded schismatic mind which yearned for heroic commitment to an ideal of love or justice, but had to acknowledge the truth that the new age demanded incessant labour and pragmatic solutions to urgent social problems. Out of idealism and scepticism together, Tennyson's best work arises, often in the form of evocations of heroic figures from classical or medieval legends, transposed into the modern mood of nervous restlessness or disgust.

But like Pre-Raphaelite painting, Tennyson's work is extremely various, and since he has poems which handle social questions explicitly, I can more usefully concentrate on them. We shall understand them best by recognizing that unlike some of the Victorian novelists Tennyson did not as a rule record industrial conditions and means of relieving them. (The two 'Locksley Hall' poems (PT, 688 and 1359) glance at such matters). He is too much possessed by the traditional culture of England, its classical affiliations, and its constitutional concern with ordered government. His voice is typically for moderation with reform. A useful comparison can be made with Ford Madox Brown, whose paintings catch the Tennysonian blend of rich coloration, sentiment, love of the familiar and unpretentious—and social concern. Brown's picture entitled 'Work', which shows two of Tennyson's friends Carlyle and F. D. Maurice watching labourers excavating in the roadway in one of his favourite London haunts, Hampstead, gives in one view an excellent insight into Victorian social relations as they might well have appeared to Tennyson himself. Brown wrote a commentary on his picture in which he praised the two 'brain-workers, who seeming to be idle, work, and are the cause of well-ordained work and happiness in others—sages, such as in ancient Greece published their opinions in the market square'.[1] The picture seems to be a 'modern'

[1] The commentary is to be found in Ford M. Hueffer, *Ford Madox Brown*, 1896, 189–195, conveniently reprinted in *The Pre-Raphaelites in Literature and Art*, ed and intr. D. S. R. Welland, 1953, 51–58. The

adaptation of Raphael's *School of Athens* in the Vatican, though in other respects Pre-Raphaelite enough.[1] This sort of gesture to tradition is everywhere apparent in Tennyson's 'idyls', which are both skilful adaptations of Theocritus and comments on the contemporary English scene, picturesquely rendered in the Pre-Raphaelite manner.

Brown's picture shows two additional groups—the poor and unemployed on one side, and two well-dressed 'idle' ladies on the other. Industrial labour is not represented at all, unless it be by a stunted beerman down from Birmingham. Again we have a parallel with Tennyson, whose poems offer plentiful studies of refined, middle-class women and of the rural poor. But another group is even more significant. A gentleman and his daughter have been obliged by the obstruction to turn back towards the Heath where doubtless they have been riding (and which Sir Thomas Wilson had for many years been selling for gravel and building lots). Brown calls him in his commentary an honest, true-hearted gentleman whom the sages could easily win over if he could only be got to hear them. He represents the gentry—probably, Brown says, a Colonel with a seat in Parliament, fifteen thousand a year and a pack of hounds. To us he may not seem particularly busy— but then how different he is to Brown from another rich man, doubtless *too* busy to be enjoying the summer sunshine in the pleasant suburb and represented only by his name displayed on billboards announcing his candidacy for a Middlesex seat. That name is Bobus, and readers of *Past and Present* (1843) would recall that his fortune derived from the profitable manufacture in Hounsditch of sausages, filled with horsemeat.

The contrast Brown makes between these two rich men reveals the profound effect upon Victorian artists of the early writings of Carlyle. It illustrates the fact that with all his eccentricity of language and apparent radicalism of purpose he did as much as anyone to sustain traditional English values, and most notably the Englishman's ingrained habit of deference towards his betters. The fact that F. D.

picture exists in two versions, to be seen in the Municipal Art Galleries of Manchester and Birmingham. It is reproduced with a long catalogue note in *Pre-Raphaelite Painters*, ed R. Ironside and J. Geve, 1948.

[1] Timothy Hilton, *The Pre-Raphaelites*, 1970, 157.

Maurice, Principal of the Working Men's College where Brown and Ruskin taught, stands next to him, 'smiling perhaps at some of his wild sallies and cynical thrusts (for Socrates at times strangely disturbs the seriousness of his auditory by the mercilessness of his jokes—against vice and foolishness)' represents a perfectly natural kinship between a large section of churchmen and the advocate of firm Government by those best fitted to govern. Carlyle looked back in *Past and Present* to an age in which feudal social values seemed to him demonstrably superior to the age of Bobus. The backward look for future guidance was characteristic of Tennyson too: for he shared Carlyle's fears of revolution even while he was crying the Whig rallying call of Liberty and linking it with the name of Hampden. Stirred by demagoguery at the hustings and some anxious experience of rick-burnings, he wrote between 1831 and 1834 a series of poems which anticipate Bagehot in their fervent recommendation of the advantages of settled government under a sound constitution.[1] His suspicion of Celtic (i.e. French) instability and detestation of Russian autocracy (looking forward to *Maud*) are poised with his heartfelt sense of the value of freedom and a fear (which is at the basis of the aristocratic system) that this freedom will be endangered by the association of the unenfranchised working class:

> *And love of novel forms avail*
> *To quench the light of Reverence.*
>
> ('Hail Briton!', 43–44: PT, 480)

Carlyle did not care for his early poetry, but on meeting him was impressed enough to recommend his giving up verse and applying himself to prose and *Work*. Tennyson, for his part, put into old James of 'The Golden Year' (1846) something of Carlyle's impatience with the Utopianism which was also part of his characteristic outlook, a belief in progress towards a state of eventual social and economic equality:

> *When wealth no more shall rest in mounded heaps,*
> *But smit with freër light shall slowly melt*

---

[1] 'Hail Briton!', 'You ask me, why', 'Love thou thy land', 'Of old sat Freedom on the heights', 'I loving Freedom for herself' (PT, 480, 489, 613, 617 and 619).

> *In many streams to fatten lower lands,*
> *And light shall spread, and man be liker man* . . . .
> (32–35, PT, 715)

Some suppressed lines reveal that Tennyson was not altogether easy about the Carlylean semi-religious belief in work, which could be used as a kind of opium for the people, or, as in Goethe's ambiguous *Faust*, a justification for self-fulfilment under the guise of public benefit: like Mill, another champion of liberty, he wondered whether progress would bring anything really much better in the long run. The doubt is very Tennysonian, and re-emerges in 'Locksley Hall Sixty Years After' (PT, 1359) in full blast.

Carlyle's vision of a nation whose estates, ranging from the highest to the lowest, laboured together in mutual cooperation under strong but provident leadership also conformed with the social outlook of many pious and industrious people who were guided by the teaching of Christian pastors throughout the land. But it was clouded by various dark and ill-understood obstructions to the clear light of hope.[1] Unemployment, for instance, resulting from the introduction of machinery or from trade-recessions, made it seem almost as if the divine plan might be an illusion, impossible of fulfilment. Then the education Carlyle believed would assist in confounding the pessimistic class of statisticians who saw no way out of the dilemma of a high population and a low production might lead to Orson demanding the privileges of Valentine. The association of work with religion (especially if it were of the Puritan variety) too often encouraged worship of success in making and manipulating money—or a suicidal despair at the threat of financial failure which appalled both Arnold and Ruskin. The competition for work depressed wages and led to clashes between unions and employers. The profit-motive, operating independently of moral and artistic principles, permitted the manufacture of tasteless and useless articles which caused men like Ruskin and Morris to turn to fundamental social questions, and away from Christian teaching on them, or rather, in Ruskin's case, to proclaim that properly understood, Christian belief

---

[1] *Chartism*, 1839, chap. 4. In chap. 6 Carlyle writes that democracy is the consummation of No-government and *laissez-faire.*

demanded an utter repudiation of a system which permitted so much less concern for social good and especially the fate of poor people than had existed centuries before. One can understand Dickens making Stephen Blackpool in *Hard Times* repeatedly cry, 'aw a muddle'.

Carlyle's *Sartor Resartus* of the beginning of the Victorian era contrasts wonderfully with Morris's *A Dream of John Ball*, of 1888, very near the end of Tennyson's life. Morris had read Marx's *Capital*, and the historical account he had found there of the development from the manorial economy and feudal society of the middle ages to the capitalist economy and bourgeois society of the modern era is cleverly translated into an exchange of views between the rebel priest of the fourteenth and the dreamer of the nineteenth century. The familiar device is remarkably effective in bringing home to the modern reader how much of Marxist theory (particularly in regard to social structure and its relation to the means of production) has become commonplace, and, correspondingly, how willing the great majority of high Victorian writers were (Tennyson included) to take ordinary Christian moral teaching, or Carlyle's radical conservatism, as their rule in questions in which economics play a main part. Mrs Gaskell, Disraeli, Dickens, George Eliot and others all register their sense that something is profoundly wrong when particular men and women find their lives denied fulfilment by a combination of seemingly immitigable economic circumstances and social attitudes cruelly at variance with them. But the resolution of their stories is usually achieved not by a revolt against the social system as in Morris, Hardy (in *Tess of the D'Urbervilles* and *Jude the Obscure*) and Samuel Butler. Frequently it is death in circumstances more pathetic than tragic (in *The Mill on the Floss, Hard Times, The Princess Casamassima*), or a resolve to accept the task of easing the burden by individual effort, (*Felix Holt, North and South*): or, finally, a wholly personal 'conversion' (often as the result of a violent encounter with death, illness, or injury). This last solution is common in Dickens, who explores the Victorian class system with a profound feeling for the relationships between it and the economic, social and educational bases upon which it rested, only in the last resort to fall back upon traditional social ideas of Christian altruism or gentlemanly prerogative which in some measure counteract the specific criticism and satire of the political system, law, the government, the church, public charity, marriage (and prostitution), and so on, with which his work abounds. Thus it comes about that his work shares that concern with personal guilt and sorrow which Tennyson's poetry has, a consequence of taking a moral view of conditions created by structural rather than by simply ethical considerations.

Brown's 'Work' and the commentary upon it illustrate this cultural inertia in all sorts of ways, but notably by the pleading tone in which the workers are justified as decent human beings, and its deferential attitude to a gentleman of the old sort. For contrast one needs to turn to Ruskin's lecture entitled 'Work', delivered to the Working Men's Institute at Camberwell, and reprinted in *The Crown of Wild Olive* (1866). Here is a passage which does something to register a more indignant reaction to the way the traditional social system was actually masking economic developments, thus dividing the nation still further. Making money was the way to lead the cultivated life of a 'gentleman', one who did not have to work, only to play. Indeed, making money has itself become a game in itself, quite as absorbing as cricket or billiards: 'So all that great foul city of London there,—rattling, growling, smoking, stinking—a ghastly heap of fermenting brickwork, pouring out poison at every pore, —you fancy it is a city of work? Not a street of it! It is a great city of play; very nasty play, and very hard play, but still play. It is only Lord's cricket ground without the turf:—a huge billiard table without the cloth, and with pockets as deep as the bottomless pit; but mainly a billiard table, after all'.[1] Ruskin was one of those whose eyes were opened, assaulting the adaptation of the traditional system as hypocrisy.

But Tennyson belonged to the larger class of writers who strove to work a spiritual revolution in individual men and women while retaining the old principle of class-subordination. *Enoch Arden* (1864: PT, 1129), near in date both to Brown's picture and Ruskin's lecture, could provide a tempting quarry for passages illustrative of the sort of self-reliance and thrift which Samuel Smiles recommended in his immensely

[1] *The Works of John Ruskin*, 39 vol., ed E. T. Cook and Alexander Wedderburn, 1902-12, XVIII, 406.

popular *Self-Help* of 1859.[1] But the incidents are put back a whole century, a circumstance suggesting that the tale has its interest in a perennial Christian concern with self-sacrifice, as in Mrs Gaskell's novel *Sylvia's Lovers* of the previous year, similarly set back in the previous century. Unlike Smiles's tales of success (actually much more capable of realisation in 1864 than in the earlier pre-industrial era of the eighteenth century), the story of Enoch Arden depends upon total *failure* to achieve commercial success. This is one of the means of intensifying Enoch's heroic self-denial on returning home from shipwreck to find his wife re-married to Philip, 'rich and well-to-do'. Interest in the sort of martyrdom which Enoch's sacrifice represents was part of Victorian culture, and is carefully dissociated from contemporary economic problems and their social accompaniments. It recurs in a more ironic, though deeply sympathetic, light in George Eliot's novels. Mrs Gaskell's story shows a direct connection with the popular versions of medieval Christian romances still read in Victorian schoolrooms. Chapter 42, entitled 'A Fable at Fault' shows Philip Hepburn, who like Enoch has to conceal his identity from his wife after long absence overseas, reading in *The Seven Champions of Christendom* the tale of Sir Guy of Warwick, who after seven years abroad fighting the Paynim 'in his own country' lived unknown at his Countess's gate until near death. But Philip withholds himself from his wife's notice because he had concealed the fact that a rival was not, as thought, dead, only pressed into the fleet. His remorse introduces a typically Victorian touch of moral realism. Happily he is reconciled with her on his deathbed because by that time she had realised that not only was he sincere and faithful but that he was in fact a better man than his rival. Tennyson's Enoch Arden is much nearer to the original tale of Sir Guy. Enoch is quite guiltless of anything underhand in his wooing, and has nothing to expiate on his return. For that matter his rival the millowner has nothing to be remorseful about either, for his conduct towards Annie during the long years of virtual widowhood before agreeing to marry him is impeccable. In fact everyone behaves so beautifully that the story is truly an 'idyl'.

The popular taste for idealised behaviour may be an index of a wish that the actual facts were in greater conformity with it. There is certainly idealisation of a similar kind in Dickens, and Thackeray's exposure of what could lie under smooth surfaces was a piece of Carlylean anti-cant which many felt to be most disagreeable. If one compares *Enoch Arden* with Byron's *Beppo* one gleans a good idea of the nature of the difference which had come over Victorian sentiments since the Regency. Byron's Beppo, another lost husband, returns from captivity to find Laura, his wife, equipped with a Count as *cavalier servente*. But does he linger without, like Enoch or Philip?

> *His wife received, the patriarch re-baptized him*
> *(He made the church a present by the way)*;
> *He then threw off the garments which disguised him,*
> *And borrowed the Count's small-clothes for a day:*
> *His friends the more for his long absence prized him . . .*
>
> *Whate'er his youth had suffer'd, his old age*
> *With wealth and talking made him some amends;*
> *Though Laura sometimes put him in a rage,*
> *I've heard the Count and he were always friends . . .*
>   (XCVIII and XCIX)

Byron's poem satirically contrasts Italian with English attitudes to marriage, Beppo's easy resumption of his marital precedence without fuss or rancour reflects upon the 'respectability' so dear to the age of Victoria and casts its shadow some twenty years before. Tennyson's poem, on the other hand, is very Victorian, very deeply moral and religious: Enoch's case is much harder than Beppo's or Philip Hepburn's in that his wife, presuming him dead, has married his old rival and rejoices in a happy home and a child. Enoch's resolve not to disturb this home is prompted by the realization that he is virtually 'a dead man come to life'. The prospect of death is enough to puzzle the will and shake the foundations of consciousness: to die and to return is to prepare for oneself a sense of arctic loneliness and desolation, to become a superfluous man in a world wherein the affections appear perilously like interests in disguise.[1] The chill this prospect makes finds a proper

[1] Hawthorne's story 'Wakefield' (*Twice-Told Tales*), typically deals

place in *In Memoriam* (xc). The lasting popularity of *Enoch Arden* must have been due to the appeal it had as a result of offering a situation of vertiginous metaphysical possibilities while at the same time treating it as if it were one of great moral simplicity, met by super-human fortitude and self-denial. Had Enoch not during his long years of loneliness

> *Spoken with That, which being everywhere*
> *Lets none, who speaks with Him, seem all alone,*
> *Surely the man had died of solitude.*   (615–17)

Rather he survives the loneliness of the ocean wastes, not once vituperating whatever Gods may be, but praying:

> *O God Almighty, blessèd Saviour, Thou*
> *That didst uphold me on my lonely isle,*
> *Uphold me, Father, in my loneliness*
> *A little longer! aid me, give me strength*
> *Not to tell her, never to let her know.*   (778–782)

It is a case of a man persistently struck down by cruel strokes of fate. Byron treated it as a little matter requiring rather unusual savoir faire. But Tennyson makes it a question of Christian faith and morals, and his poem must have won admirers (though not among the best judges of poetry perhaps) because it was a modern parable which took no regard of legal complications, metaphysical speculations or for that matter, actual circumstances of class, property and sexual attraction, which are wholly supplanted by considerations of marriage, domesticity and a religion of simple self-denial. As such it is an excellent illustration of the taste of the time for a literature which avoided the unpleasant realities of life or if it did not, made them simple moral issues, as did the Pre-Raphaelites very often. But this was compensated for by another for sensational murders and glimpses of the underworld, and corrected by the best novelists of the period, who could render moral problems and social difficulties with psychological insight and a strong sense of the

---

with the situation wherein a man may become 'the outcast of the universe' by stepping aside for a moment from the systems, nicely adjusted to one another, which govern the lives of individuals 'amid the seeming confusion of our mysterious world'.

actual. Tennyson, while generally unwilling to publish poems in the
Annuals so much beloved by middle-class readers, had for many years
gratified their refined taste with poems like 'The Sleeping Beauty' (PT,
627). From their point of view Enoch is all that a 'working class' hero
ought to be. His job-like submission actually underwrites the value of all
that is represented by the idea of home to Victorian readers—for here
is a man who glimpses it at a perfect, almost holy moment, and properly accepts that it is his duty to respect its comfort, its child-centred-
ness, its exclusiveness, all that is nowadays anathematized under the
term 'nuclear family'.[1]

The 'Victorian' quality of the poem resides, of course, in its treatment, not in its subject, for not only does the situation occur in many
ballads, novels and melodramas,[2] the very fact that the law has always
taken notice of the real possibility of disappearance for long periods
overseas leading to a presumption of death (the U.S. legislation is
actually referred to as the Enoch Arden Laws) is evidence of its
common occurrence. Enoch's situation is one which deserves sympathy; yet Crabbe's 'The Parting Hour' (which Tennyson re-read at
the time he was engaged in writing *Enoch Arden*) lacks the intense
pathetic note of Tennyson's poem despite (or because of) the fact that
Crabbe's own brother William suffered the misfortune of being carried
to Mexico by the Spanish. His imagination dwells upon the sorrow of a
life rudely broken from its familiar past. The result is a sort of numb
patience. But Tennyson's concern is to extract from Enoch's home-
coming not merely heroic self-denial but also, through having Enoch
arrange that his sacrifice be made known and his blessings conveyed to

[1] Compare Ruskin's 'Of Queens' Gardens', a lecture delivered in 1864,
reprinted in *Sesame and Lilies*. Enoch looks in upon the scene of
domestic happiness from a little garden opening 'on the waste'.

[2] See P. G. Scott, *Tennyson's Enoch Arden: a Victorian Best-Seller*,
Tennyson Research Centre, Lincoln, 1970, for a discussion. The critics
who thought the poet was joining the craze for choosing bigamy as a
subject, as were contemporary sensation-novelists, were wide of the
mark. The Offences against the Person Act of 1861, section 57, maintained the provision of the Act of 1603 which exempted from the
offence a spouse who re-married after a partner's unexplained absence
for seven years beyond the sea.

the family after his death,[1] to wring from it the maximum of pathos. This raises the emotional pitch to a point where many modern readers find it hard to linger long, and practical considerations press to enter, encouraged by the last lines of the poem:

> *And when they buried him the little port*
> *Had seldom seen a costlier funeral.*

All that has up to this been excluded from view—of class, of economic and legal considerations and so on—can now rush into mind, together perhaps with memories of other funerals in Victorian novels wherein *hypocrisy* was deliberately satirised. Many of Tennyson's first readers would have felt very differently, wholly sharing his understanding that simple people (particularly) saw funerals as sincere expressions of familial love and by no means as the trappings and the suits of woe. Enoch is acknowledged as a husband and a strong heroic soul despite the painful irony of the situation.

I have already mentioned the difference between this response and that called for by Byron's *Beppo*. With the social, economic and political changes in the period after 1870 or so we find corresponding and significant changes in response to the situation treated in the two poems. Compare *Enoch Arden* with a work by one who looked very hard at social realities, Hardy's novel *Two on a Tower* (1882), and we can find it hardly surprising that some people found the novel improper in its morals, satirical in its treatment of the Established Church, 'repulsive', 'a little short of revolting', and 'a studied and gratuitous insult'.[2] It is certainly very difficult to believe that Hardy did not write with tongue in cheek. While it is true that 'there is hardly a single caress in the book outside legal matrimony, or what was intended so to be', the plot is cleverly contrived to make the legal and social regulation of sexual love

---

[1] The effect could only have been to invalidate the second marriage and to render the child of it irretrievably illegitimate. Not until the Legitimacy Act of 1926 would the latter consequence be avoidable.

[2] Hardy's own account in the Preface written for the 1895 edition. Some reviewers found *Enoch Arden* exceptionable on grounds of dubious morality, thereby illustrating Hardy's point in *Jude the Obscure* that marriage was for respectable people a licence to love on the premises.

by marriage appear almost ridiculously inadequate to meet the circumstances of real life. Lady Constantine, a lady of warm feelings, believing on good evidence that her disagreeable husband has died on a hunting expedition in Africa, secretly marries Swithin St Cleeve, a young man of scientific temperament, only later to discover that her husband had not died until six weeks after the ceremony, which was consequently invalid.[1] Learning also that she had unwittingly deprived her scientific Adonis of an income by marrying him, she declines to remarry him for a time and packs him off to the Cape and a world tour of observatories—only to find that she is pregnant. To conceal her condition she marries the Bishop of Melchester, a pressing suitor. The novel has scenes which while technically 'proper' are really of the sort found in French bedroom farces. On the other hand it does enlist sympathy for a passionate woman who loves a younger man: and it does deal with differences in birth and income. Most important of all, it does attempt, even if unsuccessfully, to relate the lonely and terrible immensity of space revealed by astronomy to the passions of men and women in Victorian England. Swithin is actually christened by the Bishop, but in circumstances which would have struck an admirer of the serious parts of *Enoch Arden* (and in particular the description of the lonely spaces separating him after shipwreck on the 'beauteous hateful isle' from the protective familiarity of an English scene and way of life) as displaying a deplorable levity with serious spiritual concerns. *Two on a Tower* foreshadows the attack on traditional Victorian ideas on nature, sexual purity, marriage, education and class launched in *Tess* and *Jude the Obscure*. *Enoch Arden* enshrines those ideas, and we are now separated from the poem by so great a change in social attitudes that it serves as a monument to a departed era, an era which earnestly fostered a belief in the transfigurative power of idealism to make both material success and material failure equally a test of the individual soul. So the poem

[1] Moreover since she re-married after only four years had passed since her husband's supposed death she was guilty of unwitting bigamy. The action of the novel is determined by Swithin's travelling to observe the transit of Venus in 1882: it was not until 1889 (*Regina* v. *Tolson*, Queen's Bench Division) that an exception was admitted to the seven years absence provision.

has no modern shame over either humble efforts to get on in the world
or over expensive funereal demonstrations of admiration and respect.
Differences in income ought to make no difference to human relationships. In real life, of course, they often made all the difference (and
Tennyson wrote not a few poems to say so): while financial failure, as
The Mill on the Floss (1860) well illustrates, could strike many people as
a loss of respectability. Browning, in fact, thought a more appropriate
ending to the poem would be to have Enoch receive only a parish
funeral and to have slighting remarks passed about him. But Tennyson
is representing the moral heroism which English Protestantism yearned
after (and in the nineteenth century felt starved of opportunity for
showing). That he well understood the 'proud, honest egoism' which
served for religion in provincial England is shown by the 'Northern
Farmer' poems.

What Carlyle and the Christian pastors like Kingsley, who earnestly
preached optimistic faith in the redemptive power of love and work,
regularly overlooked was that industrial activity could not find an
outlet for ever in endless production, even if that activity could be
viewed as the conquest of nature. Moreover, as Ruskin pointed out, it
often meant the pollution of rivers and the disfigurement of old towns
and beautiful country. It also had to disregard or hope to preach away
the proliferation of Bobus and his kin, the adulterator of food, the
speculator and the shady joint-stock company promoter. Work like
Enoch Arden's resembled that of the navvies in Brown's picture in
exacting physical effort of a healthful though often dangerous kind,
but with the advantage of independence. Work for many factory-
employees, miners, shop-workers and others increasingly meant the
sort of serfdom which Morris's John Ball could hardly believe possible
in a country of supposedly 'free' men. It was perplexing enough to try
to bury in work the doubts and ennui that afflicted those whose childhood
faith had been challenged by scientific speculation and doubts cast
upon Christian 'evidences', and then to see that work exacted from
many people immense sacrifices of ordinary human gratifications like
decent food and shelter. Even more painfully confusing was the dis-
parity between the deceptive practices of some 'business men' and
their religious pretensions. Tennyson's poem 'Sea Dreams', first pub-

lished in 1860, and dealing with the reactions of a clerk and his wife to the loss of their fortune to a pious rogue, doubtless sprang from the bitter recollection of the loss of his own fortune in an investment in a mechanical wood-carving scheme proposed by Dr Matthew Allen, author of a work of Christian edification. But it was composed during the years when legislation limiting the liability of joint stock companies was leading to much abuse and consequent public losses. (The Companies Act of 1862, frequently amended, was passed as a means of regulating the conduct of such enterprises.) So Tennyson was responding, as Dickens did in portraying Merdle in *Little Dorrit* (1857–58) and Trollope Melmotte in *The Way We Live Now* (1875), to the fact that large-scale business activities were making 'work' take on a very different aspect from even a few decades before. Small investors could be easily duped by pious pretensions or distinguished titles into parting with money for all sorts of enterprises. Tennyson has his clerk lose his savings in an old-fashioned, rather eighteenth-century 'bubble', a Peruvian gold-mine, just as Dickens had Mr Dombey preside over an old-established family business in his novel (1847–48). His mind was really upon enforcing private morality (Christian forbearance) rather than exposing the 'System'.

Nevertheless, although the clerk's wife manages to persuade him to forgive the sanctimonious defrauder after revealing that he has died of a heart-attack, she has not had an easy part to play in her received Victorian role of a soother and pacifier of a man resentful at being cheated in the marketplace, wherein he must labour so that his wife and child may live in peace at home. Admittedly he has had a dream which has suggested the 'glorification of honest labour, whether of head or of hand, no hasting to be rich, no bowing down to any idol': this dream seems to imply that he was in part responsible for his loss out of a desire to get rich quick, yet his forgiveness is grudging; for although the man is dead, 'His deeds yet live, the worst is yet to come'.

That Tennyson should follow up this poem, in which Christian sentiments only just prevail in face of harsh financial actualities, by writing *Enoch Arden*, in which the ideal of self-abnegation is presented in so pure a form, illustrates an aspect of Victorian literature which is closely connected with middle-class ideas on women as 'angels in the house'. Victorian biographies abound in portraits of pious and devoted mothers: manuals of female conduct appear in many guises. Walter E. Houghton has given a comprehensive account of the probable reasons for the emergence of this ideal of woman and the worship of home as her shrine—the prevailing evangelical and nonconformist ethos of families which had risen in the world, fear of acknowledging the fact of large-scale prostitution, the desire to counteract the effects of French fiction—to which one might add the diffusive influence of the literature of the Renaissance, the plays of Shakespeare and the poems of Milton.[1] Most important of all, perhaps, was the *Frauendienst* which substituted, it would seem, for religious devotion. This last, particularly associated in literature with the love-poetry of Browning and Patmore, thus shares a role with Work, in serving as a surrogate, or anodyne, for religious feelings or the painful lack of them at a time when, while spirituality was counted a sign of good character and respectability, Christian belief was becoming difficult in face of controversy and recrimination. In 'Sea Dreams' the clerk's wife has a dream, prompted in part by a violently anti-Catholic sermon, which allegorically represents by way of great waves of light throwing down images on the face of cathedral-like cliffs the destruction of religion by what Tennyson termed 'The ages that go on with their illumination breaking down everything'. The last of the images to be shaken down are the Virgin and her Child, whose cry of alarm blends with that of the real child in the room of the dreaming mother. We are here presented with a good example of the process also seen in the novelists (in *Adam Bede* for example) whereby Christian belief is adapted to a vague religious humanism, sometimes centring on 'feminine' virtues.[2] This explains the important place for women in the 'social' novels of Mrs Gaskell, Disraeli, Kingsley and Dickens, and the deep concern with the adequacy of the received conception of the life of women in the fiction of George Eliot and Meredith. The connection of the great issues of work and of woman is often apparent in nineteenth-century literature (in the

[1] Walter E. Houghton, *The Victorian Frame of Mind 1830–1870*, New Haven and London, 1957, chap. 13.
[2] See U. C. Knoepflmacher, *Religious Humanism and the Victorian Novel*, Princeton, New Jersey, 1965.

Prologue of *The Princess*, for example, and *Maud*): the dissociation in our own century is to be seen in various degrees of violence in the novels of E. M. Forster, Virginia Woolf and D. H. Lawrence, which in rejecting the ethos of Work in its modern forms of imperialism and business autocracy reopen the whole question of the relation of the sexes and the values of society. In Dickens it leads to the constant return from large questions of social justice and developments in the fields of politics and economics to small ones of supposed feminine wisdom in questions of personal unselfishness and charitable concern. In Tennyson it takes a somewhat similar, but much more explicit form, notably in *The Princess, Maud* and the *Idylls of the King*, which between them show the different ways in which frustration at the contradictions of modern life is resolved by attributing to women a *moral* healing-power for economic ills and their social consequences.

Kate Millett puts Tennyson's *The Princess* (first published in 1847) in the same camp with Ruskin's 'Of Queens' Gardens' in opposition to J. S. Mill's *The Subjection of Women* (1869), and exposes it to her scorn.[1] But she writes from the standpoint not merely of an age which can challenge the 'Victorian' qualities of mind in Freud, but as one who recognizes the male arrogance in the major work of Lawrence, whose detestation of Freud is a creative impulse. Tennyson and Ruskin were certainly not men of the speculative and analytic power of Mill. Faced with social change of immense proportions they turned from their concerns with art to matters of a social kind, and Tennyson's work bears the stamp of uncertainty and timidity. Ruskin shirks the main issue, as Mill did not, when after having shown that Homer, Dante, Chaucer, Spenser, Shakespeare, Wordsworth and Scott demonstrate in their works the superior sense, courage and wisdom of their women characters, he answers the question, 'But how, you will ask, is the idea of this guiding function of women reconcileable with a true wifely subjection?' by resort to the familiar doctrine of separate characters and separate spheres:

> The man, in his rough work in the open world, must encounter all peril and trial;—to him, therefore, must be the failure, the offence,

[1] Kate Millett, *Sexual Politics*, 1971.

the inevitable error: often he must be wounded, or subdued, often misled; and *always* hardened. But he guards the woman from all this; within his house, as ruled by her, unless she herself has sought it, need enter no danger, no temptation, no cause of error or offence. This is the true nature of home—it is the place of Peace; the shelter, not only from all injury, but from all terror, doubt, and division.[1]

Clearly this conception of things was practically very convenient to the male portion of the nation possessed of legal rights over its wives of intimidating completeness: and it offered small consolation to those whose 'home' was a slum. But on the other side there is also something to be said. Ruskin, like Tennyson, is addressing a middle-class audience which was not going to change its fundamental character overnight: accepting that, he makes proposals, which, if adopted, promise some lively domestic scenes:

> You bring up your girls as if they were meant for sideboard ornaments, and then complain of their frivolity. Give them the same advantages that you give their brothers— appeal to the same grand instincts of virtue in them; teach *them* also that courage and truth are the pillars of their being . . .'

> Is a girl likely to think her own conduct, or her own intellect, of much importance, when you entrust the entire formation of her character, moral and intellectual, to a person whom you allow your servants to treat with less respect than they do your house-keeper (as if the soul of your child were a less charge than jams and groceries), and whom you yourself think you confer an honour on by letting her sometimes sit in the drawing room in the evening?

> There is not a war in the world, no, nor an injustice, but you women are answerable for it . . . There is no suffering, no injustice, no misery in the earth, but the guilt of it lies lastly with you.

As with Ruskin, so with Tennyson. *The Princess* will strike most modern readers as almost overwhelmingly literary—it parades its artificiality in pretending to be the sort of narrative round-game played by young men at College, inevitably displaying thoughtless prejudices

[1] *Works*, XVIII, 122.

concerning the female sex while at the same time succumbing to the allure of a haughty beauty. Like Ruskin's 'Queens' the princess is treated with chivalric devotion (quite literally) as well as to insensitive and rumbustious comment by the upholder of male pre-eminence. And in the end she is forced by circumstance to accept that change cannot be introduced overnight, very much as a more convincing aspirant to freedom and independence, Dorothea Brooke in *Middlemarch*, has to accept the harsh fact that time had still a long way to run before those gifts were ceded. Her university for women, with its curriculum ranging over all fields of modern knowledge, is broken up: her fate is to be marriage and children after all. But the point that can be easily over-looked by a modern reader of the fanciful tale is established by a more careful look at both the poem and Ruskin's writings. It is this: the sympathetic, even chivalrous, attitude towards women is part of a strategy a main object of which is to attack the commercial ethos and to replace it by one having human welfare as its goal. Women are re-quired to represent and defend the precious concerns of private feelings and public morality. Tennyson goes further. He suggests in the charac-teristically semi-scientific poetic diction which Yeats found so un-palatable that women are the guardians of the springs of life itself. It may be the case that Mill's pragmatism is more persuasive and realistic than the idealism of Tennyson and Ruskin, but it is not altogether different in intention. Ruskin is fiercer than both in his denunciation of the Goddess of Getting-On and all her works. In his lecture on 'War' in *The Crown of Wild Olive* (1866), operations in the Crimea, India, America and Italy in mind, he makes it abundantly clear that the chival-ric demeanour towards women he expects English soldiers to make their principal norm of conduct is not merely another example of a sort of Platonic remoteness from reality. Quite the contrary. He denounces modern war and colonialism, castigates a mean-minded commercial ethos, and rebukes the exclusively domestic and family preoccupations of English ladies. He puts all his confidence, in fact, in the natural good-ness of men—and more particularly of women—and their improveabil-ity through education in the principles of social justice. *The Princess*, for all its laboured lightness and uncertainty over what note to sound, is on the same track, appealing to its readers by phrases like 'an universal culture for the crowd' and 'ourselves are full of social wrong' to the need to remould social attitudes in order to do justice to those denied their rights in the commonwealth—women and the workers. The ideal of social responsibility is embodied in the concluding portrait of Sir Walter Vivian, who might well have served as Brown's model for his modern gentleman:

> *In such discourse we gained the garden rails,*
> *And there we saw Sir Walter where he stood,*
> *Before a tower of crimson holly-hocks,*
> *Among six boys, head under head, and looked*
> *No little lily-handed Baronet he,*
> *A great broad-shouldered genial Englishman,*
> *A lord of fat prize-oxen and of sheep,*
> *A raiser of huge melons and of pine,*
> *A patron of some thirty charities,*
> *A pamphleteer on guano and on grain,*
> *A quarter-sessions chairman, abler none;*
> *Fair-haired and redder than a windy morn . . .*
>
> (Conclusion, 80–91: PT, 843)

This passage appeared in the first edition (1847), and is matched by the portrait of Lord Minchampstead, industrialist turned landowner, in *Yeast.* In 1850 were added the self-congratulatory words—attributed to 'The Tory member's elder son'—on Britain's good fortune at having nothing to do with events like those of 1848 in France, words which afford a sort of chauvinistic chiaroscuro to the portrait. In point of fact the repeal in 1846 of the Corn Laws signalled the beginning of the gradual dissociation of the aristocracy (who still had real political power) from an exclusively land-owning preoccupation; thenceforth they and independent large-scale farmers increasingly maintained agricultural production with fewer and fewer labourers (because of the efficiency of new farming methods). *They* were driven from the land by the effect of the New Poor Law, and swelled the ranks—if employment offered—of those 'mechanics' and townworkers who in *The Princess* enjoyed on a single day a year the pleasures of private pleasure-grounds.[1] So Tennyson's hale Sir Walter is perhaps no more hopeful a repre-

[1] Alice Wilson in *Mary Barton* (1848) is an illustration from fiction.

sentative of social progress than Brown's true gentleman. But the poem's spirit of tolerance and consent to the loosening of traditional social constrictions (without much awareness of the forces which were gathering towards the eventual overthrow of the inherited pattern of political and economic power)[1] is representative of the more hopeful if only mildly liberal mood of the mid-nineteenth century, just as in some sense the conclusion of *In Memoriam* reflects a temporary stay to the doubting spirit of earlier years, abundantly displayed in the preceding parts of the poem. Its refinement is more striking nowadays than its liberalism: but even that refinement is indicative of a most important development in English social life, though not particularly new in 1847 —the superimposition upon the often proud and dictatorial ruling caste (the 'quality freedom' of the Prince's father in the tale is an illustration) of gentler manners and more enlightened views. What we take as half-hearted concessions to those who demanded great changes in attitude towards women and the working-class are really important first steps in a programme intended to leaven middle-class opinion but at the same time also to preserve a rich culture associated with church, university, and learned professions, a culture felt to be endangered if reform, that is, liberal democracy, were undertaken too fast. But with the decline of the economic importance of agriculture, and the assumption of the style of gentleman by Bobus and Veneering, (as well as honest manufacturer and worthy member of society, of course) the question of defining the qualities of the possessor of this culture became acute. The question 'what are the qualities of a gentleman?' is agitated with varying degrees of personal detachment by novelists from Jane Austen to Thomas Hardy—among high Victorian authors Trollope and Dickens perhaps represent the two extremes. George Eliot's Grandcourt is unsurpassed as a specimen of detestable arrogance and indifference which could be produced by the English landed gentry almost exclusively. Ruskin did find a Russian competitor for the palm of lordly extravagance among the reports of extremes of wealth and poverty

[1] See E. J. Hobsbawm, 'Agriculture 1750–1850', chap. 5 of *Industry and Empire*, in *The Pelican Economic History of Britain*, III, From 1750 to the Present Day, Harmondsworth, 1968, 97–108: and G. Kitson Clark, *The Making of Victorian England*, 1962, 217.

which like Arnold, he savagely snipped from the newspapers. He banked up his fires of prophetic denunciation for a middle class which aspired to the exaltedness of landed status while depending in reality on a mill 'not less than a quarter of a mile long, with one steam engine at each end, and two in the middle, and a chimney three hundred feet high. In this mill are to be in constant employment from eight hundred to a thousand workers, who never drink, never strike, always go to church on Sunday, and always express themselves in respectful language'.[1]

Tennyson knew little of mills and factories—he was born in Lincolnshire, and resided most of his life in London or the southern counties. Like Queen Victoria, who built Osborne when the Royal Pavilion, Brighton, ceased to be private enough for seaside residence, he took refuge (in 1853, at Farringford) in the Isle of Wight, and when that became popular in summer, in the lonely heathlands of Surrey at Aldworth. 'Aylmer's Field', published in the *Enoch Arden* volume of 1864, is placed in Kent:

> *A land of hops and poppy-mingled corn,*
> *Little about it stirring save a brook!*   (31–32: PT, 1161)

whence France can be felt as a presence, 'out yonder'. Sir Aylmer Aylmer is no Sir Walter Vivian, but one of those 'county Gods' who 'saw from his windows nothing save his own'. His pride of ancestry is matched by pride of wealth—and it leads to the death of his only child and her young, poor, but well-born suitor whose brother, rector of the place, is left to preach against the hypocrisy of mammonism consorting with worship 'Of One who cried, "Leave all and follow me"'. The story, despite its charming descriptions of the labourers' homes, or huts, almost hidden by jasmine, roses and hollyhocks, is rather like a highly-compressed novel, and too much must not be inferred from a production showing so many features of conventional fiction—unfeeling parents, Indian kinsman bearing gifts (a jewelled dagger among them), youthful ardour in legal studies, aristocratic pride. It must be admitted that Sir Aylmer's disdain for the pretensions of the youthful suitor hardly needed the setting-back of the tale to the period of the French

[1] 'Traffic', *The Crown of Wild Olive, Works*, XVIII, 453.

Revolution indicated by the date 1793 below the title, for the old system of society remained largely unchallenged until the last quarter of the century, though it was intruded upon by new people, many of whom sought assimilation to it, and were even more jealous of its privileges. The central and most literary feature, the Romeo and Juliet aspect of marriage to further (profitable) alliances was, if anything, more true in the mid-nineteenth century than half a century before. The talk of 'woman markets of the west' and 'This filthy marriage-hindering Mammon' which makes for city-prostitution was not meant to be wasted on *contemporary* readers.[1] Nor for that matter was the bereaved preacher's incredulity at the conduct of Sir Aylmer in view of the atrocities befalling his class so near at hand in France: the old order of things in face of the Niagara soon to be approached seemed full of danger. The Carlylean touches in the poem show how the old prophet's influence remained strong, as *A Tale of Two Cities* (1859) also shows.

With the advent of fortunes derived from other sources than land, and to men who had not the justification of birth and county connections for their exercise of influence in the country as well as the city, the confusion in the social system in the sixties and seventies created problems of morals and manners much more subtle than could be recorded by writers of Carlylean temper, didactic and moralistic in approach. Sir Aylmer and Sir Leicester Dedlock are types of pride, Mr Thorne of Ullathorne a man proud in quite another manner. Trollope registers the social scene with a fine sense that truth lies in particulars and that character and morality operate within social forms. When the forms are going, behaviour becomes more and more indeterminate, and the question of what is right and wrong more difficult to answer. But Trollope's uneasiness concerning the simplifications which Carlyle's criticism of institutions inevitably involved does not mean that he differs from his contemporaries in not sharing their fundamental concern (owing much to Carlyle) with the moral qualities demanded of the upper ranks of society. He admires what only wealth can achieve, and

---

[1] 'Edwin Morris' deals with family pride on the part of

new-comers in an ancient hold,
New-comers from the Mersey, millionaires . . . (9–10: PT, 708)

if he were to allow an objector to speak it would be 'with the voice not
of Marx or of Chartism but of the gospels'. This is quite as true of
Tennyson, even if his religious tone (so obtrusive in the sermon in
'Aylmer's Field'), as well as his exaggerated idealism, is wholly foreign
to Trollope's temperament.

The poem's rather melodramatic story of disappointed love shows
clearly enough the age-old theme of high station affecting love or
marriage, a theme which Tennyson treated in jaunty early poems like
'Lady Clara Vere de Vere', 'Lady Clare' and 'The Lord of Burleigh'
(PT, 636, 638, 603): the popular, even novelettish sentiments of these
poems doubtless appealed to the readers of Susan Ferrier's stories, on
which 'The Lord of Burleigh' is based. Though still preoccupied with
traditional models he adapted the popular motif of love frustrated by
station to more realistic and contemporary situations in his 'English
Idyls'. 'Walking to the Mail' (1842) treats of Sir Edward Head who
like the Earl of Burleigh married beneath him: but unlike him made his
wife, as well as himself, deeply unhappy:

> *She was the daughter of a cottager*
> *Out of her sphere. What betwixt shame and pride,*
> *New things and old, himself and her, she soured*
> *To what she is: a nature never kind!*
> *Like men, like manners: like breeds like, they say:*
> *Kind nature is the best: those manners next*
> *That fit us like a nature second-hand;*
> *Which are indeed the manners of the great.*   (51–8: PT, 703)

Thus the Tory speaker, who also relates how mortified Sir Edward was
by the Reform Act:

> *I once was near him, when his bailiff brought*
> *A Chartist pike. You should have seen him wince*
> *As from a venomous thing: he thought himself*
> *A mark for all, and shuddered, lest a cry*
> *Should break his sleep by night, and his nice eyes*
> *Should see the raw mechanic's bloody thumbs*
> *Sweat on his blazon'd chairs; but, sir, you know*
> *That these two parties still divide the world—*

> *Of those that want, and those that have: and still*
> *The same old sore breaks out from age to age*
> *With much the same result.* . . .   (62–72)

'Edwin Morris' (1851) takes the landscape-painter motif of 'The Earl of Burleigh' and fits it into a modern story in which it is not *he* who proves owner of a splendid house to which he brings his bride but the nouveau-riche 'cotton-spinning' family to which the sentimental Letty Hill belongs—and he is sent packing:

> *and in one month*
> *They wedded her to sixty thousand pounds,*
> *To lands in Kent and messuages in York,*
> *And slight Sir Robert with his watery smile*
> *And educated whisker.* . . .   (125–129: PT, 713)

The 'rent-roll Cupid of our rainy isles', the God worshipped in Vanity Fair, is he who conducts the 'woman markets of the west', and prepares his victims by an education in accomplishments to attract a buyer. The irony is that she upon whom the modern Wertherish young man reposes his distressed soul is herself subjected to social pressures to marry money: succumbing, she is made the object of pitying contempt in this poem and in 'Locksley Hall', a poem in which many threads are drawn together to compose a brilliantly representative tapestry of Victorian social attitudes. The Tennysonian skill in working into a single pattern traditional popular motifs and contemporary issues —so as to highlight the effect upon the love-relation of the gulf between rich and poor which was deepening exactly as Shelley had foretold—is rivalled only in *Maud*; and that for the simple reason that the popular materials assembled in this and other poems are used again, but with the variation of having Maud prove faithful and true. About both poems there is an air of heady excitement produced by the skill with which, as in Dickens, the popular elements are dextrously associated to produce a glamour tempting to smile at, but hard to resist—if only because extremes of love, hate, wealth and dependency are undeniably a part of Victorian life and feeling. The romantic idealism that dreams of Utopia, a return to Eden—admonished in 'The Golden Year'—is in these poems chastened by a loss of the Eve who should have lent it reality. So we have a touch of Hamlet in both 'Locksley Hall' and *Maud*. In these poems young men revolting against a mercenary society seek escape through the oblivion of action, the questionable value of which, judging by 'The Lotos-Eaters', Tennyson himself must have been aware. When 'progress' and war are offered as anodynes by a poet who elsewhere expresses his doubt about the validity of both, the case may seem desperate.[1] Indeed, his pessimism was never wholly assuaged throughout his career. But 'Locksley Hall' and *Maud* illustrate a hope in the possibility of progress, national unity and international justice and peace which was shared by many in the years before and after 1851.

To reviewers of political inclination, *Maud* seemed to suffer from morbidity, bloodthirstiness and confused thinking. Goldwin Smith wrote in the *Saturday Review* from a position of scornful common sense, making two crushing rejoinders to the poem's apparent recommendations: 'Strahan, Paul and Co. did not change their ways when we sat down before Sebastopol. Swindling, burglary, adulteration of food, wife-beating, are as rife as ever. To the common list of rogueries you have to add those of commissaries and contractors. The poor are more ground than ever when taxes drain the charities, and bread is high. As for stock-jobbing, which drove the father of the hero to suicide, and the hero himself to misanthropy, war is the element in which it revels. . . . To wage "war with a thousand battles and shaking a hundred thrones", in order to cure a hypochondriac and get rid of the chicory in coffee, is a bathos'.[2] The Liberal point of view (which Arnold later sought to moderate in *Culture and Anarchy*) is well-displayed in these observations, which assume that the poem is actually proposing a course of practical action. But Tennyson is writing at an altogether different level, attempting to give a voice to the depths beneath the surface of practical consciousness. In *Nostromo* Conrad registers the tragic inadequacy of material interests as an object upon which to found a personal life by showing a failed marriage: in *Maud* Tennyson has his hero, his mind poisoned by disgust at having to belong to a society founded on principles of remorseless competition, restored by a brief

[1] See the Epilogue to 'The Charge of the Heavy Brigade'.
[2] 'The War Passages in "Maud"' in CH, 187.

experience of love, a flowing-outward of feeling which creates an impulse of self-forgetfulness and a desire for commitment. To readers of today, aware of the indecision of the Aberdeen government and the Radical war fever, and also familiar from modern Russian novels with the tragic discrepancy between the political systems supposed to achieve the overthrow of class-exploitation and the actual sufferings of individuals yearning for social justice, the resolution of the poem in which the protagonist commits himself heart and soul to the Crimean War will seem ironic or naive. But it is deeply Tennysonian. The rebuke to Bright's peace-policy (which was based on Manchester free-trade principles) anticipates that to the anti-imperialists like Robert Lowe, in 'To the Queen' of 1873. Imperial and foreign activities were for Tennyson the field in which his vision of an Albion devoted to virtue and sacrifice could hope for fulfilment. Concluding the last chapter of Vol III of *Modern Painters*, published in 1856, Ruskin glances at the war which occupied all thoughts at that time. He is not blind to the possibility that historians may show it to have resulted from intrigue, ignorance, party-feeling or even misunderstanding. But 'the cause of this quarrel is no dim, half-avoidable involution of mean interests and errors, as some would have us believe'. Even if this were true, 'that which brings swift punishment in war, must have brought slow ruin in peace; and those who have now laid down their lives for England, have doubly saved her; they have humbled at once her enemies and herself; and have done less for her, in the conquest they achieve, than in the sorrow that they claim'.[1] Ruskin's passionate conviction that a deep desire for justice underlay the trivial apparent causes of the war is fully shared by Tennyson (even though the latter certainly did not see reconciliation with France and Napoleon III as one of the war's great benefits).

At the end of his lecture 'Of Queens' Gardens', Ruskin quotes *Maud* in support of his belief that women ought to equip themselves not merely for marriage, home and children but for a part in public life. The spoliation of the 'garden' of England by industry and by the neglect of its indigent city populations is an offence against religion and

[1] *Works*, V, 412, 414.

humanity which it is the duty of women to condemn and repair—'Did
you ever hear, not of a Maud but a Madeleine, who went down to her
garden in the dawn, and found One waiting at the gate, whom she
supposed to be the gardener? Have you not sought Him often;—
sought Him in vain at the gate of that old garden where the fiery sword
is set? He is never there; but at the gate of *this* garden He is waiting
always. . . .'[1] Ruskin is not hypocritical in interpreting the poem as a
religious allegory when it concludes with war, for as his lecture on war
in *The Crown of Wild Olive* (1865) makes out quite clearly, he execrates
modern mass warfare (lately seen in America) as an exploitation of the
masses akin to the exploitation they have always suffered from the
earliest civilisation—'the population of the earth divides itself, when
you look at it widely, into two races: one of workers, and the other of
players—one tilling the ground, manufacturing, building and otherwise
providing for the necessities of life:—and the other part proudly idle,
and continually therefore needing recreation, in which they need the
productive and laborious orders partly as their cattle and partly as their
puppets or pieces in the game of death'. But he also *still* believes in the
just war, like Augustine and Thomas Aquinas before him: and inci-
dentally thinks it preferable that a man slay his neighbour rather than
cheat him. War for dominion, mere increase of numbers, is no better
than the variety which entertains idle men: but 'as it is at their own
peril that any race extends their dominion in mere desire of power, so
it is at their own still greater peril that they refuse to undertake
aggressive war, according to their force, whenever they are assured
that their authority would be helpful and protective'. 'I tell you that the
principle of non-intervention, as now preached among us, is as selfish
and cruel as the worst frenzy of conquest, and differs from it only by
being, not only malignant, but dastardly.' War, being taken further
along lines all too characteristic of the nineteenth century by the adoption in 1866 of the *mitrailleuse* by the French, was still a noble enterprise
for men of high mettle and an invariable condition for the production of art. Echoing Carlyle in *Sartor Resartus*, he writes: 'Peace and
the *vices* of civil life only flourish together. We talk of peace and learn-

[1] *Works*, XVIII, 143–4.

ing, and of peace and plenty, and of peace and civilization; but I found that those were not the words which the Muse of History coupled together: that, on her lips, the words were—peace, and sensuality—peace, and selfishness,—peace and death'. And Ruskin asks his soldiers, too proud to be shopkeepers, whether they are satisfied to become the servants of shopkeepers. 'You imagine yourselves to be the army of England: how, if you should find yourselves at last, only the police of her manufacturing towns, and the beadles of her Little Bethels?'

Ruskin shares Tennyson's yearning after justice and honour, and associates these virtues with a chivalric life, even to the extent of advising his soldiers 'that the highest law of this knightly truth is that under which it is vowed to women. . . . Believe me, every virtue of the higher phases of manly character begins in this; . . . in truth and pity, or truth and reverence, to all womanhood'.[1] The greatest good fortune was thus, for both writers, that a man be able to lose himself in the noble dream of knightly submission to the moral insight of one chosen woman and to conquer evil, if necessary, by force of arms on behalf of a nation united and inspired, as was the family, by her sense of justice and pity. Maud is the begetter in her love of a fervent patriotism, an act of self-sacrifice for the cause of social order and law between nations. How hard it is now to do justice to the idealism, compassion and generous feeling which underlay these aspirations! To us Ruskin's (and Tennyson's) refusal to admit that human nature is anything but 'a noble and beautiful thing' must seem an act of faith more fortunate than well-founded. The complications introduced into ethics and politics by the availability of huge financial resources, industrial power, modern weapons, and rapid communication: in other words, the capacity of the modern state to mislead or subdue even its own citizens, makes us view with concern the ambition of Victorian intellectuals and leaders of opinion like Ruskin, Carlyle, and Arnold to establish strong governments[2]—and to overlook *their* concern. The desire for justice and order

---

[1] *Works*, XVIII, 464, 480, 483, 489.
[2] Cf *Maud*:

> *One still strong man in a blatant land,*
> *Whatever they call him, what care I,*

has its own peculiar dangers—notably an insensitiveness to human weakness and over-reaction on encountering it. Ideals,

> *Presences*
> *That passion, piety or affection knows,*
> *And that all heavenly glory symbolise*

can easily turn into 'self-born mockers of man's enterprise'. The idealism which Tennyson's poetry expresses is part of a national effort to control and humanise the changes inexorably brought about by industrialism, an effort seen in public-school and eventually popular education, in trade-unionism, in improved cities. Tennyson's passion for liberty, truthfulness, justice and self-denial sometimes leads him to a warmth of expression which is a sign of the string being drawn a little too tight: he lacks the healthy scepticism of a Clough which could temper patriotic enthusiasm with mistrust of the heroic impulse. Unlike Ruskin to whom the air of France was as if from Paradise, Tennyson's suspicions of France, or rather her leaders and notably Napoleon III, were unbounded: and in 1852 and 1859, before and after the Crimea when the Emperor was our ally, he could write poems very unlike the statesmanlike verses of the period of the Reform Act:

> *Let your reforms for a moment go!*
> *Look to your butts and take good aims!*
> *Better a rotten borough or so*
> *Than a rotten fleet and a city in flames!*
> *Storm, storm, Riflemen form!*
> *Ready, be ready against the storm!*
> *Riflemen, Riflemen, Riflemen form!*

(PT, 1111)

The four *Idylls of the King* published in 1859 show the characteristically romantic tendency of Tennyson's imagination reappearing strongly by way of poems which both sharpen the outlines of the idealised role of

---

> *Aristocrat, democrat, autocrat—one*
> *Who can rule and dare not lie.*
>
> (Part I, X, v, 392–95: PT, 1060)

1. Blind Man's Buff, *by David Wilkie*

2. The Doubt: 'Can These Dry Bones Live ?', *by Henry Alexander Bowler*

3. The Cottage, *by David Wilkie*

4. Interior of an English Cottage, *by William Mulready*

women in representing virtue and at the same time try to raise it from a pious ideal to the status of myth. The pathos, devotion and self-sacrifice of Enid and Elaine contrast with the wickedness of Vivien and the adultery of Guinevere. The whole cycle, not finished until 1885, shows the progressive corruption of Arthur's court by the effect of Guinevere's infidelity. The tension between the literal and the symbolic elements is very great, for in some respects the narratives have the prosaic quality which Tennyson was at such pains to realise in his numerous idyls of English life. The Arthurian elements on the other hand have associations with imperial destiny and religio-political ideals which are given a metaphysical glamour far exceeding that of any of the many earlier poems touching on such interests—perhaps 'Ode on the Death of the Duke of Wellington' comes nearest. The *Idylls* are the consummate expression of a moral idealism forced into service as a substitute for religious faith, a myth not actually in conformity with visible facts but essential as a support for a whole system of social aspirations terribly exposed to collapse:

> *take withal*
> *Thy poet's blessing, and his trust that Heaven*
> *Will blow the tempest in the distance back*
> *From thine and ours: for some are scared, who mark,*
> *Or wisely or unwisely, signs of storm,*
> *Waverings of every vane with every wind,*
> *And wordy trucklings to the transient hour,*
> *And fierce and careless looseners of the faith,*
> *And softness breeding scorn of simple life,*
> *Or Cowardice, the child of lust for gold,*
> *Or Labour, with a groan and not a voice,*
> *Or Art with poisonous honey stolen from France. . . .*
>   ('To the Queen', 1873: PT, 1756)

Arthur's rejection of Guinevere offended Swinburne as priggish and at entire variance with Malory's treatment of the fatal passion of these two great ones: it must have given pain to all those who had been taught by the novelists to sympathise with the actual sufferings of women in and out of marriage. Trollope, in fact, explicitly reflected upon the unreality of the treatment of the wicked Vivien in *The Eustace Diamonds* (1873), a novel which attempts to deal fairly with the behaviour of women in a corrupting environment. But while many readers in the sixties and seventies were awakening through the writings of Swinburne and Pater to the limitations of the Hebraic view of love and art, Tennyson's stern dissociation of sense from soul was made abundantly clear in the *Idylls* and in 'Lucretius' (1867). He displays through these works the ultimate stage of the culture which had its origins in the heroic past of western Europe, an order which originally rested upon personal supremacy in war, but was overlaid with rational values in the epic literature of Greece and Rome and transfigured by Christianity during the middle ages. This culture was sustained by the extraordinary power over men's imagination during the Renaissance and Reformation of the writings of the classical poets and the Church Fathers, despite the changes in the economic base of society during the sixteenth and seventeenth centuries, and the accompanying developments in science and philosophy. At the end of the sixteenth century, in which science took its first great steps and historians shook off the superstitions of a Trojan origin and an Arthurian destiny for Britain, Spenser produced in *The Faerie Queene* a fragment of a work which typically sought to conflate in a timeless setting the imperial preoccupations of the present, Puritan moral ardour (masquerading as Aristotelian ethics) and, beneath the ever-changing surface of revived Arthurian romance, a sensuous depth of feeling which occasionally bring the breath and stir of myth. But in the *Idylls*, the nineteenth-century counterpart, there is no more genuine mythic experience than in Burne-Jones's painting, only the result of taking thought. The Grand Betrayal of national culture consists, in Tennyson, in turning aside from the great work in hand, the daily work which is a sublimation of the yearning of spirit and flesh, and a recognition that man is born to bring civilization out of his own discontents. Heroism is fighting the enemy within, putting to death the monster which seeks to defile.

By the last quarter of the nineteenth century the values of the Puritan culture—self-denial, deference and patriotism—were exposed to the unprecedented challenge which has continued into the twentieth century. 'Locksley Hall Sixty Years After' (1886: PT, 1359) cunningly exploits the old age of its speaker to protect itself from the charge of despair in face of the new age, with its democracy and demagoguery, its doctrine of Art for Art's Sake, its Zolaism, its Irish land-war, its city-slums. It is certainly quite impossible to identify the poet himself on all points with the speaker, who represents what must have been the mood of those who recognized that the Second Reform Act and all that flowed from it was but one aspect of a great cultural change, long prepared and long resisted. The old man remains true to his Whig ideals of common sense and pragmatism: the 'anarchy' of the new age is at entire variance with his belief in sound government supported by a responsible landowning class who 'Served the poor, and built the cottage, raised the school, and drained the fen' (268). Locksley Hall is hopefully to continue, under its latest 'lord and master', into an age in which, unforeseen by him, liberal values are to be assaulted from both left and right and the ideals of puritan culture threatened.

Tennyson was remarkably self-consistent through his career, even if his consistency lay in entertaining simultaneously idealism and doubt. This was recognized in a tribute by Walt Whitman on the appearance of this poem. Some of his remarks so admirably sum up Tennyson's position in regard to the society of his time that they will serve as a conclusion.

'His very faults, doubts, swervings, doublings upon himself, have been typical of our age', he wrote, and continued in Tennysonian vein: 'We are like the voyagers of a ship, casting off for new seas, distant shores.' Tennyson was one of those who saw the perils of the voyage and sought to awaken the embarkers upon the democratic adventure to the dangers of irresponsibility: 'The course of progressive politics (democracy) is so certain and resistless, not only in America but in Europe, that we can well afford the warning calls, threats, checks, neutralizings, in imaginative literature, or any department, of such deep-sounding and high-soaring voices as Carlyle's and Tennyson's. Nay, the blindness, excesses, of the prevalent tendency—the dangers of the urgent trends of our times—in my opinion, need such voices almost more than any'.[1]

---

[1] 'A Word about Tennyson', in CH, 349 and 350.

7: 'Story Painters and Picture Writers': Tennyson's Idylls and Victorian Painting

JOHN DIXON HUNT

IT WAS Hallam in a review of *Poems, Chiefly Lyrical* in 1831 who first identified Tennyson's 'picturesque delineation of objects'. And modern criticism of his poetry owes much to H. M. McLuhan's essay of 1951 which used Hallam's perception to annex Tennyson's picturesque vision to the symbolist and imagist modes of modern poetry.[1] Yet however strongly we would wish to stress the continuities between the Victorian and modern imaginations, it is also crucial to identify how such a poet as Tennyson worked within the artistic contexts of his own age. The purpose of this essay is to read mainly his English idylls—and to touch upon the idyllic elements of poems like *The Princess* and *Maud* —in the light of Victorian painting.

The debt of Victorian artists to Tennyson's poetry seems to indicate the scope it offered for their painterly structures.[2] And the poetry in its turn was obviously shaped in part by a painterly instinct. However it is less specific influences that are my concern than the more general effect on Tennyson's poems of a dialogue between word and image during the nineteenth century that Beardsley captured in the phrase used as a title for this essay, 'story painters and picture writers'.[3] It is a phrase that signals a certain *rapprochement* between the arts: pictures that seek

[1] Hallam's review is reprinted in CH, 34 ff, and McLuhan's essay in *Critical Essays on the Poetry of Tennyson*, ed John Killham, 1960, 67 ff.
[2] See George Wesley Whiting, *The Artist and Tennyson*, a monograph issued as *Rice University Studies*, 50, Summer 1964. Several of the paintings referred to in the present chapter are reproduced in *Pre-Raphaelite Painters*, ed R. Ironside and J. Gere, 1948.
[3] *The Letters of Aubrey Beardsley*, ed Henry Maas, J. L. Duncan & W. G. Good, 1970, 61.

to announce the past and future of narrative in the present of their painterly image; poems that order their events in the picturesque mode of visual focus. *In Memoriam* would not usually be associated with such poetic manoeuvres. But at various stages in the sequence of lyrics Tennyson seems to look to a painterly structure, similar to those of the *genre* picture, as a means of rendering more public, more available, his highly individual experience. At such points *In Memoriam* invokes, as *The Spectator* noticed in its review, 'pictures of common landscape and of daily detail'. The rather rambling, speculative Epilogue seeks to focus its intuitions of a new growth and larger future in a wedding scene, which since it is only a type or metaphor at this point cannot dominate but must be offered in glimpses with a firm visual insistence: twice we are required to notice some visual contrast between the bride and the 'pensive Tablets' dedicated to the dead or between the married couple and the grave of Hallam. Frequently, if fleetingly, the occasion is caught through visual detail—the village girls throwing flowers in the porch; the lights of the house seen from the park as wedding guests roam in the dusk; the glance of 'her blissful eyes' towards the bridegroom. It is as if the larger abstractions—'That God, which ever lives and loves'—need the tentative identification of their vastness with visible Victorian circumstance.

The 'subtle thought' (XXXII) of *In Memoriam*, that both torments and sustains the poet, needs constantly to 'fix itself to form' (XXXIII). One such form that readily yields itself to Tennyson is that of ordinary Victorian life, the circumstances, as *The Spectator* saw, of 'daily detail'. This invocation of contemporary contexts was never perhaps for Tennyson more than the need to solve certain difficulties of expression in his poetic vision. Unlike some Victorians, he was not readily drawn to the details of a common environment for their own sakes, his attention being rather fixed upon those 'imperishable presences serene/ Colossal, without form, or sense, or sound,/Dim shadows but unwaning presences'. Yet Tennyson was obviously alert to the need to articulate in a language shared by his audience those subjects which *The Christian Remembrancer* thought 'all equidistant from himself and from us'. Since a language he readily chose was the visual and pictorial, it must have

been congenial to him to find this common idiom in *genre* painting, those
accounts of daily life that we may find at their best in the Dutch
seventeenth century and in Victorian England. So that in *In Memoriam*
we are aware of a process by which the 'thoughts of a metaphysician
[come to be] expressed by a painter'.[1] Because (in Hazlitt's words)
'Painting is essentially an imitative art; it cannot subsist for a moment on
empty generalities'.[2] And hence Tennyson's fascination for it, with the
added attraction that the visual structures, by their attention to things
seen outside the poet's mind, would also curb the dangerous subjective
tendencies of his imagination.

So that in *In Memoriam* the visual language finds a vital place,
providing an occasional structure in which to focus both visionary
generalities and intense introspection: hence the images of the 'Old
Yew' (II), the 'Dark house . . . On the bald street' (VII), the 'Witch-
elms that counterchange the floor/Of this flat lawn' (LXXXIX), or the
Christmas 'pastimes in the hall' (XXX) that recall some picture like
David Wilkie's *Blind Man's Buff* (plate 1). The sections that introduce
and centre upon the Tennysons' removal from Somersby in 1837
(XCV CIII) are redolent with visual image, with what Hallam had
himself called the 'picturesque delineation of objects . . . *fused* . . .
in a medium of strong emotion' (*CH*, 42). The comparison of certain
later Victorian pictures with some of the picturesque structures in this
sequence of the poem will perhaps serve to illuminate a characteristic
Tennysonian strategy.

Four paintings suggest themselves. Frederick Waller's *Old Letters*,
where the girl in the window-seat on a summer's day re-reads the letters
of an old lover, provides a close parallel with

> *I read*
> *Of that glad year which once had been,*
> *In those fallen leaves which keep their green,*
> *The noble letters of the dead.*   (XCV)

[1] Hazlitt, quoted Roy Park, *Hazlitt and the Spirit of the Age*, Oxford,
1971, 95. Especially the second section of this study, on Hazlitt as a
painter, is an extremely useful account of the attitudes towards the relations of poetry and painting in the early nineteenth century.
[2] Park, 104.

Frank Dicksee's *A Reverie* shows a man listening to a melody from the pianoforte and recalling how 'Lips that are dead/Sang me that song'. Bowler's *The Doubt: "Can These Dry Bones Live?"* (plate 2) is directly derived from *In Memoriam*. A fourth relevant painting, though obviously its narrative of ruin brought on by drink and gambling is totally at odds with Tennyson's poem, is Robert Martineau's *The Last Days in the Old Home*. All four paintings come into that category of which Henry James wrote in 1877:

> The pictures, with very few exceptions, are 'subjects'; they belong to what the French call the anecdotical class. You immediately perceive, moreover, that they are subjects addressed to a taste of the British merchant and paterfamilias and his excellently regulated family. What this taste appears to demand of a picture is that it shall have a taking title, like a three-volume novel or an article in a magazine; that it shall embody in its lower flights some comfortable incident of the daily life of our period, suggestive more especially of its gentilities and proprieties and familiar moralities, and in its loftier scope some picturesque episode of history or fiction which may be substantiated by a long explanatory extract in the catalogue.[1]

James testifies to the movement of much Victorian painting towards the literary—the catalogue words needed with Dicksee's *A Reverie* to enlarge one's sense of the visual image; the suggestion by the visible scene of some larger meaning, moral, sentimental, poetic.[2] Conversely,

[1] *The Painter's Eye. Notes and Essays on the Pictorial Arts*, selected and with an introduction by John L. Sweeney, 1965, 148.

[2] For some indication of the prevailing taste for paintings with such larger suggestions and of the fashion in which non-visual material was often the inspiration of a picture see the catalogue entry for H. P. Parker's *The Burial of Sir Francis Chantrey in Norton Churchyard* in *British Life: Catalogue of an Exhibition of Paintings showing Life in Britain*, The Arts Council, London, 1953. Chantrey's biographer, John Holland, was struck by the contrast between Chantrey—'the unnoticed village boy'—and the large gathering of gentry that accompanied him to his final resting place, and it was apparently at his suggestion, excited by his own *verbal* description of the scene, that Parker undertook the picture. (I am grateful to John Ingamells for drawing my attention to this item as for other assistance in the preparation of this Chapter.)

Tennyson's poetry moves towards a visual focus of high points of his spiritual narrative: often, as in the hundred and third section of *In Memoriam*, the visionary excitement is carefully placed in a context of Victorian circumstances, a country house with distinct landscapes of blossom, maple and stream. And whereas the pictures need our verbal explanations to enhance and expand the significance of one visual moment, Tennyson's meditations in time (which we share in the process of reading) are frequently formed into distinct visual prospects 'Of all the landscape underneath' (C).

But this convergence of structures in poem and picture is not all. Again, we may invoke Hazlitt: 'Painting gives the object itself; poetry what it implies. Painting embodies what a thing contains in itself: poetry suggests what exists out of it, in any manner connected with it. But this last is the proper province of the imagination.'[1] Although Tennyson seeks to give us intimations of the 'object itself'—the rather grotesquely foreshortened perspective of the bats (XCV) or the 'foliaged eaves' (XCIX)—he has finally more control over the implication than the painter. When he provides us with the prospect of

> *the doubtful dusk revealed*
> *The knolls once more where, couched at ease,*
> *The white kine glimmered, and the trees*
> *Laid their dark arms about the field* (XCV),

the commonplace is finely spiritualized and the controlling excitement of 'boundless day' is suggested by words that refer doubly to visible fact and emotional mood. With the Victorian paintings analogous to these sections of *In Memoriam* there is a much more precarious control over the latter element. I suspect that our satisfaction with them is in direct proportion to how we control our own associations—of leaving a home, reading old letters, listening to tunes from the past—and to the tact with which we as spectators of the pictures bring these into dialogue with the visual images. Only perhaps Bowler's painting manages to control in *visual* terms our emotional response to it: the delicate play of light and shade that picks out the word 'Life' on the tombstone, the butterflies, and the luminous exit from the churchyard

[1] Park, 122.

contrasted with the dark severity of the tree trunk at the right, all work upon us and shape our ambiguous reading of the painting. And it is in such qualities that Bowler acknowledges his debt to *In Memoriam*, especially the play with darkness and light (XCVI), with the graves and flames (XCVIII) recorded among the garden boughs and the 'circle of the hills' (CI).

In Memoriam is perhaps the most concentrated attempt by Tennyson to heed the advice of his reviewers to 'aspire to the rank of a prophet' (in the words of *The Christian Remembrancer* in 1849). It is all the more fascinating then to watch him trying to shift its intellectual endeavours into a pictorial idiom; yet it seems no accident that he does this in a poem dedicated to Hallam's memory. The coincidence of his friend's death with a series of hostile reviews in the early 1830's exercised a profound effect upon the remainder of Tennyson's career as a poet. Nowhere more than in his 'picturesque' imagination is this so conspicuous, and I do not believe that he could ever forget how his friend had identified this as one of his best poetic effects.

In one of the last letters received from Hallam in Vienna Tennyson was told:

> and oh Alfred such Titians! by Heaven, that man could paint! I wish you could see his Danaë. Do you just write as perfect a Danaë! Also there are two fine rooms of Rubens, but I know you are an exclusive, and care little for Rubens, in which you are wrong: although no doubt Titian's imagination and style are more analogous to your own . . . (*Mem.*, I, 104)

And just before Hallam's departure from London Tennyson had joined him on a visit 'to see Rogers' (the poet's) gallery of paintings: superb Titian, very beautiful Raphael Madonna, and in fact all art gems . . . There were many proofs of the engravings that will appear in his (Rogers's) forthcoming volume' (*Mem.*, I, 104-5). Such shared encounters with the visual arts could only have confirmed Tennyson's respect for what Hallam had written of *Poems, Chiefly Lyrical*. Besides the famous description of 'the picturesque delineation of objects', Hallam had shrewdly identified the 'feeling of art' in the poetry and praised both 'a perfect gallery of pictures' and effects similar to those of 'Venetian colouring'. We have further testimony of how he emphasized these qualities in a letter of 1831 where he defended 'Mariana in the South' for its pictorial qualities and argued that 'poetry cannot be too pictorial'. Even if Tennyson was able to recognize the extravagance of his friend's claims (the comparisons with Titian seem notably over-enthusiastic), he must still have realized that this picturesque habit was central to his imagination: others besides Hallam were attentive to it. J. S. Mill in the *London Review* (CH, 84 ff) noted Tennyson's 'art of painting a picture to the inward eye' and praised 'his power of creating scenery, in keeping with some state of human feeling'. W. J. Fox in the *Westminster Review* (CH, 21 ff) discovered the 'best pictorial qualities of poetry' in the 1830 volume and invoked Lawrence's portraits as well as landscapes by Wilson and Gainsborough in his examination of poems. And that it was this distinct and usually admired pictorial focus that Tennyson did *not* choose to curb during the disciplines of the ten years' silence is attested by the renewed praise for his picturesque vision in the late 1840's.[1] George Gilfillan saw that Tennyson painted 'in words vivid as colours' and that his poems were 'vivid and complete pictures'. *Hogg's Weekly Instructor* hailed the poet as a 'mighty painter', combining the palpable power of Raphael, the grandeur of Michelangelo, the richness of Titian, and the softness of Claude: 'Mariana' was a 'perfect picture . . . framed in every circumstance of life's and love's cold sorrow'.

That last phrase is, however, more interesting than the rather excessive catalogue of old masters: it signals Tennyson's success in using his picturesque vision, not after the rich vein of Titian, but in the interests of 'common feelings and thoughts of men'. For it was precisely that area of human concern over which he had been accused of having little power—notably by 'Christopher North' (CH, 52). And it is my own feeling that from the 1830's onwards Tennyson's particular effort was to utilize his talent for the picturesque to satisfy those Victorian contemporaries who urged him from the Palace of Art to 'a cottage in the vale'. And for this elaborate compromise he drew upon

---

[1] The following three quotations are all cited by Whiting, 2.

that branch of painting which is dedicated to ordinary subjects—including cottages (see plate 3): namely, *genre painting*.[1] By the 1860's and the publication of *Enoch Arden* it is abundantly evident that he had succeeded. *The Art Journal* exclaimed:

> "Enoch Arden" for Artists—No poem to which the century has given birth is so full as this of *pictures*; none to which the artist can turn with surer certainty of harvest . . . Here, then, is a rare gallery for the painter: every page supplies a subject—nay, subjects more than one—for the pencil; and, no doubt, "the exhibitions" will be full of evidence that the Poet has conferred an incalculable boon on Art.[2]

It is perhaps because critics have not been ready enough to follow Hallam's hint about Tennyson's ineluctably picturesque vision through the more domestic Victorian poems that the English idylls have been neglected.

It is not possible to discover what *genre* works Tennyson actually knew. But we can find testimony enough to the early nineteenth-century taste for such pictures. It was, of course, the Dutch influence that predominated at first and Coleridge is on record (not insignificantly for my purposes here) as deploring the literature that emulated Dutch painting: 'we have had many specimens of this sort of work in modern poems, where all is so dutchified . . . by the most minute touches, that the reader naturally asks why words, and not painting, are used?'[3] The vogue for Dutch and Flemish pictures was given a strong impetus by the collecting of George IV and Sir Robert Peel[4] and it was a work by Teniers, seen after his arrival in London in 1805, that led David Wilkie to paint the first of his *genre* pictures, *The Village Politicians*. His attention to the incidents and ingredients of everyday life

---

[1] For further discussion of Victorian painting see Jeremy Maas, *Victorian Painters*, 1969, Raymond Lister, *Victorian Narrative Painting*, 1966, and Graham Reynolds, *Victorian Painting*, 1966.

[2] Whiting, 2.

[3] *Shakespearean Criticism*, ed T. M. Raysor, 1960, II, 134.

[4] See *Dutch Pictures from the Royal Collection*, with an introduction by Oliver Millar, 1971–72.

made him the foremost of early *genre* artists—an engraving of *The Cottage Door* (plate 3) shows both his loving care with the paraphernalia of common circumstance and—in the detail of the dog scratching its ear—the painterly capture of one passing moment. But Wilkie's most impressive contribution to *genre* painting came from his study of psychological interplay, which can be seen at work in the groups of *Blind Man's Buff*. For the kind of attention we need to pay to such a work—identifying, understanding and articulating the responses between characters—is close to the approach we must take with a narrative painting.

Much Victorian painting devoted to contemporary life extends itself readily into narrative. William Mulready, with Wilkie the most important and influential of early Victorian painters, subtly modulates his Dutch *genre* idiom into suggestive and sentimental narrative. Although *The Mall, Kensington Gravel Pits* of 1811 is a beautiful formal composition in which the painstaking detail is yet held in the larger patterns of light and shade, our attention is eventually drawn to the children playing and to identifying their games. And comparing Mulready's *Interior of an English Cottage* (plate 4) with Wilkie's similar piece we can detect in its more sentimental colouring of the figure and her surroundings an invitation to indulge a narrative response. In later paintings, like *The Wolf and the Lamb* (plate 5) or *The Sonnet* (plate 6), Mulready's narrative instincts are more pronounced. The first requires its viewers to construct a story antecedent to and maybe even subsequent to the moment of the picture in which a little girl calls upon the woman to intervene in the boys' fight. The second makes an especially subtle use of its eponymous sonnet to elicit and sustain our 'reading' of its narrative: the story here is rather one of emotional scope than of plot, as in *The Wolf and the Lamb*. A boy has written the sonnet and bends to try and catch his girl's reactions, while she bates her breath (or maybe stifles her giggles) till she has finished. The visual structure—the glance, the hand held to the mouth—is enforced by our knowledge from the title that the span of time they will be so is short. Yet the picture also requires something akin to the verbal structure of the sonnet itself, something that will explain the process of the event depicted and our understanding of the picture's larger time when the reading has finished and the poised relationship has been resumed.[1]

These *genre* narratives are, of course, a prominent feature of much Pre-Raphaelite painting. *The Blind Girl* (plate 7) is Millais's passionately coloured poem on the sadness of lost sight: the sharply-lighted landscape is what a visual structure can readily offer, but this is extended by our own need to 'explain' the scene, to 'read' the girl's inner response to her companion's telling of the double rainbow, even perhaps to recall the biblical language of a rainbow and accommodate it to our sense of the modern scene. The Pre-Raphaelite dedication both to detailed observation and to meanings that seem to need more than a merely visual language to explain themselves make this group of painters important mediators of *genre* and narrative art in the mid-century. Arthur Hughes is in some ways the most instructive among their number: for he keeps firmly to the range and vocabulary of *genre*, yet manages to suggest whole areas of story or emotion beyond the specific event in the painting. *The Art Journal* of 1862 commented on the 'dull solemnity' and 'cheerless piety' of *Bed Time*, two remarks which perhaps miss the careful and even tender assimilation into a crowded frame of the family details: but the criticism rightly attends to the painting's larger effort of meaning. Hughes's more famous picture of the following year, *Home From Sea*, more successfully balances the cheerful texture of the outward world against the inner grief of the young boy at his mother's grave.

These narratives suggest a major Victorian preoccupation with the problem of attending to the details of their daily life as well as to a more than mere circumstantial significance. A reviewer of the Royal Academy exhibition of 1863 listed 'Scenes Domestic' as one element of Victorian art and then commented: 'England, happy in her homes, and joyous in her hearty cheer, and peaceful in her snug firesides, is equally fortunate in a school of Art sacred to the hallowed relations of domestic life'.[2] The sentimental emphasis is precisely an expression of the need of

[1] Cf Jonson: 'It is a noble and just advantage that the things subjected to understanding have of those which are objected to sense that the one sort are but momentary and merely taken, the other impressing and lasting': *The Complete Masques*, New Haven and London, 1969, 75.

[2] Quoted Jeremy Maas, 104.

Victorian art to pay tribute to some species of higher truth—in this case, 'hallowed traditions of domestic life'. An increasing tendency in Victorian visual art was to depict some genre scene—a young seamstress seated at a table by the attic window, a shirt and workbox before her— and then by way of a title or catalogue entry to lift the daily details onto a 'higher' or more 'significant' plane—in the case of the seamstress, by a quotation from Thomas Hood:

> *For only one short hour*
> *To feel as I used to feel,*
> *Before I knew the woes of want*
> *And the walk that costs a meal!*

The proliferation of paintings with abstract titles—*Love, Prayer, Praise, Hope in Death*[1]—show this same urge to root the larger meaning in the smaller circumstance. The abstractions, at least until we encounter the grandiloquent rhetoric of Rossetti's *Astarte Syriaca* or Watt's *Love Steering the Boat of Humanity*, have the benefit of being focused in detailed visual accounts of ordinary life. It was, as I shall show, an analogous, if converse, problem for Tennyson—attempting to anchor in verbal descriptions of *genre* scope the larger visions from the 'labyrinth of the mind' (PT, 950) that words could barely make accessible in more than a general and abstract fashion. These dialogues between abstraction and *genre* idiom have their more strenuous formulation in such works as *Modern Painters*, where Ruskin is preoccupied with both the careful delineation of the physical scene and the larger truths for which Turner is praised, or Carlyle's seminal essay, 'Signs of the Times'. Carlyle specifically identifies the nineteenth-century loss of the invisible, which he celebrates in abstract terms:

> the primary, unmodified forces and energies of man, the mysterious springs of Love, and Fear, and Wonder, of Enthusiasm, Poetry, Religion, all which have a truly vital and *infinite* character.[2]

---

[1] All these, as well as the picture of the seamstress, are by Ruskin's correspondent, Anna Blunden: see *Sublime and Instructive*, ed Virginia Surtees, 1972, 80 & 87.

[2] *Selected Writings*, ed Alan Shelston, 1971, 74 & 72; the third quotation is from 61.

Yet the essay was forced to begin by recognizing a more accessible Victorian sentiment: 'Happy men are full of the present, for its bounty suffices them; and wise men also, for its duties engage them'.

It was Tennyson's preoccupation in the years following the early, hostile reviews and Hallam's death, to learn ways of accommodating what Carlyle calls 'invisible, mystic and ideal' aims to that present world of happy and dutiful men that seemed a particularly fruitful territory for the early *genre* painters. There were undoubtedly moments of mistrust, even despair:

> *What hope is there for modern rhyme*
> *To him, who turns a musing eye*
> *On songs, and deeds, and lives, that lie*
> *Foreshortened in the tract of time?*
>
> *These mortal lullabies of pain*
> *May bind a book, may line a box,*
> *May serve to curl a maiden's locks.*   (PT, 926)

Yet the struggle to bring significance to such mundane details, to see Carlyle's larger abstractions manifested and realized in ordinary Victorian circumstance, was continuous and not always unsuccessful. And it was a struggle that seemed to draw strength and solace from his long-established picturesque vision.

As early as 1833–4 Tennyson composed 'The Gardener's Daughter; or the Pictures'. Though the narrator is an artist, which accounted— according to the poet (PT, 508)—for the pictures which compose the poem, this pictorial structure comes just as readily from Tennyson's own imagination. The poem's narrative, like that of genre paintings, seem to bring past and even future (see lines 231 ff) into the focus of a seen and visible moment of the present—'This morning is the morning of the day' and, later—

> *And sure this orbit of the memory folds*
> *Forever in itself the day we went*
> *To see her.*

Not only is that day a sharply pictured event, but its scenery and its actors ('My Eustace might have sat for Hercules') are the figures of a painterly imagination. The scenery that leads the men into a Victorian rose-garden has a precise visual focus that is strangely reminiscent (or prophetic) of Holman Hunt's *Love at First Sight* in its landscape of slanting meadow and 'dark-green layers of shade' beyond. The garden caught between the busy world and a pastoral and painterly seclusion may be identified as almost emblematic of Tennyson's effort in these English idylls. But it is the central picture that is most brilliantly rendered:

> till *close at hand,*
> *And almost ere I knew mine own intent,*
> *This murmur broke the stillness of that air*
> *Which brooded round about her:*
> *   'Ah, one rose,*
> *One rose, but one, by those fair fingers cull'd,*
> *Were worth a hundred kisses press'd on lips*
> *Less exquisite than thine'.*
> *   She look'd: but all*
> *Suffused with blushes—neither self-possessed*
> *Nor startled, but betwixt this mood and that,*
> *Divided in a graceful quiet—paused,*
> *And dropt the branch she held, and turning, wound*
> *Her looser hair in braid, and stirr'd her lips*
> *For some sweet answer, tho' no answer came,*
> *Nor yet refused the rose, but granted it,*
> *And moved away, and left me, statue-like,*
> *In act to render thanks.*

The immobility not only of that final 'statue-like' but also of the 'pause' with which Rose greets the narrator's extravagant courtesy has the poise and momentarily apprehended structure of a narrative picture. The richness and intensity of its retrospective emotion anticipates the paintings of Arthur Hughes, where similar fleeting encounters are caught on canvas. The later scene of the lovers seated 'upon a garden mound,/Two mutually enfolded' has a similar focus: the lines direct us first to them, then over a 'range' of scenery that encompasses their story, upon which we are required finally to 'settle'.

Certain of Tennyson's revisions of the poem seem to have contrived these picturesque elements more emphatically. The poem was originally

5. The Wolf and the Lamb, *by William Mulready*

6. The Sonnet, *by William Mulready*

7. The Blind Girl, *by John Everett Millais*

'The moving whisper of huge trees that branch'd
And blossomed in the zenith, or the sweep
Of some precipitous rivulet to the wave . . .'

'So past the strong heroic soul away
And when they buried him the little port
Had seldom seen a costlier funeral.'

8. *and* 9. *Two original designs for* 'Enoch Arden', *by Arthur Hughes*

much longer (*Mem.*, I, 509) and it seems a fair inference that some passages (see especially PT, 512) were deleted because they blurred the discrete painterly images. Yet if the original leisurely verses, more apt for verbal than simulated visual narrative, were cut, Tennyson also betrays the urge, that I have already noticed as prompting later Victorian painters, for explaining visual images in rather grandiloquent abstractions—

> *But while I mused came Memory with sad eyes,*
> *Holding the folded annals of my youth;*
> *And while I mused, Love with knit brows went by,*
> *And with a flying finger swept my lips.*

The visual sense is there perhaps, but only as in the uneasy allegories of a Watts that lack entirely the poem's earlier attention to Victorian circumstance. They are lines that remind us of Leigh Hunt's strictures on 'Lilian' in 1842—'that injudicious crowding of *images* which sometimes results from Mr Tennyson's desire to impress upon us the abundance of his *thoughts*' (PT, 182–3, my italics). It is Tennyson's chosen success in the English idylls to subdue his thoughts and offer precisely the images that may suggest the larger mental territory. One particular example is Tennyson's evident fondness for the older meaning of the word, 'circumstance'; namely its implication of 'the totality of surrounding things' and hence 'the heavens'. But in his own verses titled 'Circumstance' it is not the abstract totality nor the idea of the 'hollow orb of moving Circumstance' that he strives to articulate: it is the simplicities of English *genre*—

> *Two children in two neighbour villages*
> *Playing mad pranks along the heathy leas;*
> *Two strangers meeting at a festival;*
> *Two lovers whispering by an orchard wall;*
> *Two lives bound fast in one with golden ease;*
> *Two graves grass-green beside a gray church tower,*
> *Washed with still rains and daisy blossomed*
> *Two children in one hamlet born and bred;*
> *So runs the round of life from hour to hour.*   (PT, 250–1)

It is this dedication through such *genre* idiom to unaffected implication that characterizes 'Dora'. The simplicities of this poem are argu-
ably the effect of Tennyson's attempt to offer everything in idyllic
picture (we should recall that the name—εἶδος—implies compactness
and quickly apprehendable form). Sentiment, human feeling and moral
concerns are *seen* items and they are almost deliberately repressed as
spoken ideas:

> *the boy's cry came to her from the field,*
> *More and more distant. She bow'd down her head,*
> *Remembering the day when first she came,*
> *And all the things that had been. She bow'd down*
> *And wept in secret; and the reapers reap'd,*
> *And the sun fell, and all the land was dark.*   (PT, 643)

What she remembers at this highpoint of the poem is less crucial than
our sight of her in the landscape: it is a scene that has a tone almost
more reminiscent of Poussin's *Summer*, where the biblical dignity of
Ruth and Boaz is set against the men working in the corn, than of Victorian *genre*—perhaps because of this over-ambitious scope the passage
reads somewhat portentously. The opening (the farmer seen glancing
at his son) and close (the reassembled household) are images that
neglect all but the barest details because, I think, *we* are encouraged to
visualize the actors in terms of Victorian pictures of family life. There
are other such painterly moments when the two women peep through
the open door:

> *and saw*
> *The boy set up betwixt his grandsire's knees,*
> *Who thrust him in the hollows of his arm,*
> *And clapt him on the hands and on the cheeks,*
> *Like one that loved him: and the lad stretch'd out*
> *And babbled for the golden seal, that hung*
> *From Allan's watch, and sparkled by the fire.*
> *Then they came in . . .*
>   (PT, 645)

That picture is held as long as poetic *sequence* will allow, when the
action ('Then they came in') resumes, but only to refocus again as

soon as possible in another picture:

> Then they clung about
> The old man's neck, and kiss'd him many times.
> And all the man was broken with remorse;
>
> (PT, 646)

it is such moments that hold the reader and not, for example, the direct speech of Mary in the preceding section.

The effect of other domestic poems of the 1830s is similar. When Aubrey de Vere talked of these poems as 'a gift such as no other writer . . . had ever given to his countryman', he in part certainly identifies Tennyson's aim: for, as he goes on

> No Englishman can read them in far lands without
> the memory coming back to him of the days when
> he sat on an English stile, and watched English
> lambs at play, or walked beneath hedgerow trees
> in a 'land of ancient peace' listening to the
> last note of the last bird-song as the twilight
> deepened into night.   (*Mem.*, I, 508 & passim)

But the poet was not, I suggest, dedicated to 'depicting the country life in England' for its own sake. Like Will Waterproof who may canvass the platitudes of tap room and chop-house, he has dim apprehensions of larger themes:

> Ten thousand broken lights and shapes,
> Yet glimpses of the true.
>
> (PT, 669)

Only through attending to the phenomenal fragments of this world may we learn to recognize the noumenous and what Carlyle called the 'invisible'.

In such poems as 'Walking to the Mail' (1837–8) or 'Audley Court' (1838) we may perhaps be excused suspicions of merely superficial description. But the larger motives are still just conspicuous—the conventional, by no means unimportant, critical insistence upon the presence of Theocritus in 'Audley Court' is one means of pointing to them. Another would be to note how Tennyson concentrates upon pictures in the poem—the bustle of the 'narrow quay' or its companion nightpiece:

> *The town was hushed beneath us: lower down*
> *The bay was oily calm; the harbour-buoy,*
> *Sole star of phosphorescence in the calm,*
> *With one green sparkle ever and anon*
> *Dipt by itself,*
>
> (PT, 707)

and especially the landscape that, lying at the centre of the poem, sharply controls its visual narrative ('There, on a slope of orchard . . .'). It is then through these *genre* scenes that we are allowed access to the larger human aspirations and motives that the songs celebrate: Tennyson's invocation of music here to amplify the narrative perhaps recalls Giorgione's *Le concert champêtre* in the Louvre. Without the pictures, the poet would scarcely earn the right to that last half line—'and we were glad at heart'—for it draws upon the seen idyll of picnic, upon the visible companionship and the freedom of the two friends from the 'hive' of 'Audley feast'. In 'Walking to the Mail' the narrative's reflections upon quixotic humanity are made to arise directly from the noticed, pictured landscapes, the Mulready-like glimpses of Jocky Dawes or James's Etonian pastimes.

All of these poems from the 1830s were to be placed after 1853 among the 'English Idyls', thus reaffirming both their formal picturesque structures and their common strategy of using English domestic detail as the vehicle of a larger motif. And after the poet's attention had been given during the 1840s and 1850s to *The Princess, In Memoriam* and *Maud,* the *genre* idiom of the 1842 volume was recovered and consolidated in two poems of the 1860s—'Enoch Arden' and 'Aylmer's Field'.

There would be little point in enumerating the extraordinary scope of Tennyson's picturesque imagination in the first of these: *The Art Journal,* already cited, was absolutely accurate in its acclaim for 'a rare gallery for the painter'. What perhaps it could not envisage was that Tennyson's illustrators might fail to take advantage of the gallery simply because the poet had accomplished the visual structures adequately in words; that it was the careful tension between what words could properly do and what words could equally contrive by way of painterly effects that allowed the poem its occasional and peculiar successes. Arthur Hughes, whom one might think of as the ideal Tennysonian illustrator, is quite unsuccessful with his designs for 'Enoch Arden' (plate 8). They are poor because they must either invent pictures where there are none in the poem or they are forced to fill out their own visual space, whereas the poetry allows more suggestive and tantalizing visual hints (it was Beardsley, learning maybe from his 'picture writers', who recognized the proper role of blank space in graphic art).

Tennyson is manifestedly uninterested in narrative for its own sake: 'things seen are mightier than things heard' is his conviction as well as his hero's. Enoch's most intense moments are his visions, either of an impoverished future for his family after the accident or of the redolent English scene when he is alone on his desert island:

> *the small house,*
> *The climbing street, the mill, the leafy lanes,*
> *The peacock-yewtree and the lonely Hall,*
> *The horse he drove, the boat he sold, the chill*
> *November dawns and dewy-glooming downs,*
> *The gentle shower, the smell of dying leaves,*
> *And the low moan of leaden-coloured seas.*
>
> (PT, 1144)

It is a more elegiac version of the vision that de Vere thought Tennyson's verse would conjure up for the expatriate Englishman. Throughout the poem Tennyson deliberately neglects any narrative that cannot afford him such picturesque opportunities: thus Enoch making his way in the world (ll. 45 ff) or Annie's decline after his departure (ll. 244 ff) are telescoped as much as possible, the poetry expanding more leisurely and more interestedly only at a point where the story can be focused in pictures—the lovers agreeing ('Then, on a golden autumn evening . . .') or Philip pausing 'for a moment at an inner door' which is replaced quickly by Annie turning away from his entry to weep. The account of Enoch's travels (ll. 523 ff) is rendered cavalierly, only the rhythmic mastery disguising the brisk dispatch of uncongenial material.

Like the earliest of English narrative artists, Hogarth, Tennyson finds it rewardingly economical to allow visible details to announce

future events.[1] The children playing house in the cliff cave could be a
Wilkie genre scene did it not also envisage later history—'Enoch was
host one day, Philip the next,/While Annie still was mistress'. Similarly,
the marvellously detailed scene upon the beach tells emblematically the
changes and waste of the ensuing story:

> *And Enoch Arden, a rough sailor's lad*
> *Made orphan by a winter shipwreck, played*
> *Among the waste and lumber of the shore,*
> *Hard coils of cordage, swarthy fishing-nets,*
> *Anchors of rusty fluke, and boats updrawn;*
> *And built their castles of dissolving sand*
> *To watch them overflowed.*

(PT, 1130)

Where Tennyson falters, apart from the sections of uncongenial
narrative, is where he neglects pictures for words. The momentary
success of the image of Annie,

> *as the village girl*
> *Who sets her pitcher underneath the spring,*
> *Musing on him that used to fill it for her,*

or the Millais-like farewells of the family—'And kissed his wonder-
stricken little ones'—depend upon the words suggesting pictures and
controlling the extra-visual meanings. In contrast, the verbal insistence
of these lines is merely rather bathetic:

> *Yet Enoch was a brave God-fearing man,*
> *Bowed himself down, and in that mystery*
> *Where God-in-man is one with man-in-God,*
> *Prayed for a blessing on his wife and babes*
> *Whatever came to him.*

(PT, 1134)

[1] See Ronald Paulson, *Hogarth's Graphic Works*, 2 vol., New Haven and
London, 1970, or, for a shorter account, the same author's essay,
'Hogarth and the English garden: visual and verbal structures', *Encounters: Essays on literature and the visual arts*, ed John Dixon Hunt,
1971.

The *genre* idiom cannot sustain such explicit celebration of more resonant mysteries. Similarly Philip's speech to Annie (II. 285 ff), without any picturesque structuring, has little of the impact of the scene some lines later (II. 369 ff) where the emotional histories are held in a suggestive conversation piece by the 'prone edge of the wood'. Both the sentiments for the 'sacred old familiar fields' and the undertow of satire[1] in the poem are suggested in that carefully and deliberately exaggerated *genre* scene which Enoch Arden sees in Philip's house:

> *For cups and silver on the burnished board*
> *Sparkled and shone; so genial was the hearth:*
> *And on the right hand of the hearth he saw*
> *Philip, the slighted suitor of old times,*
> *Stout, rosy, with his babe across his knees;*
> *And o'er her second father stoopt a girl,*
> *A later but a loftier Annie Lee,*
> *Fair-haired and tall, and from her lifted hand*
> *Dangled a length of ribbon and a ring*
> *To tempt the babe, who reared his creasy arms,*
> *Caught at and ever missed it, and they laughed;*
> *And on the left hand of the hearth he saw*
> *The mother glancing often toward her babe,*
> *But turning now and then to speak with him,*
> *Her son, who stood beside her tall and strong,*
> *And saying that which pleased him, for he smiled.*
>
> (PT, 1147–48)

The passage, consciously framed between 'Enoch saw' and 'Now when the dead man came to life beheld . . .', is a picture of almost grotesque poignancy for Enoch. But it is our own ability in our turn to watch him contemplating its hearty *genre* aplomb that ensures a subtle distancing of his predicament. The painterly device briefly restrains the poem from a perspective it would otherwise share with the 'good and garrulous' Miriam Lane.

The need to curtail the merely verbal obviously perplexed Tennyson

---

[1] See T. J. Assad, 'On the Major Poems of Tennyson's *Enoch Arden* Volume', *Tulane Studies in English*, XIV, 1966.

too in 'Aylmer's Field'. He is reported as finding 'how incredibly difficult the story was to tell, *the dry facts of it so prosaic in themselves'* (PT,
1160, my italics). It has been suggested[1] how in 'Aylmer's Field' we may
discover common ground between Tennyson and Victorian novelists
and how the poet sought to communicate his own sense of modern life
in varying the narrative pace and scale of the poetry. Yet we might also
notice how he struggles, less successfully than in 'Enoch Arden', to
accommodate his verse to the demands of pictorial rhythms.

The tense and rather unrelenting progress of the first eighty lines
suddenly relaxes into the charming children's scene of the next twenty,
a picture of a 'couple, fair/As ever painter painted, poet sang'. There
are other such painterly moments during the poem—the congregation
gathered for the sermon, the 'wife, who watched his face,/Paled at a
sudden twitch of his iron mouth', Sir Aylmer 'desolate' beneath his
ancestral portraits. But the temptation to overdramatise renders others
as awkward as those Victorian pictures which also attempt a larger
rhetoric than their circumstances allow—the Lear-like stance of Sir
Aylmer banishing Leolin or his stumbling exit from the church after his
wife's collapse. What really redeem the poem from its 'prophet's
righteous wrath' (*Mem.*, II, 9) and from the too intense demands of its
verbal indignation are the 'icons' of landscape description. The title
rightly celebrates the poem's true hero: the 'land of hops and poppy-
mingled corn', which at the start seems doomed, despite its annual
freshness and rejuvenation, to the same 'old rut', but which by the end
reassumes its natural role:

> *Then the great Hall was wholly broken down,*
> *And the broad woodland parcelled into farms;*
> *And where the two contrived their daughter's good,*
> *Lies the hawk's cast, the mole has made his run,*
> *The hedgehog underneath the plaintain bores,*
> *The rabbit fondles his own harmless face,*
> *The slow-worm creeps, and the thin weasel there*
> *Follows the mouse, and all is open field.*
>
> (PT, 1183)

[1] P. Drew, '"Aylmer's Field": a Problem for Critics,' *The Listener*,
LXXI, 1964.

It is a Pre-Raphaelite landscape of exquisite, preternatural detail—and almost rescues the poem.

By the time Tennyson was composing these later English idylls he had of course already published the first of his Arthurian poems,[1] in which the same painterly structures were to find an assured role. The occasional conjunction of the two modes—domestic and Arthurian—tends to double the painterly effect. 'Godiva' juxtaposes the 'ancient legend', sharply seen in a series of tableaux, with the Victorian *genre* picture of the poet hanging 'with grooms and porters on the bridge,/To watch the three tall spires', while he waits for his train at Coventry. The story of 'Morte D'Arthur', which Sterling rightly saw was 'full of distinct and striking description' (CH, 120), is conjured up amid the deliberately empty image of a modern Christmas Eve—'The game of forfeits done—the girls all kiss'd/Beneath the sacred bush'. The effect intended by such doubling of picture—and the most ambitious effort in this way is *The Princess*—is to contrive an even more forceful presence of meaning in the seen events.

As we saw in *In Memoriam*, Tennyson not only will endeavour to focus his more abstract thinking in *genre* pictures that speak with a recognizable and shared language to his Victorian readers—thus the forlorn debate of the 'Two Voices' is suddenly steadied against the sight of the group on its way to church, reminiscent of Richard Redgrave's *Sunday Morning—the Walk from Church*. He is also alert to the way in which images of the present may be given a typological emphasis, enlarging their meaning without seeming to explain or resorting to narrative sequence. In both *In Memoriam* and the *Idylls of the King* Hallam emerges as a type of Christ and King Arthur and they of him. When Gladstone reviewed the first book of *Idylls of the King* in 1859 he

[1] It is this closeness of painterly aim in both sorts of idyll and, as a result of this shared endeavour, my sense of their similarity that has led me to refer throughout this essay to the idylls, not distinguishing the English variety by the poet's preferred spelling of 'idyl'. For a more detailed account of the matter canvassed in these last paragraphs see my essay, 'The Poetry of Distance: Tennyson's *Idylls of the King*', *Victorian Poetry*, ed M. Bradbury and D. J. Palmer, Stratford-Upon-Avon Studies 15, 1973.

saw how Tennyson had achieved a 'refined analogy which links the manifold to the simple and the infinite to the finite' (CH, 261). Bagehot in the same year saw Tennyson's ornate art as dedicated to surrounding 'the type with the greatest number of circumstances which it will bear' (CH, 284). Doubtless this encouraged Tennyson to use the biblical allusions and quotations to enlarge the significance of 'Enoch Arden', just as he had hinted at the garden of the *Roman de la Rose* as a type of the Victorian encounter in 'The Gardener's Daughter'. The constant presence of Theocritus within all these idylls is surely another form of Tennyson's typological manoeuvre.

But our own tendency to overlook such strategy and perhaps Tennyson's failure, generally, to sustain it in the English idylls may once again be related to Victorian painting. By the nineteenth century any typological structures, possible for the Renaissance mind, for example, had been lost: only the Pre-Raphaelites managed anything approaching its multiple meanings when—among themselves—they delighted in recognizing their own friends and contemporaries in the mythical and biblical scenes of their paintings. But the *genre* pictures of Wilkie, Mulready and their successors that I have offered as precedents or analogues for Tennyson's picturesque delineation of objects and men did not have this kind of potency. It was perhaps no wonder then that Tennyson's typological attempts could not rely upon shared responses to an art that proposed the same device. In fact, one could argue that his most successful and indeed radical use of visual imagery did not contrive any meanings by analogy or typology: the sharply seen pictures of *Maud* are there because they define a highly subjective vision with no regard beyond itself—'And the whole little wood where I sit, is a world of plunder and prey'. *Maud* is a poem where, in Hallam's words to W. B. Donne,

> poetry cannot be too pictorial, for it cannot represent too truly, and when the object of the poetic power happens to be an object of sensuous perception, it is the business of the poetic language to paint (*Mem.*, I, 501).

8: *Tennyson as Poet Laureate*

SIR CHARLES TENNYSON

TENNYSON WAS without doubt the most successful of all our Poets Laureate, even if we include Spenser and Ben Jonson in the list, as, strictly speaking, we should not. Spenser was the representative poet of the Elizabethan age; he dedicated his greatest poem to the great Queen and paid her many exquisite compliments, but he wrote no 'laureate' verse and was never in fact her Poet Laureate. Ben Jonson was the chosen poet of the Court by reason of the series of masques which he wrote for its entertainment, but he too was not Poet Laureate and wrote no 'laureate' poetry in the sense that Tennyson wrote it. The greatest amongst Tennyson's official predecessors was John Dryden. He held the office from 1668–1680, but seems to have taken a very restricted view of his duties, regarding himself as the King's poet-advocate, bound by his position to place his unrivalled powers of argument and satire at the Monarch's service, which he did with resounding success. Of later Laureates much the most successful was Robert Southey (1814–1843) who is now chiefly remembered for the merciless fun which Byron made of his poem on the death of George III, 'The Vision of Judgment'. Southey was an honest, vigorous and skilful versifier, who did much to raise the office from the disrepute into which it had fallen during the eighteeenth century when the Laureate's duties had dwindled to the provision of New Year and Royal Birthday odes to be performed with music, which, as contemporary critics observed, mercifully made the words inaudible. But Southey, though industrious and skilful, lacked genius and sparkle. He claimed to have written more laureate verse than any Poet Laureate before him—even if Ben Jonson's Masques are taken into account—but he produced no laureate poem which retains any interest today.

Tennyson owed his success as Laureate to the circumstances of the time and the character of the Sovereign no less than to his own character and abilities. He had the immense advantage, which no previous Laureate had enjoyed, of being Poet Laureate to a constitutional monarch. It is true that both Southey and Wordsworth had been Laureates under Queen Victoria, but, in 1837, when Queen Victoria came to the throne, Southey was already suffering from incipient softening of the brain, and Wordsworth, who succeeded him in 1843, in his 74th year, was already a spent force and was to be totally inactive as Laureate.[1] Tennyson, who succeeded Wordsworth in 1850, had been an ardent supporter of the Reform Movement in the late 1820s and early 1830s and he had fully shared the enthusiasm of the British people at the accession of the eighteen-year-old Princess and the hopeful contrast which she presented to her Hanoverian uncles: to quote Lytton Strachey, 'the nasty old men, debauched, selfish, pig-headed and ridiculous, with their perpetual burden of debts, confusions and disreputabilities'. So much is clear from the light-hearted lines to 'The Queen of the Isles' which he dashed off at the time of her accession, but which were not published until they appeared in PT (1969):

THE QUEEN OF THE ISLES

My friends since you wish for a health from the host,
Come fill up your glasses; I'll give you a toast.
Let us drink to the health that we value the most—
To the health of the Queen of the Isles.

The reigns of her fathers were long or were short,
They plagued us in anger or vext us in sport,
Let them sleep in their good or their evil report—
But a health to the Queen of the Isles.

[1] Wordsworth was invited by the Prince Consort in 1847 to write an ode to celebrate his election as Chancellor of Cambridge University. The request came when Wordsworth's sister Dorothy lay dying, and finding himself unable to compose the ode, he got his son-in-law Edward Quillinan to write it under his supervision.

May those in her council that have the chief voice
Be true hearts of oak that the land may rejoice
And the people may love her the more for her choice—
So a health to the Queen of the Isles.

No slaves of a party, straightforward and clear,
Let them speak out like men without bias or fear
That the voice of her people may reach to her ear
With a health to the Queen of the Isles.

That the voice of a satisfied people may keep
A sound in her ear like the sound of the deep,
Like the voice of the sea when the wind is asleep
And a health to the Queen of the Isles.

Let her flag as of old be the first on the seas,
That the good of the land and the world may increase
And Power may balance the nations in Peace
With a health to the Queen of the Isles.

But if despots and fools must be taught with the rod,
Let her soldier tread firm as his fathers have trod,
And her cannon roar out like the judgement of God
With a health to the Queen of the Isles.

My brothers and friends! may the days that commence
Be so fruitful in genius, in worth and in sense
That a man's eye shall glisten, a thousand years hence,
When he reads of the Queen of the Isles!

And since Time never pauses but Change must ensue,
Let us wish that old things may fit well with the new,
For the blessing of promise is on her like dew—
So a health to the Queen of the Isles.

God bless her! and long may she hold the command
Till the hair of the boy shall be grey in the land
And the ball and the sceptre shall pass from her hand
To the race of the Queen of the Isles.

So fill up your glasses and hold them on high,
Were the health fathoms-deep I would drink it or die,
And send out your voices and join in the cry
To the health of the Queen of the Isles.

(PT, 665)

The Laureateship which came to him thirteen years later marked a turning point in his career. Only five years before Sir Robert Peel had granted him a pension from the Civil List, on the ground that he could never expect to earn a living from his poetry. Then in 1850 he published *In Memoriam,* a long poem in memory of his friend who had died seventeen years before, issued anonymously, in what might have seemed a monotonous stanza-form and without any explanation of the title or identification of the friend to whom the poem referred. Almost overnight the book became a best-seller. Tennyson was at last enabled to marry the woman to whom he had become engaged twelve years previously, and before the end of the year he was appointed Laureate.

Tennyson's great achievement as Laureate was not in the quality of his laureate verse (though this was technically high and includes one outstanding poem—the 'Dedication' prefixed to the 1862 edition of *Idylls of the King*), but in the fact that he added a new element to the Laureateship in the relationship which he established with the Queen as a result of this poem. This relationship, however, was not established until more than eleven years after his appointment. Tennyson was morbidly shy and retiring. He avoided London and general society so far as he could. The Queen had little interest in contemporary literature, Tennyson's appointment having been due entirely to the Prince Consort's admiration of *In Memoriam.* His publication of Laureate verse during the eleven years immediately succeeding his appointment had been confined to the 'Dedication' to the Queen, which he prefixed to the new edition of his two volumes of 1842 issued in March 1851 and which is still printed at the beginning of his collected works, and two additional stanzas to 'God save the Queen' commissioned for use at the State Concert which was to be given at Buckingham Palace in January 1858, on the evening before the wedding of the Princess Royal to Crown Prince Frederick William of Prussia. Nor was there any personal contact during these years with the Queen, who was absorbed by the care of a growing family and left as much as possible of the official work to her energetic and capable Consort.

Tennyson did however make acquaintance with the Prince, who visited him at his home in the Isle of Wight in the spring of 1856. Tennyson was deeply impressed during this visit by the Prince's sincerity, modesty and intellectual power.

Then in December 1861 came the shock of the Prince's death. For the Queen, deeply emotional as she was, the blow was crushing. After more than twenty years of marriage she still loved Albert as passionately as ever and she had, as the years went by, passed on to him more and more the political and business responsibilities which she found so distasteful. Now she was called on to face her huge world and the care of her large family alone.

It is clear that Tennyson and his wife already felt a close personal involvement with the royal couple. 'A terrible blow,' wrote Emily Tennyson in her diary, 'one fears for the Queen, for the nation the loss is unspeakable.' Almost immediately afterwards Tennyson received a message through one of the Royal Household expressing Princess Alice's wish that he should write something about her father. The request caused him acute distress. He hated to write to order—'Poetry is as inexorable as death itself', he used to say—yet he ardently desired to comply with the Princess' wish. The draft of a reply, which he prepared but did not send, shows (particularly in its alternative endings) his extreme perturbation:

> Hearing of your Royal Highness's strong desire that I should write something on the memory of the Prince Consort, I answer that at present I am unwell and the subject wh. I have tried is too exciting to me, but that in my own way & at my own time I trust I may be enabled to do honour to the memory of as gracious, noble & gentle a being as God has sent among us to be a messenger of good to his fellow-creatures. We all honour him—We all love him —more and more since we lost him: there is scarce an instance in History of a person so pure & blameless—is not that some comfort to Her Majesty & Her Children, some little comfort in the midst of so great a sorrow? But I wished to say to your R.H. that when I was some three or four years older than yourself I suffered what seemed to me to shatter all my life so that I desired to die rather

than to live. And the record of my grief I put into a book; & (of this book) I continually receive letters from those who suffer, telling me how great a solace this book has been to them. Possibly if by & by Your R.H. would (look into this book) consider this record it might give you some comfort. I do not know. I only know that I write in pure sympathy with your affliction & that of your R. mother—

1) & if I sin against precedent in so doing
2) & if I have seemed in any way to have violated the sanctity of your sorrow
3) & if I trouble you (have troubled you) in vain forgive as your Father wd have forgiven me.

A. Tennyson
(cf. Mem., I, 479)

But his hesitation was shortlived. Before Christmas he had finished his poem—the 'Dedication' which has been printed at the beginning of *Idylls of the King* ever since. By the middle of January 1862 he had obtained favourable opinions from two of the Queen's most esteemed Ladies, had submitted the poem to Princess Alice and heard from her how much the Queen had been moved in reading the lines and how they had 'soothed her aching, bleeding heart'. The Queen had already turned to *In Memoriam* for consolation and written in her diary for January 5 : 'much pleased and soothed with Tennyson's *In Memoriam*. Only those who have suffered as I do, can understand these beautiful poems'. As a result she formed an earnest desire to meet and speak with Tennyson and on April 14th with some reluctance ('I am a shy beast and like to keep in my burrow') he drove over from Farringford to Osborne. The meeting was an instantaneous success—in spite of Tennyson's shyness and the Queen's surprise at his shagginess and the eccentricity of his dress. He spoke to her directly and entirely without affectation of the great problems of life and death, spiritual survival, and human free will, which had so much obsessed his thoughts since the death of Arthur Hallam—questions the insolubility of which most people take for granted but which he would discuss with extraordinary simplicity and earnestness, even seeking the opinion of old men and women in the cottages at Freshwater, who, he thought, might by some instinct be nearer to the truth than more sophisticated inquirers. At parting the Queen asked whether there was anything that she could do for him, to which he replied, 'Nothing, Madam, but shake my two boys by the hand. It may keep them loyal in the troublous times to come'. This interview with the poet and his family took place on May 9th 1863, a few weeks after the wedding of the Prince of Wales to Princess Alexandra of Denmark. Tennyson's light-hearted poem 'A Welcome to Alexandra' (PT, 1152) had appeared in *The Times* of March 10th and delightfully expressed the enthusiasm and optimism with which both Queen and people greeted the coming of the simple, beautiful Princess.

Tennyson and the Queen only met three more times before his death —in 1867, 1872 and 1883—always of course on her invitation. She had also asked him to visit her at Osborne earlier in 1883 and she invited him to the wedding of her youngest daughter, Princess Beatrice, in 1885, but on neither of these occasions did he feel well enough to accept.

A list of Tennyson's poems which may fairly be attributed to his position as Laureate will be found at the end of this chapter. The list shows that there were only four laureate poems between 1864 (the year in which the Queen turned to Tennyson, in the second great sorrow of her life, for some lines to inscribe in the Mausoleum for her mother the Duchess of Kent: PT, 1183) and 1882, and nine in the last eleven years of Tennyson's life (1882–1892). The course of his friendship with the Queen is fully traced and documented in *Dear and Honoured Lady* (ed. H. Dyson and C. Tennyson, 1969) where it is pointed out that 1864 was the year in which John Brown was brought down from Balmoral to be the Queen's personal attendant and 1883 the year of his death. During the years 1864–1882—the John Brown years (which also included Benjamin Disraeli's two premierships)—the Queen's friendship with Tennyson was by no means in abeyance and the period included two of his most important Laureate poems, the dedicatory Epilogue to *Idylls of the King* in 1872 and the 'Welcome to Marie Alexandrovna' (PT, 1755 and 1223) two years later, but she looked to him for support and consolation less than she had done in 1861–4 and than she was to do from 1883 onwards when both John Brown and Benjamin Disraeli were dead.

The editors of *Dear and Honoured Lady* emphasize the fact that the last and most intimate phase of Tennyson's friendship with the Queen began with the letter of sympathy which he wrote to her on John Brown's death. They point out that Brown gave her, what must always be difficult for a reigning sovereign to enjoy, a direct human relationship on a different level from that on which she met her ministers and courtiers and even her own family (the intimate relation of wife with husband she had not known since 1861). Brown treated her as a woman—even sometimes called her 'wumman'—and supplied in his rough human way her need for affection and support *as a woman*. Tennyson also met her on a different level from Court and family— though of course not on the John Brown level. He could never have called her 'wumman' but he instinctively understood her spiritual needs and spoke directly to them, with that extraordinary simplicity and earnestness which sophisticated people were apt to find embarrassing.

During this final phase she began in 1883 to write to him in the first person and in her own hand. By 1885 she was signing 'yours affection- ately' in place of 'yours truly'. She corresponded with him intimately, and sometimes indiscreetly, on political matters and he celebrated in verse the main events, whether tragic or joyful, of ten highly emotional years of his highly emotional Sovereign. In 1883 Gladstone conferred a peerage on him—the Queen's part in this is obscure but she must surely have known about and approved of the proposal. He signalized his admission to the Second Chamber by one of the most important of his political poems, 'Freedom' (PT, 1889) which showed how little his views that changed since Reform Bill days. In 1887 he lavished all his metrical virtuosity on an ode in honour of her Jubilee.

The tragic domestic events of those years he felt acutely. In 1884 came the death of her thirty-three-year-old haemophiliac son Prince Leopold, a young man of ability, energy and independence—'the dearest of my dear sons' his mother called him. Tennyson's lines on this event are characteristic of the tone which prevailed in his relations with the Queen:

> *Early-wise, and pure and true,*
> *Prince, whose father lived in you,*
> *If you could speak, would you not say:*
> *'I seem, but am not, far away;*

Wherefore should your eyes be dim?
I am here again with Him.
O Mother-Queen, and weeping Wife,
The Death, for which you mourn, is Life!

(PT, 1330)

In January 1892, when Tennyson, who had not recovered wholly from a severe illness which had nearly carried him off in the winter of 1888-9, was still struggling with an attack of influenza, came news of the death of the Duke of Clarence, eldest son of the Prince of Wales, in his twenty-eighth year and within six weeks of the announcement of his engagement to Princess Mary of Teck, afterwards Queen of King George V. Tennyson, though still far from well, threw himself into the composition of a poem of consolation for the bereaved family, concluding with the well-known lines:

The face of Death is toward the Sun of Life,
His shadow darkens earth; his truer name
Is 'Onward', no discordance in the roll
And march of that Eternal Harmony
Whereto the worlds beat time, tho' faintly heard
Until the great Hereafter. Mourn in hope!

(PT, 1450)

From the strain of this effort he never recovered, and on October 6th 1892 he died. The Queen, who had been in close touch with Hallam Tennyson, recorded the news in her diary for that day: 'I heard that dear old Ld Tennyson had breathed his last, a great national loss. He was a great poet and his ideas were ever grand, noble, elevating. What beautiful lines he wrote to me for my darling Albert, and for my children and Eddy'. To Gladstone, his old friend and her old enemy, she wrote perceptively: 'A Tennyson we may not see again for a century, or—in all his originality—ever again'.

Many critics have expressed the view that Tennyson's acceptance of the Laureateship was a mistake, that it led him to forsake the higher reaches of the imagination, where his lyric gift could have full play, and to interest himself in politics and philosophy, subjects which he was not intellectually suited to deal with, and for which his peculiar poetic gift was not adapted. I do not share this view. To me Tennyson's outstanding quality is his immense variety, and his capacity for change. Great poets do not repeat themselves and Tennyson did not (indeed could not) repeat 'The Lady of Shalott', 'The Lotos-Eaters' and *In Memoriam*. The Laureateship was among the influences—perhaps the chief influence—which brought him into the midstream of Victorian life, giving him a new interest and involvement in the tendencies of his time, both political and social, and helping him to become the representative poet of the Victorian Era.

This of course is apparent not only in his strictly laureate verse. In addition one must take into account both the poems which he would not have written—or would not have written in the same form—if he had not been Laureate, and the effect of his Laureateship on the general tone and content of his work.

Oddly enough the first poems which he composed in the former category were issued under a pseudonym for fear of compromising the Queen and her Government by the violence of his reactions.

On December 2nd, 1851, Prince Louis Napoleon, who had been elected President of the French Democratic Republic soon after the fall of Louis Philippe, carried out a *coup d'état,* with what the wife of the British Ambassador called 'dreadful and undiscriminating bloodshed', and had himself proclaimed 'Emperor of the French'. Early in 1852 it became known that he was restoring the Imperial Eagles to the uniforms and flags of the French army. A wave of apprehension swept through Britain.

Tennyson caught the infection as did his young friend, the poet Coventry Patmore. Patmore launched a plan for setting up Volunteer Rifle Clubs all over the country. The idea appealed to Tennyson, who sent him three stanzas entitled 'Rifle Clubs!!!' for use in his campaign. Though Patmore published a letter advocating his scheme in *The Times* of January 22nd 1852, Tennyson's exceedingly spirited lines were not published until Ricks included them in his comprehensive edition:

RIFLE CLUBS!!!

Peace is thirty-seven years old,
Sweet Peace can no man blame,

> *But Peace of sloth or of avarice born,*
> *Her olive is her shame;*
> *And I dreamt of Charon alone in my bed—*
> *His boat was crammed and he rose and said*
> *'I carry the dead, the dead, the dead,*
>   *Killed in the Coup d'Etat'.*
>
> *Half a million of men in arms,*
> *Yet peace we all require,*
> *Half a million of men in arms,*
> *And the head of them all a liar*
> *'They wronged him not', the ferryman said,*
> *'Yet look at his bullets in heart and head—*
> *So I carry the dead, the dead, the dead,*
>   *Killed in the Coup d'Etat'.*
>
> *Some love Peace for her own dear sake,*
> *Tradesmen love her for gain,*
> *But in France the rifle is all-in-all,*
> *And the crimson trousers reign—*
> *'Children and women—their wounds are red,*
> *And I wait for Louis', the ferryman said,*
> *To follow the dead, the dead, the dead,*
>   *Killed in the Coup d'Etat'.*

                                                      (PT, 996)

This was by no means the end of Tennyson's burst of political
activity. On January 31st 1852, he published in his friend John Forster's
paper, *The Examiner,* a poem of extraordinary violence under the title
'Britons, Guard your Own'. The first and last stanzas of this not very
distinguished poem will give an idea of its quality:

> *RISE, Britons, rise, if manhood be not dead;*
> *The world's last tempest darkens overhead;*
>   *The Pope has bless'd him;*
>   *The Church caress'd him;*
> *He triumphs; maybe, we shall stand alone:*
> *Britons, guard your own. . . .*
>
> *Should he land here, and for one hour prevail,*

> There must no man go back to bear the tale:
> No man to bear it—
> Swear it! We swear it!
> Although we fought the banded world alone,
> We swear to guard our own.

(PT, 997)

This poem appeared over the signature 'Merlin', because Tennyson feared that if he used his own name his views might be taken as official, and compromise the Queen and the government who had decided to remain passive on the issue.

On February 7th *The Examiner* published a less violent and more statesmanlike poem by Tennyson (also over the signature 'Merlin') called 'The Third of February—1852'. This poem was occasioned by the action of the House of Lords, which on February 3rd had rejected the Bill for the organisation of the Militia that had been brought forward because of the crisis. Four stanzas out of the eight will show the poem's tone and quality:

The Third of February 1852

> My Lords, we heard you speak; you told us all
>   That England's honest censure went too far;
> That our free press should cease to brawl,
>   Not sting the fiery Frenchman into war.
> It was our ancient privilege, my Lords,
> To fling whate'er we felt, not fearing, into words. . . .
>
> As long as we remain, we must speak free,
>   Tho' all the storm of Europe on us break:
> No little German state are we,
>   But the one voice in Europe; we must speak;
> That if to-night our greatness were struck dead,
> There might be left some record of the things we said.
>
> Shall we fear him? our own we never fear'd.
>   From our first Charles by force we wrung our claims.
> Prick'd by the Papal spur, we rear'd,
>   We flung the burthen of the second James,
> I say, we never feared! and as for these,

We broke them on the land, we drove them on the seas. . . .

Tho' niggard throats of Manchester may bawl,
  What England was, shall her true sons forget?
We are not cotton-spinners all,
  But some love England and her honour yet,
And these in our Thermopylae shall stand,
And hold against the world this honour of the land.

(PT, 1000)

In the same number *The Examiner* printed yet another poem by Tennyson (still over the signature 'Merlin'), entitled 'Hands All Round'. Walter Savage Landor, reading this in *The Examiner,* called it, perhaps rather extravagantly, 'incomparably the best (convivial) lyric in the language'. It is of special interest today for the two concluding stanzas addressed to the United States, and the terms in the second stanza about the Queen:

Gigantic daughter of the West
  We drink to thee across the flood,
We know thee most, we love thee best,
  For art thou not of British blood?
Should war's mad blast again be blown,
  Permit not thou the tyrant powers
To fight thy mother here alone,
  But let thy broadsides roar with ours.
      Hands all round!
  God the tyrant's cause confound!
To our great kinsmen of the West, my friends,
  And the great name of England round and round.

O rise, our strong Atlantic sons,
  When war against our freedom springs!
O speak to Europe through your guns!
  They can be understood by kings.
You must not mix our Queen with those
  That wish to keep their people fools;
Our freedom's foemen are her foes,
  She comprehends the race she rules.
      Hands all round!

God the tyrant's cause confound!
To our kinsmen of the West, my friends,
And the great name of England round and round.

(PT, 1002)

Even this was not the end. In *The Examiner's* issue of February 14th appeared the most singular of all the series. It had the title 'Suggested by Reading an Article in a Newspaper' and was preceded by a letter signed over a new pseudonym 'Taliessin', in the following terms:

To the Editor of *The Examiner*

SIR,—I have read with much interest the poems of Merlin. The enclosed is longer than either of those, and certainly not so good: yet as I flatter myself that it has a smack of Merlin's style in it, and as I feel that it expresses forcibly enough some of the feelings of our time, perhaps you may be induced to admit it.

TALIESSIN

This singular poem is addressed to the Press, urging it to match up to its great responsibilities. The connection with the *coup d'état* crisis only appears in the last stanza, but the poem is of interest as an effective example of a kind of satire in which Tennyson very rarely indulged. Here are six of the concluding stanzas:

I feel the thousand cankers of our State,
I fain would shake their triple-folded ease,
The hogs who can believe in nothing great,
Sneering bedridden in the down of Peace
Over their scrips and shares, their meats and wine,
With stony smirks at all things human and divine!

I honour much, I say, this man's appeal.
We drag so deep in our commercial mire,
We move so far from greatness, that I feel
Exception to be character'd in fire.
Who looks for Godlike greatness here shall see
The British Goddess, sleek Respectability.

Alas for her and all her small delights!
She feels not how the social frame is rack'd.

She loves a little scandal which excites;
A little feeling is a want of tact.
For her there lie in wait millions of foes,
And yet the 'not too much' is all the rule she knows.

Poor soul! behold her; what decorous calm.
She, with her week-day worldliness sufficed,
Stands in her pew and hums her decent psalm
    With decent dippings at the name of Christ!
And she has mov'd on that smooth way so long,
She hardly can believe that she shall suffer wrong. . . .

Alas, our youth, so clever yet so small,
    Thin dilettanti deep in nature's plan,
Who make the emphatic One, by whom is all,
    An essence less concentred than a man!
Better wild Mahmoud's war-cry once again!
O fools, we want a manlike God and Godlike men!

Go, frightful omens. Yet once more I turn
    To you that mould men's thoughts; I call on you
To make opinion warlike, lest we learn
    A sharper lesson than we ever knew.
I hear a thunder though the skies are fair,
But shrill you, loud and long, the warning-note—
Prepare!

(PT, 1004)

This series of poems, particularly the last, shows an attitude towards national affairs entirely different to any displayed by Tennyson before. It also indicates his recognition of the conventions by which he conceived that the Laureate should be governed.

On 14th September 1852 the great Duke of Wellington died. Tennyson, who remembered the London coach driving into Spilsby decorated with white ribands in honour of the Victory of Waterloo, now set about what was to prove one of his grandest achievements, unrivalled for sustained emotion, metrical originality, grandeur of melody and imaginative force. Although the fear of a French invasion had waned, Tennyson repeated the warning urged in the previous poems against

the lack of military preparation, which has so often landed our country
in almost fatal difficulties. Of particular interest for our present purpose
is the brief reference to the British monarchy:

> O Statesman, guard us, guard the eye, the soul
> Of Europe, keep our noble England whole,
> And save the one true seed of freedom sown
> Betwixt a people and their ancient throne,
> That sober freedom out of which there springs
> Our loyal passion for our temperate kings . . .
>   ('Ode on the Death of the Duke of Wellington': PT, 1013)

A strange reference, for it could hardly be said that the English people
had ever shown much 'passion' for its Hanoverian Kings, or that the
epithet 'temperate' was conspicuously appropriate to them. In fact I
think Tennyson must have had his mind fixed on a Queen, not a King,
and that perhaps he meant to include in his reference that Queen's
Consort, Prince Albert.

Tennyson himself rather indignantly repudiated suggestions that the
great ode was a 'laureate poem', maintaining, no doubt rightly, that it
was a perfectly spontaneous tribute to a great and long-admired hero.
Yet one cannot but feel the new and 'laureate' note in the poem, as
though the poet was not making a purely personal utterance but
realized that he was speaking for the British people, just as he had in
fact done in the greatest of all his acknowledged laureate poems, the
'Dedication' of 1862.

Tennyson's next publication, Maud, was the least understood and the
most controversial of all the poems issued by him after 1850. This is not
surprising for it is the wildest both in form and content and must have
seemed to his contemporaries strangely inappropriate for their official
poet, settled in an idyllic country home and enjoying a happy married
life after years of frustration and unhappiness. Yet it is easy for us today
to see how Maud came to be written. As John Killham has pointed out
(Critical Essays on the Poetry of Tennyson, 1960, 228–35), one theme of
the poem is 'the attainment through sexual love of a psychic balance
in a world where violence, rapine and greed exist naturally in the
hearts of men and nations'. The violent attacks on the growing material-

ism of the age and on the exploitation of the poor by the rich, come no doubt from the interest which Tennyson's new position had given him in the social problems of the time and the talks which he had on the subject with F. D. Maurice, Charles Kingsley and other leaders of the Christian Socialist Movement, while the discussions of individual and collective violence are the culmination of thoughts which had animated the squibs about Napoleon III and the great Wellington Ode and were further stimulated by the sudden flare-up of the Crimean War.

The outlines of the *Maud* story had been in Tennyson's mind for perhaps twenty years, but if he had written the poem before 1850 it would surely have been very different—much more inward looking and subjective—than the strange and complex work which he produced in 1855.

Tennyson's next publication after *Maud* was *Idylls of the King* in 1859. This volume contained only five of the twelve Idylls which ultimately (in 1885) completed the poem. He had made a beginning with 'Morte d'Arthur', written in 1833-4 and published in 1842, and it is clear that he had then had in mind the possibility of proceeding immediately with the completion of an Arthurian epic. The reasons why he decided against this need not concern us here. It is also probable that when he wrote 'Morte D'Arthur' he had already determined that his epic should be a parable of man's need for a spiritual ideal and his unending and never to be successful pursuit of it. When he took up the subject again after the publication of *Maud* he changed his method of approach, abandoning the idea of a continuous epic treatment in favour of a succession of Idylls. Each Idyll was to be a separate unit, but each was to fit into the general pattern and the general parabolic drift. The public and critical reception of the book was enthusiastic, but when he endeavoured to continue the poem he found himself in difficulties—chiefly about the Holy Grail legend. He felt that he must include this, but did not know how to treat it. Mediaeval writers had believed in the legend as a modern poet could not, and without belief how could the theme be treated sincerely? The Queen, the Princess Royal and many of his friends urged him to continue the Idylls, but it was only after the publication of the *Enoch Arden* volume in 1864 that he found a solution of his problem. By this time his grasp of the whole

subject had matured and the parabolic drift had widened so as to sym-
bolize the decay of a civilization in which 'the cynical indifference,
intellectual selfishness, sloth of will, and utilitarian materialism of a
transition age' are allowed to override the spiritual ideal, as he feared
was happening in the western civilizations of the nineteenth century.
He made this point so fiercely in 'Locksley Hall, Sixty Years After',
published in 1886 (the year after the first publication of the completed
Idylls of the King), that his friend Gladstone, who had been responsible
for so much of the progressive legislation of the past generation, pro-
tested in an elaborately deferential article in *The Nineteenth Century*, at
the end of which he appealed directly to the poet not to mar the Queen's
forthcoming Jubilee with 'Tragic Notes'. Tennyson accepted this suggestion, but his Jubilee ode contained some warning lines, inserted it is
said with Victoria's expressed approval:

> *Are there thunders moaning in the distance?*
> *Are there spectres moving in the darkness?*
> *Trust the Hand of Light will lead her people,*
> *Till the thunders pass, the spectres vanish,*
> *And the Light is Victor, and the darkness*
> *Dawns into the Jubilee of the Ages.*
>
> ('On the Jubilee of Queen Victoria': PT, 1372)

During the interval in the 1860s, when Tennyson found himself
unable to proceed with the *Idylls*, he turned his energies in a new
direction; the result of this was the publication in 1864 of *Enoch Arden
and Other Poems*. Tennyson's wish to call this Volume *Idylls of the
Hearth* (frustrated by Emily's dislike of the title) shows the direction in
which his thoughts were turning. He had attempted popular poems
before, for instance the 'May Queen' series, 'The Charge of the Light
Brigade' in 1855, 'The Grandmother' in 1859. Now he determined to
devote the whole of his powers to a major poem which should go
straight to the hearts of the largest possible public. The result was
Enoch Arden, the most popular poem he ever wrote, the most widely
translated and the most widely adapted for use on stage and film. This
poem has on the whole been badly received by the critics, but its
popularity and the pains which Tennyson lavished on it cannot be

ignored. A careful study and evaluation by P. G. Scott has recently been issued by the Tennyson Society (*Tennyson's 'Enoch Arden': A Victorian Best-Seller*, Tennyson Research Centre, Lincoln, 1970). '*Enoch Arden*,' says Mr Scott, 'was the first of Tennyson's poems to make an impact on the whole of the reading public.' Its success encouraged him to have a series of his poems published in threepenny numbers so that they might reach the widest possible audience. The Queen cordially approved the idea, expressing her satisfaction that her Laureate's work would 'be brought within the reach of the poorest among her subjects'.

This attempt of Tennyson's to become 'the Poet of the People' must have owed something to his position as Laureate. If it did not result in any new work of the highest class, it produced at least one volume of controversial vitality and it may well be that we owe to it the great ballads of the 1870s and 1880s, 'The Revenge', 'The Relief of Lucknow' and 'The Charge of the Heavy Brigade'.

I do not think it has been suggested that Tennyson's position as Laureate had anything to do with the last experiment of his long career —the endeavour to establish himself as a poetic dramatist, which occupied him for ten years after the completion of his creative work on the *Idylls*. This experiment, which has generally been regarded as unsuccessful and has received little attention from the critics, is treated at length in another chapter of this volume so I will not attempt to evaluate it here. I will only point out that it occupied ten vital years of Tennyson's life, at a period when it could not be expected that his creative powers would be long maintained, that it produced in *Queen Mary* an armchair-drama of outstanding power and interest, and in *Becket* provided Henry Irving with the outstanding success of the last twelve years of his life. It cannot therefore be dismissed as unimportant.

Tennyson's first idea was to supplement the history plays of Shakespeare with three dramas on themes which Shakespeare had not handled. These, *Harold, Becket* and *Queen Mary* all dealt with important crises in the history of the English monarchy and its relation to the papacy. It seems reasonable to suppose that Tennyson's position as Poet Laureate had at least some influence on his choice of these subjects, the last of which (*Queen Mary*) left England on the hopeful verge of the reign of the young Elizabeth, no doubt reminding him of the time when, some forty years before, he had dashed off those hopeful lines to the young 'Queen of the Isles'.

To one so steeped as Tennyson in English history and the English tradition, the *mystique* of the British monarchy must have been a powerful influence, affecting much more than the choice of subjects for his dramatic experiment. The peculiar exaltation of his personal feeling for the Queen was no doubt due largely to the same cause. And here there were other mystical, or should one say, intuitive, influences. 'Locksley Hall', written not long after Victoria's accession, had contained the famous reference to 'The Parliament of Man, the Federation of the World' (PT, 696). Nearly fifty years later, in the second 'Locksley Hall', he was still able to look forward to:

> *Earth at last a warless world, a single race, a*
> *single tongue—*
> *I have seen her far away—for is not Earth as*
> *yet so young?* . . .   (PT, 1366)

It was this ideal that made him so strongly deprecate any weakening of the British Empire—particularly Gladstone's Irish policy. Multiracialism he held to be a source of strength, vital in the struggle towards 'a single race, a single tongue', and he strongly advocated some form of Imperial Federation (see for instance *Mem.*, II, 376 and Stanza IV of 'Opening of the Indian and Colonial Exhibition by the Queen' PT, 1358), no doubt hoping that the British, whom 'the roar of Hougonmont/Left mightiest of all peoples under Heaven' might in this way lead the world forward in the quest of his ideal.

Tennyson's feeling for Queen Victoria (Queen and Empress after May 1st 1876) no doubt gained additional force from his poetic vision of this progress, under British leadership, towards the 'warless world'. And there was, I think, another visionary element in his devotion. Tennyson shared to the full the domestic sentiment of his age, but characteristically he gave this too a mystical quality.

He saw in the ideal family relationship the surest basis for that spiritual evolution of mankind, which he formulated fifteen years before

Darwin announced his theory of biological evolution. In lines 271–279 of the last Canto of *The Princess* (1847), he had written:

> *And so these twain, upon the skirts of Time,*
> *Sit side by side, full-summed in all their powers,*
> *Dispensing harvest, sowing the To-be,*
> *Self-reverent each and reverencing each,*
> *Distinct in individualities,*
> *But like each other even as those who love,*
> *Then comes the statelier Eden back to men:*
> *Then reign the World's great bridals, chaste*
> *and calm:*
> *Then springs the crowning race of humankind.*
> *May these things be!*

(PT, 839)

and at the end of the Epilogue to *In Memoriam* he described 'the crowning race':

> *Of those that, eye to eye, shall look*
> *On knowledge; under whose command*
> *Is Earth and Earth's, and in their hand*
> *Is Nature like an open book;*
>
> *No longer half-akin to brute,*
> *For all we thought and loved and did,*
> *And hoped and suffer'd, is but seed*
> *Of what in them is flower and fruit;*

(PT, 987)

Tennyson's naive humanity enabled him to speak and write to the Queen directly and without reserve or affectation. His vision of her as symbolic leader of 'the Federation of the World' and symbolic mother of this 'Crowning Race' added overtones to a remarkable friendship which cannot be fully understood unless both elements are taken into account.

Appendix

Tennyson's Laureate Poems

1851 March	'To the Queen'	
	Printed as the Dedication of Tennyson's	
	Collected Works	PT, 990
1856	'Harp, Harp'	
	first published in 1969	PT, 1094
1857 December	Additional Stanzas for the National	
	Anthem	
	(*Dear and Honoured Lady*, London,	
	1969, p. 45)	
1861–2	'Dedication' of *Idylls of the King*	PT, 1467
1862 April	'Ode Sung at the Opening of the	
	International Exhibition'	PT, 1127
1863 March	'A Welcome to Alexandra'	PT, 1152
1864 March	Lines for the Statue of the Duchess of	
	Kent	PT, 1183
1872 December	Epilogue to *Idylls of the King*	PT, 1755
1874 March	'A Welcome To Her Royal Highness	
	Marie Alexandrovna, Duchess of	
	Edinburgh'	PT, 1223
1879 April	Dedicatory Poem to the Princess Alice	PT, 1250
1880 April	'To Princess Frederica on Her Marriage'	PT, 1281
1882 March 15	'Hands All Round'	
	adapted from an early poem and	
	published with musical setting by Emily	
	in honour of the Queen's birthday.[1]	PT, 1310

[1] According to Hallam Tennyson (*Mem.*, II, 264) Tennyson adapted the poem (quoted on p. 215) at the request of Sir Frederic Young. This was probably Sir Frederick Young K.C.M.G. (1817–1913) an enthusiast for Imperial Federation, who had written a book on the subject in 1876. He must have been the only man who attended the Coronations of both William IV and George V. (Information communicated by Miss Jane Langton of the Royal Archives, Windsor Castle)

1883 September	Lines for a Memorial Statue of John Brown (*Dear and Honoured Lady*, p. 107)	
1884 March	'Prince Leopold, an Epitaph'	PT, 1330
1884 December	'Freedom'	PT, 1339
1885 July	To H. R. H. Princess Beatrice	PT, 1345
1886 May	'Opening of the Indian and Colonial Exhibition by the Queen'	PT, 1357
1887 April	'On the Jubilee of Queen Victoria'	PT, 1369
1890 February	'Remembering Him who waits thee far away'	PT, 1430
1891 June	'Take, Lady, What Your Loyal Nurses Give'	PT, 1440
1892 February	'The Death of the Duke of Clarence and Avondale'	PT, 1450

9: Tennyson's Plays and Their Production

PETER THOMSON

IF WE include the astonishing but unfinished boyhood composition, *The Devil and the Lady*, Tennyson wrote eight plays. Of these, five were performed during his life, and he died exactly four months before the brilliant opening night of a sixth. Only one can be said certainly to have failed in production. This is a theatrical record second to no nineteenth-century poet's, rivalled only by Byron's. Tennyson's dealings with the theatre are, moreover, remarkably free from bitterness. His respect for Irving survived the laceration of the text of *Queen Mary*, the rejection of *Harold*, the protracted negotiations over *Becket*, the actor's interpretation of Synorix in *The Cup*, his tantalizing interest in and eventual dismissal of *The Foresters*, and his refusal to help vindicate *The Promise of May* after its disastrous production by Thackeray's volatile goddaughter, Mrs. Bernard Beere. That failure and his faith in Irving were in his mind less than sixty hours before he died. 'They did not do me justice with *The Promise of May*,' he told his doctor, but 'I can trust Irving—Irving will do me justice.'[1] It was not just Irving, though; his negotiations with the Kendals, with Lawrence Barrett, with Ada Rehan and Augustin Daly were mutually respectful. Tennyson, unlike too many writers of superior talent in the years between the Collier controversy and *The Importance of Being Earnest*, perceived that the success of a play in the theatre is properly separable, though not necessarily separate, from its literary quality. The perception is not matched by the achievement, but it was Tennyson's awareness of theatrical possibilities beyond his own expertise that allowed him to make so many (too many?) concessions, particularly but not uniquely to Irving.

[1] There are various versions of Tennyson's words. I quote here from Charles Tennyson, *Alfred Tennyson*, 1949, 535.

For the last eighteen years of his life he was never able to forget for long one or other of his plays. And yet there is no sign, through all the disappointments and disputes, of the kind of deep outrage that Browning could not finally conceal from Macready. Even when accepting Macready's suggestions, Browning preserved a conviction of his own rightness. Tennyson seems genuinely to have recognized the alternative rightness of the actor. Nor was there in his attitude to any of his dramatic work that coyness about performance through which Byron built up his conspicuous defences before any attack was proposed.[1] Tennyson wrote unashamedly in the hope of performance, recognizing, implicitly at least, that the life of a play is delivered by the actor. To Granville-Barker 'Tennyson's modest approach to playwriting' seemed obviously flawed, and even its modesty suspect. He refers to the passage in the *Memoir* (II, 175) in which Hallam claims that 'his dramas were written with the intention that actors should edit them for the stage, keeping them at the high poetic level', and comments pertinently that Tennyson 'speaks—or his son speaks for him—of drama and the theatre as a sort of House of Lords and House of Commons, with the play as a Bill sent down to be pulled about a bit, rewritten a little and at last turned out as an effective Act.' But the objectionable passage is, after all, Hallam's, and Tennyson's modesty seems to me, in its full Victorian context, more notable than the flaws. Granville-Barker is finally less concerned with debunking than with the recognition of 'something of the absolute dramatist in him, for he can project a scene, fully significant only in its action, conceived so, evidently, not plotted out on paper.'[2] He is thinking primarily of the short penultimate scene of *Queen Mary*, in which five 'voices of the night' describe the dying of the queen, representing at the same time the crisis of religious divisions in a terrified country. But there are further outstanding examples in this and other plays, the confrontation of Becket and the Council (*Becket* I. iii), the Bayeux oath (*Harold* II. ii), and Stigand's commentary on the Battle of Senlac (*Harold* V. i) being among the best. The presence of

---

[1] For an examination of Byron's attitude to the staging of his plays, see D. V. Erdmann, 'Byron's Stage Fright', *ELH* VI, 1939.

[2] Granville-Barker discusses Tennyson's plays in *The Eighteen-Seventies*, ed Harley Granville-Barker, Cambridge, 1929, 164–75.

strong scenes is, of course, insufficient tonic for a weak play, but such scenes do provide evidence of Tennyson's mature awareness that narrative must be enacted in the theatre rather than merely translated into dialogue. It is this awareness that I am concerned to explore, admitting at the outset (look anywhere in *The Foresters*) that there is too much mere translation.

From his early years Tennyson progressed easily and emotionally from the writing to the speaking of his verse. It led his family and friends to talk of him as an actor. Fitzgerald remembered occasions in 1842 when he showed some skill in mime. 'He used also to do the sun coming out of a cloud, and retiring into one again, with a gradual opening and shutting of the eyes, and with a great fluffing up of his hair into full wig and elevation of cravat and collar' (*Mem.*, I, 184). But such displays were exceptional. His performing instinct was best satisfied by the famous readings to friends, when 'the roll of his great voice acted sometimes almost like an incantation, so that when it was a new poem he was reading, the power of realizing its actual nature was subordinated to the wonder at the sound of the tones'.[1] It is above all a precocious delight in words that characterizes *The Devil and the Lady*. I do not know why the fourteen-year-old Tennyson should have been inspired by an article read in the *Quarterly Review* to write 1675 lines of a play in blank verse on the theme of marital jealousy, nor why, having got so far, he left the piece unfinished. Whatever the cause, the effect is remarkable. Old Magus, a necromancer whose black art is never subjected to moral attack during the play, summons the Devil to guard the chastity of his young wife while he goes on a short journey. The Devil proves to be not at all a nursery nightmare, but a resourceful ironist with a self-confessed moralizing tendency. He announces himself to Magus like Ariel to Prospero (more extraordinary than the borrowing in the play is the young Tennyson's skill in adopting the stance to his own language of a writer willing to borrow. As a result he seems to be borrowing more often than he is):

> *I come, O I come, at the sound of my name*
> *From the depths and the caverns of Hell where I lie,*

[1] The description is Emily Ritchie's, quoted in *Mem.*, II, 87.

> *I can rush through the torrent and ride on the flame*
> *Or mount on the whirlwind that sweeps through the sky.*
>
> (I. i. 41–44: PT, 12)

The play's characteristic concern with the human body's comedy is initiated at once, as the Devil continues:

> *What wilt thou have me do for thee? Shall I weave*
> *The sunbeams to a crown for thy bald brows?*
> *Shall I ungarter the Pleiades for thee*
> *And twist their glittering* periscelides
> *To keep the hose up on thy 'minishing calves?*
>
> (I. i. 45–49: PT, 12)

Behind the parade of language the plot struggles to survive. Magus goes, having first cautioned his girl wife Amoret against the 'querulous serenade or flute/Wooing the dewy wings o' the midnight air . . .' (I. iv. 100–101) and having offered as a final blessing the comically unsuitable 'may Heaven/And the good Saints protect thee!' (I. iv. 108–109). Amoret reviles her husband in a soliloquy whose images are spirited even where they are not precise, and is recovering boldly from the initial fright of the Devil's appearance when she is sent to bed to 'Lie quietly,/Without the movement of one naughty muscle . . .' (I. v. 153–154). The Devil does not relish his task, and Tennyson allows him a number of unfelt gibes at the shrewishness of women. These and the jokes about noses, which vary from the vulgar to the quirkily observant, betray the author's youth more surely than anything else in the play. Act Two, which the Devil begins with a long philosophical soliloquy inspired by the night sky, is centrally concerned with the introduction of Amoret's six would-be lovers. They are, successively, lawyer, apothecary, sailor, mathematician, soldier, and monk, each speaking the jargon of his profession in grotesque courtship of the Devil in female disguise. The repeated elaboration of the situation does nothing to propel the plot, and the central sequence of five scenes gathers into an often exhilarating game with words, interrupted by occasional exits and frequent entrances. The rivals take a Gilbertian delight in scoring comic points off each other's ugliness. Thus, the lawyer Antonio describes the apothecary:

> *This Ipecacuanha, this emetic,*
> *This wall-eyed monster, this anomaly,*
> *This piece of speckled parchment, this vile patchwork,*
> *Whose sallow and carbuncled face resembles*
> *A red design upon a yellow ground.*
>
> (II. iv. 30–34: PT, 37)

and thus the mathematician:

> *His thin dry lips seem parallel straight lines,*
> *His red and angular and shapeless nose*
> *Shows like a Gyron gules in Heraldry,*
> *And his sharp chin so narrowed to a point,*
> *That if 'twere possible his neck could bend*
> *'Twould perforate and pierce his collar bone.*
>
> (II. v. 48–53: PT, 44)

The presence of an actor would be a disappointment. Such detailed description is not for the stage. A made-up man is unequal to it. I doubt whether Tennyson intended *The Devil and the Lady* for anything more than family theatricals, but it is likely that he had some such presentation in mind, and that he abandoned writing when the hope of performance dwindled, perhaps as a result of his father's breakdown of health in 1824. Certainly the breaking off of the manuscript as the Devil is on the point of selecting one of his deceived 'lovers' owes nothing obvious to a loss of creative energy. Act Three, with the return of Magus, the farcical concealment of the terrified suitors ('Pharmaceutus, /Stow your long body cheek by jowl with Angulo/Within the closet yonder.' III. i. 242–244), and the Devil's imminent unveiling, moves purposefully towards a comic conclusion. Nor is there any decline in verbal inventiveness. Magus's exuberant mockery of the Devil-in-drag may stand finally for Tennyson's enjoyment of the expressiveness of his own blank verse:

> *What jejune undigested joke is this?*
> *To quilt thy fuscous haunches with the flounced,*
> *Frilled, finical delicacy of female dress.*
> *How hast thou dared to girdle thy brown sides*

> *And prop thy monstrous vertebrae with stays?*
> *Speak out, thou petticoated Solecism.*
>
> (III. ii. 27–32: PT, 57)

Fifty years separate *The Devil and the Lady* from *Queen Mary*, and even a cursory comparison of a vignette from the later play with those already quoted from the other will show how far Tennyson's dramatic blank verse has travelled. The Princess Elizabeth is confiding to Lord William Howard:

> *I am of sovereign nature, that I know,*
> *Not to be quell'd; and I have felt within me*
> *Stirrings of some great doom when God's just hour*
> *Peals—but this fierce old Gardiner—his big baldness,*
> *That irritable forelock which he rubs,*
> *His buzzard beak and deep-incavern'd eyes*
> *Half fright me.*
>
> (I. iv: CPW, 545)

The use of the monosyllable to steady the speaking voice, the spreading of the sentence across the limits of the lines, and the manipulation of the verse to accommodate rather than to exhibit the choice word, these are major departures from *The Devil and the Lady*. The contrast is, in large part, a reflection of Tennyson's general poetic development. Still, there are signs as early as the ten year silence of a particular pull towards the drama. There is, for example, the dialogue poem 'Walking to the Mail', published among the 'English Idyls' in 1842 but written about five years earlier. The conversation of James and John as they walk to meet the mail-coach mixes gossip, ghosts, triviality, and self-revelation, but even more interesting than Tennyson's 'dramatic' concern to set two characters moving at a distance from himself is the obvious wish to experiment with a blank verse that shaves the prose of daily conversation.[1] The confidence that blank verse could be drawn into familiar dialogue increased the range of Tennyson's mature plays:

---

[1] Two tiny changes in later editions of 'Walking to the Mail' illustrate the detail of Tennyson's pursuit of a colloquial blank verse. 'I myself' replaces 'I, that am' in line 72, and 'Sets out' is preferred to 'Sets forth' in line 34.

JOHN.   *I'm glad I walk'd. How fresh the meadows look*
         Above the river, and, but a month ago,
         The whole hill-side was redder than a fox.
         Is yon plantation where this byway joins
         The turnpike?
JAMES.   *Yes.*
JOHN.   *And when does this come by?*
JAMES.   *The mail? At one o'clock.*
JOHN.   *What is it now?*
JAMES.   *A quarter to.*

                                              (PT, 701)

Part of the poem's gossip refers to the daughter of a cottager, transformed from exemplary sweetness to 'a woman like a butt, and harsh as crabs' by ten years of marriage 'out of her sphere' to Sir Edward Head. The situation, against which the urbanity of the poem revolts, is a melodramatic one. Tennyson's narrative poems are not usually so reticent, and it is in the affecting treatment of domestic crisis that they approach contemporary dramatic modes most closely. 'Dora' reads almost like a poetic paraphrase of a domestic melodrama plotted in three distinct acts. It is the completest example, but there are vivid moments in many other poems that constitute perfect melodramatic insets. Sometimes Tennyson's prime endeavour is to hold the picture still, as in the staged tableau. At other times he looks towards the decisive action of the *scène à faire*. What seems clear is that he himself had a histrionic temperament that was gratified by melodrama. Melodrama is a constituent of such works as 'Locksley Hall', 'Maud', 'Sea Dreams', 'Enoch Arden', and 'Aylmer's Field'. They might be set against the decision not, after all, to individualize the seven story-tellers of 'The Princess', a significant formal step away from the drama towards the novel. The telling of the story in 'The Princess' is less dramatic than the arrangements made for its narration. More to the point is the detailed imitation of the speaking voice in, for example, 'The Grandmother' and the two 'Northern Farmer' poems, but it was above all the strenuous composition of the *Idylls of the King* that led Tennyson decisively towards the drama. Properly to present the sequence of Arthurian legends, he chose to imagine a set for them, and to select and deploy his own cast. Moreover, the narrative conventions he had to establish led through ritual towards drama rather than through suspense towards the short story or the novel. The connections were brought vividly home to him during the writing in early 1872 of 'Gareth and Lynette'. 'If I were at liberty, which I think I am not,' wrote Tennyson to Knowles on 5 April 1872, 'to print the names of the speakers "Gareth" "Linette" over the short snip-snap of their talk, and so avoid the perpetual "said" and its varieties, the work would be much easier' (*Mem.*, II, 113n.). The extreme difficulty of composition arose partly from the irritated consciousness that he was being slowed down by the narrative convention of reported speech. Mere translation of narrative into drama was not, at this point, a possibility. Tennyson was reaching his story through its dialogue.

The public is generally sceptical when an established writer ventures into a new *genre*. Tennyson was, moreover, sixty-five, an old dog defiantly setting about the learning of new tricks. There was no shortage of cautionary advice during the next few years. Surprisingly perhaps, he decided against extending Arthurian legend into drama (Comyns Carr did that for Irving in 1895).[1] From a number of considered subjects, which included certainly Lady Jane Grey, Elizabeth, William the Silent, and the Armada, he chose the reign of Mary Tudor. He read Froude's *Mary* to his wife in April 1874, finding Froude too unsympathetic to his subject, but evidently caught up in the presentation of history through persons. This was history as Tennyson saw it too, and as he read it in Shakespeare. As for Roman Catholicism, Tennyson joined consciously in the great nineteenth century debate. The authority of the Roman church is the only issue common to the three plays that compose what he later called his 'historical trilogy'. Particularly in *Queen Mary,* he hoped to make a personal contribution to historical and religious understanding. To this end he read widely and thoughtfully, preparing portraits of his protagonists which may be contentious but are never glib. The turning to Shakespeare for guidance in the dramatic handling of English history was as carefully considered. Tennyson had not much

[1] An Arthurian scenario in five acts exists in the 1833–1840 MS books. It is reproduced in *Mem.*, II, 124–5 where it is described as a musical masque.

admired Lytton's theatrically resourceful *Richelieu* when he saw Irving in it in November 1873, and though he respected the plays of his friend Henry Taylor he told Lecky that 'they were too uniformly stately' (*Mem.*, II, 202). He was determined to give *Queen Mary* a Shakespearean variety. Unfortunately, he was equally determined not to sacrifice his historical insights. The published play suffers from a lack of authorial editing. Considering the amount of material it contains, it is surprisingly short; but, quite simply, it should not contain so much. There are twenty-three scenes, and almost as many subjects—the enmity of France and Spain, the death of Cranmer, Courtenay's brief credit at court, Wyatt's rebellion, the return and fall of Cardinal Pole, the joyless marriage of Philip and Mary, Gardiner's ascendancy and death, Elizabeth's political and amatory adventures, the fall of Calais, and the plight of the plain patriot in a divided country are only the most important. The real flaw is not that so much is covered, but that, because each theme is given independent treatment, each is required to deflect our attention for a certain duration from all the others. There are trees (the portraiture is generally so lively that it engages us fully), but is there a wood? Is there an action that is other than the sum of the episodes?

The final answer, probably, is no. *Queen Mary* is, as Jerome Buckley has declared it, 'not . . . a single dramatic structure but . . . a sprawling panorama'.[1] Yet Tennyson worked much harder on the structure than has generally been allowed. The play is written in five movements, corresponding with its acts. Act One opens with Mary's queenship and England's Catholicism in the balance, and concludes with both confirmed. Act Two deals with Wyatt's rebellion, the major *military* challenge to Mary's authority. Act Three—how late Philip is introduced, and even then in how reticent a scene—is primarily concerned with the marriage of Philip and Mary, though its two long central scenes touch that marriage with ceremonial and debate. Act Four, in parallel with Act Two, deals with Cranmer's death, the major *spiritual* challenge to Mary's authority. Act Five moves through the dissolution of Mary's queenship towards a Protestant England. This, certainly, is the pattern, but it remains pattern rather than structure. Lopped off, as virtually they

[1] Jerome Hamilton Buckley, *Tennyson: the Growth of a Poet*, Cambridge, Mass., 1960, 200.

were in the Lyceum production of 1876, the second and fourth acts approach a separate existence as short plays, with Wyatt and Cranmer as their tragic heroes. They are not integrated; nor is there any convenient accommodation in the play as planned for the rival interest of Elizabeth's career. Tennyson has not sufficiently concentrated on his heroine. This is all the more a pity because the portrait of Mary is so poignant. As she initially perceives it, her task is honourably to fulfil her role as Catholic Queen of England, but that fulfilment is impeded from the outset by a private agony. To Tib and Joan, the two gossips resting in St Mary's Church whilst Cranmer is led to the stake, the private and the public will are indistinguishable, and 'Queen Mary gwoes on a-burnin' and a-burnin', to get her baaby born' (IV. iii). But the Mary of I. v, is resolved to be as merciful as she may, resisting Renard's advice to have Elizabeth beheaded as confidently as she later resists the pleas for Cranmer's life. Hysterical pregnancy has intervened, and the coldness towards her of the husband she immoderately loves. Tennyson gives us a Philip who is soulless, worthless, and lecherous, a strange man to inspire love; but as the Spanish Ambassador explains to the puzzled Alice:

> . . . *you should know that whether*
> *A wind be warm or cold, it serves to fan*
> *A kindled fire.*
>
> (I. v: CPW, 552)

The excesses of Mary's vulnerable maturity reach a climax in the hysterical exaltation of III. ii. The ingenuous identification of herself with the Virgin Mary is one of a number of references to this coincidence of names. It is inspired here by the belief that a child has moved inside her:

> *The second Prince of Peace—*
> *The great unborn defender of the Faith,*
> *Who will avenge me of mine enemies—*
> *He comes, and my star rises.*
> *The stormy Wyatts and Northumberlands,*
> *The proud ambitions of Elizabeth,*
> *And all her fieriest partisans—are pale*
> *Before my star!*

> *The light of this new learning wanes and dies:*
> *The ghosts of Luther and Zuinglius fade*
> *Into the deathless hell which is their doom*
> *Before my star!*
> *His sceptre shall go forth from Ind to Ind!*
> *His sword shall hew the heretic peoples down!*
> *His faith shall clothe the world that will be his,*
> *Like universal air and sunshine! Open,*
> *Ye everlasting gates! The King is here!—*
> *My star, my son!*
>
> (III. ii: CPW, 568)

If we set against this the measured way in which she introduces the
great debate on the burning of heretics (III. iv), the range of Tennyson's verse and characterization in this play may emerge:

> *The King and I, my Lords, now that all traitors*
> *Against our royal state have lost the heads*
> *Wherewith they plotted in their treasonous malice,*
> *Have talk'd together, and are well agreed*
> *That those old statutes touching Lollardism*
> *To bring the heretic to the stake, should be*
> *No longer a dead letter, but requicken'd.*
>
> (CPW, 572)

This scene and the whole conduct of Act Four endorse Tib's view of
Mary, burning heretics because of her own agony. Joyless and doomed
('I see but the black night, and hear the wolf.' I. v), Mary dies surrounded by loyal ladies-in-waiting, but threatened by nightmares and
madness. Her reign has been an illustration of the argument put forward
by Pole during his inadequate resistance to the zeal for burning of
Gardiner and the sadistic Bonner:

> *. . . when men are tost*
> *On tides of strange opinion, and not sure*
> *Of their own selves, they are wroth with their own selves,*
> *And thence with others; then, who lights the faggot?*
> *Not the full faith, no, but the lurking doubt.*
>
> (III. iv: CPW, 573)

The lurking doubt, and the tides of strange opinion which were flowing again over Tennyson's England, bewilder Lords and commoners alike. The very Shakespearean crowd of the opening scene is puzzled about the meaning of 'legitimate'; the women of London promise to support Wyatt, but beg him to 'kill the Queen further off' because 'little Dickon, and little Robin, and little Jenny—though she's but a side-cousin' are here (II. iii.); Tib sees the Catholic zealots 'A-burnin', and a-burnin', and a-makin' o' volk madder and madder'; and Paget and Howard, the most moderate of the Catholic lords, see 'Action and re-action,/The miserable see-saw of our child-world . . .' (IV. iii). On this background of confused values leading to violence (*Queen Mary* follows soon after 'The Last Tournament', and lies full in the gloom with which Tennyson contemplated England in the seventies) Tennyson has sketched an Hegelian outline, with Mary's thesis that England should be under Rome met by a bewildering quantity of antithesis, and the synthesis provided by the simple patriotism of which Lord Howard is the courtliest and Sir Ralph Bagenhall the bluffest embodiment. Howard, catholic but not papist (a distinction which the play allows), holds firm his love of Cranmer, though driven to fury by Tib's prophecy that 'the burnin' o' the owld archbishop 'll burn the Pwoap out o' this 'ere land vor iver and iver' (IV. iii). Bagenhall, 'black-blooded' like a Tennyson, stands more or less where John Bull must on every issue. He has the closing words of II. ii, when his confusion is everyman's:

> *I am for England. But who knows*
> *That knows the Queen, the Spaniard, and the Pope,*
> *Whether I be for Wyatt, or the Queen?*

(CPW, 559)

He refuses to league himself with Stafford in a French-led rebellion against Mary (III. i), but two scenes later is the only Member of Parliament who will not kneel while Cardinal Pole pronounces the absolution ('A Parliament of imitative apes! . . . /I am ashamed that I am Bagenhall,/English'), an offence for which he is sent to the Tower. Released at the suit of Lord Howard, he is finally present to pronounce an Englishman's benediction over the new queen:

God save the Crown! the Papacy is no more.

(CPW, 606)

Before going on to consider the Lyceum production of *Queen Mary*, I must deal briefly with *Harold*. Modestly conscious that his first play bore the marks of his theatrical inexperience, Tennyson preceded the writing of *Harold* with a reading of several contemporary plays (his son does not say which) likely to help him 'meet the conditions of the modern drama' (*Mem.*, II, 188). The play is of a practical length, and the cast is much smaller (twenty-three against *Queen Mary's* forty-five), but there are few other advances. After the promise of *Queen Mary*, *Harold* is unexpectedly lame. It has moved away from the impassioned analysis of historical forces that distinguishes *Queen Mary* from the mass of contemporary 'historical' dramas, and taken refuge among that mass. The romantic triangle of Harold, Edith, and Aldwyth has a stale stage smell about it. Only the fact that history has been distorted separates the play from the popular period pieces (after Scribe but not necessarily *bien faites*) in which history was invented. I have already referred to the play's two fine scenes. There is nothing more ambitious in Tennyson's drama than the end of V. i, when Archbishop Stigand's commentary on the battle is counterpointed by the Latin chant of the Waltham Canons. In Stigand and the rebellious Tostig, Tennyson provided attractive acting roles, and Harold combines an Arthurian spiritual authority with an acceptable manliness. But the play fell between two theatrical stools. To heroic actors, Harold's defeat in battle was an impossible climax; and there was no appeal to Irving, the most likely English producer. His physique excluded him from traditional heroic roles—after 1880 they became the Lyceum property of William Terriss—and William, the only plausible alternative for a star actor, has too little to say and do.

Harold was never seen on the nineteenth-century stage. Something resembling *Queen Mary* was. There is some mystery about events prior to its opening at the Lyceum on 18 April 1876. 'Colonel' Hezekiah Bateman, manager of the theatre, had bought an option on the play shortly before his death in March 1875. Final negotiations were left to his widow, who wrote a helpless letter in early December 1875: 'Dear

Mr. Tennyson, After reading over Mr. Searle's commentaries and comparing his suggestions with those formerly proposed by Mr. Knowles, Mr. Irving and yourself last summer, I have thought it best to write and ask if you will undertake the requisite curtailment yourself. It is always an onerous task to propose the alteration of beautiful language but the exigencies of the stage demand that the play be reduced in length and that it may not be longer than *Hamlet* (and it ought to be half an hour shorter) and not fuller of characters, Hamlet being well known to be the *fullest play on the stage.* I should like to receive this acting copy as soon as possible as I propose doing the play at Easter or a little before. . . .' Tennyson's reply was less verbose: 'Dear Mrs. Bateman, Why do you beat about the bush? If you have repented of your proposal freely made to me in the spring, would it not be better to say so at once? You know very well that I have always said one and the same thing, i.e. "let me know what changes you want making in *Queen Mary* and I will do my best to make them". . . .' Despite the assurance, it is hard to reconcile the belief of Irving's biographer that Tennyson did the revisions himself[1] with the poet's known hope that Irving would play Pole. Pole is cut completely from the stage version. So are Cranmer, Wyatt, Bonner, and even Bagenhall. The twenty-three scenes of the original are reduced to nine, more by excision than conflation. Portions remain of I. iv. and I. v (*Act One* of the stage version), II. ii (*II. i*), II. iv (*II. ii*), III. v (*III. i*), III. ii and III. vi (*III. ii*), IV. iii (*IV. i*), V. i (*IV. ii*), V. iii (*V. i*), and V. v (*V. ii*). Almost nothing of the roles of Philip and Elizabeth is lost. Instead, as Clement Scott observed, the religious controversy is 'carefully eliminated from the story'.[2] The theatrical aims of the adaptation can be clearly seen in the preservation of the colourful Tib and Joan (Tib played by a man) despite the total removal of their original context, the last bravery and burning of Cranmer. Virginia Francis, second of the Bateman daughters, seems to have wasted the opportunities for play-stealing furnished by the new prominence of

---

[1] See Laurence Irving, *Henry Irving: the Actor and His World*, 1951, 266–7. The Bateman-Tennyson letters are also on these pages.

[2] Clement Scott's reviews of Lyceum productions are conveniently collected in *From 'The Bells' To 'King Arthur'*, 1897. I am quoting here from p. 94.

Elizabeth. Irving wasted nothing as Philip. His entrance in both versions is delayed until Act Three, but carefully prepared for particularly in the heavily stressed curtain-lines of the first two acts. Irving could always create space around himself on stage. Almost all the reviewers singled him out, commenting with unreserved admiration on the 'high-bred heartlessness'[1] with which he reassured Mary at the end of III. vi:[2]

> *By St. James I do protest,*
> *Upon the faith and honour of a Spaniard,*
> *I am vastly grieved to leave your Majesty.*
> *Simon, is supper ready?*

(CPW, 581)

This was a high point of the play in performance, a moment of characterization caught in Whistler's chilly portrait. But Philip, even in the stage version, does not sustain the play. Kate Bateman, an efficient actress, was not adequate for Mary, and several of the minor roles were sketchily played. After a run of five weeks, *Queen Mary*'s dwindling houses led to its replacement by a revival, first of *The Bells*, and later of *The Belle's Stratagem*. Not quite a failure, but not a success. There is, however, a limit to what might be learnt from the fate of such a travesty. Responsible cutting of the play should begin with the slicing out of Elizabeth and Courtenay, perhaps of Le Sieur de Noailles and the peripheral French interest. The removal of Wyatt, Cranmer, and Bagenhall, and the complete omission of the great debate in III. iv are inexcusable. My view that *Queen Mary* is the most likely of all Tennyson's plays to repay revival cannot be susbtantiated by anything that happened at the Lyceum. That version cannot have been Tennyson's work. I find it hard to believe that it was Irving's.

The association of Tennyson and Irving, which began with *Queen Mary*, lasted without intensity until Tennyson's death. Few men were more eagerly sought by the curious public, though they reacted very differently to the pursuit. There is a story, whose source I have not

---

[1] The phrase is from 'Frederic Daly', *Henry Irving in England and America 1838–84*, 1884, 46, but it could be matched in many other accounts of the play in performance.
[2] III. ii in the stage version.

traced, of an occasion when they were walking together in London. 'I wish people wouldn't stare at me so,' said Tennyson, to Irving's certain chagrin.[1] Irving took over the management of the Lyceum in 1878, and for the next twenty years it was a National Theatre *avant la lettre,* though with a repertoire to antagonize the highbrow. Of the twenty-nine plays first staged at the Lyceum under Irving's management, nine were Shakespearean, and almost all the others brittle theatre pieces of the kind Ibsen was already making archaic. In the Lyceum play there needed to a be part for Irving (stately, malignant, secretly guilty, *strong*), and a part to suit the gently seductive energy of Ellen Terry. There was no shyness of scenic and musical effect, and Irving enjoyed deploying actors and extras on a crowded stage. He would not have mounted *The Cup* and *Becket* if he had been unable to see how they might be made to suit his company and the idiom of his *mise en scène.* By the end of 1877, Tennyson was fully occupied with *Becket,* the last of his historical trilogy, which he sent to the printers in early 1879. Irving served him, as Macready had served Browning during the composition of *The Return of the Druses,* as a notional collaborator, whose acting style and production methods Tennyson bore constantly in mind. The version of 1879 is shorter than the one eventually published in 1884. Sir Charles Tennyson is surely right that 'it was especially prepared for submission to Irving'.[2] Irving did not believe it stageworthy, and fended Tennyson off as kindly as he could by talking of costs of production. The invitation to write a shorter play for Lyceum production was a further softening of the blow. That shorter play, *The Cup,* opened at Irving's theatre in January 1881, eleven years before the more ambitious piece that Irving initially rejected.

Becket was no less inspired by an enthusiasm for history than *Queen Mary* had been. Tennyson did not believe his hero faultless, but he felt a profound sympathy with the man he saw sustaining in brave isolation the spiritual standards of a threatened civilization. There is some uncertainty in Becket's attitude to Rome, and Tennyson may be betraying his own patriotic prejudices when he has Becket align himself, after the

[1] Joanna Richardson, *The Pre-Eminent Victorian: A Study of Tennyson,* 1962, 251, tells the story, but gives no source.
[2] *Alfred Tennyson,* 446.

meeting of the Kings at Montmirail, with those Englishmen who are Catholics before they are papists:

> *Save for myself no Rome were left in England . . .*
> *. . . Why should this Rome, this Rome,*
> *Still choose Barabbas rather than the Christ,*
> *Absolve the left-hand thief and damn the right?*
> *Take fees of tyranny, wink at sacrilege,*
> *Which even Peter had not dared?*

(II. ii: CPW, 674)

Harold's legacy of

> *war against the Pope,*
> *From child to child, from Pope to Pope, from age to age,*
> *Till the sea wash her level with her shores,*
> *Or till the Pope be Christ's.*

(*Harold*, V. i: CPW, 639)

seems to survive, in *Becket*, in the unlikely person of the Archbishop himself. Becket is, however, consistent in his opposition to the secularization of England which Henry proposes by his exhumation of the customs of the realm; and he realizes as early as the Council meeting of I. iii that his death may be more effective in the struggle than his life:

> *Strike, and I die the death of martyrdom;*
> *Strike, and ye set these customs by my death*
> *Ringing their own death-knell thro' all the realm.*

(CPW, 658)

This view of the martyrdom as a spiritual triumph over a rational but ultimately impoverishing political movement is at the centre of Tennyson's reading of history, but his presentation of the arguments falls some way short of his hopes. The play lacks the vigour of intellectual clarity. The quarrel between Henry and Becket, finely begun in the chess game of the Prologue, is not sustained on a level of realized opposition. Neither character is won by argument into shifting his ground, and Henry in particular falls easy prey to an unimpressive emotionalism. Becket, on the contrary, is given a sequence of carefully contrasted opportunities to elaborate on a theme of single-mindedness. Contemporary dramatic critics, who heard in Irving's voice the Tennysonian melody, seem often to have admired the play for love of its hero. Certainly Becket has his fine moments. The opening of I. i, for instance, in which the self-questioning 'Am I the man?' recurs like a refrain, is a rare point of nine-teenth-century poetic drama when the weight of thought is equal to the expressiveness of the verse. But the play *Becket* is deeply flawed. Tenny-son's wish to reach contemporary theatre audiences led him to provide here, as in *Harold,* an alternative 'dramatic' approach. Once again he tried to marry history and romantic legend, once again disastrously. To give room to the story of Rosamund de Clifford and the jealousy of Queen Eleanor, he compresses to confusion the dispute of Henry and Becket. He even makes it the rivalry of Eleanor and Rosamund that provokes the fatal question, 'Will no man free me from this pestilent priest?' (V. i). A large part of Act Three and the whole of Act Four are set in or near Rosamund's Bower, and it is Rosamund who is left on stage, kneeling beside Becket's body, when the slow final curtain falls. The isolation of the Bower and the pathos of its occupant had intrigued Tennyson for many years,[1] but Rosamund is scarcely more acceptable than the Lady of Shalott in the realized world of the drama. Only in the unnecessary contrivance of the dropped letter in V. iii does *Queen Mary* make any patronizing step towards the theatre of Scribe, whereas the whole treatment of Rosamund and Eleanor is patronizingly Scribean. 'I don't know what to do with her,' Ellen Terry admitted, faced with the role of Rosamund. 'She is not there, She does not exist. I don't think that Tennyson ever knew very much about women, and now he is old and has forgotten the little that he knew. She is not a woman at all.'[2] Like Eleanor, Rosamund has only the plot-flattened life of bad melo-drama. If Tennyson had learnt from Shakespeare the use of sub-plots, the damage might be reparable in performance. As it is, there is some-thing in *Becket* of the savaged masterpiece.

[1] Rosamund appears in 'A Dream of Fair Women', and is the subject of the short poem first published in *Mem.,* II, 197, where it is stated that it was 'written before 1842'. Christopher Ricks points out that 'the legend is told in the *English Encyclopaedia* (1802), of which there was a copy at Somersby' (PT, 735)

[2] Quoted in Roger Manvell, *Ellen Terry,* 1968, 210.

Having failed with Irving, Tennyson offered the performing rights of *Becket* to the American actor, Lawrence Barrett. Not until 1889, though, and when Barrett died two years later leaving an unperformed adaptation, Tennyson sent it to Irving. At last Irving saw how the play might be made to 'go'. There was never any doubt of the appeal of playing Becket, nor that the three big scenes (the Council, Montmirail, the assassination) fed Irving's strength as a director. The version he made shows clearly the marks of a practical theatrical intelligence. The four leading roles had be to raised further above the level of the play if audiences and actors were to be satisfied. That meant, inevitably, the retention of almost all of Eleanor and Rosamund for Genevieve Ward and Ellen Terry, and it meant also a heavier underlining of the progress of the quarrel between Henry and Becket. None of this need involve more than the cutting of lines here and there and the emphatic linking of episodes. There was one other preliminary problem. A prologue and five acts required one interval too many. The play must be shuffled into a prologue and four acts. As for the prologue itself, there was one error of theatrical tact to be corrected. No nineteenth-century leading actor liked to be discovered at the first raising of the curtain. Either an entrance must be made, or lesser actors used to silence the settling audience. Irving divided the prologue into two scenes, opening with Eleanor and Fitzurse, and leaving the discovery of Henry and Becket at chess until scene two. His Act One begins, like Tennyson's, with Becket's questioning 'Am I the man?', retains scene two (the confrontation of Eleanor and Becket), and adds a four-line scene to *point* the four knights to the audience. Then comes the first big change. Tennyson had ended his first act with a challenging and determinedly theatrical scene (I. iv), in which Becket is protected from the knights by the beggars he is feeding at his table. Irving cut it completely, choosing to end the act with the first of the big scenes, the meeting of the Council at Northampton Castle (I. iii in Tennyson). Wanting a longer curtain for his exit to the cheering crowd, he asked Tennyson for a speech to follow the crowd's shout, 'Blessed is he that cometh in the name of the Lord'. Tennyson wrote it during the spring of 1892.[1] Act Two is a tidying up of the

[1] There are several textual variations between this speech as Hallam Tennyson quotes it (*Mem.*, II, 197), and as it appears in Bram Stoker,

original. It consists simply of a conflation of the two scenes (Tennyson's II. i and III. i) in which Henry and Rosamund talk and sigh in Rosamund's Bower. The second big scene, the meeting of the Kings at Montmirail, is held over to open Act Three. There is more tidying up to follow. Tennyson had separated the scene in which Eleanor and Fitzurse begin looking for the way through the maze to Rosamund's Bower (III. ii) from the two scenes in which they find it (IV. i and IV. ii). By cutting the intervening scene, Irving achieved two things. He omitted the brief reconciliation of Henry and Becket, which, bereft of consequence as it is in Tennyson, would certainly have confused an audience, and he makes consecutive the hunting and the finding of Rosamund, thus avoiding the artless hiatus of the original. By cutting short Tennyson's IV. ii, he does nothing to redeem the mediocre melodrama of that callow scene, but he does give Becket the last lines (slow curtain and tableau) of his Act Three:

> *Daughter, the world hath trick'd thee, leave it, daughter.*
> *Come thou with me to Godstow nunnery.*
>
> (CPW, 686)

The arrangement has been adept enough to allow Act Four to coincide, scene by scene, with the original Act Five. Collation of texts confirms the impression that Irving preferred regular small excisions to infrequent larger ones. The only notable character to be removed is Walter Map, for whose prose commentary on two dramatic confrontations Tennyson cherished an exaggerated fondness. Irving's famous reading of his own version of *Becket* in the old Chapter House of Canterbury Cathedral in 1897 lasted ninety-five minutes. Tennyson's 'original, would have taken him a full hour longer.

The production of *Becket* was in preparation when Tennyson died. It opened at the Lyceum on 6 February 1893, Irving's fifty-fifth birthday. Overture and entr'acte music had been commissioned from Stanford, who also provided a Becket theme by orchestrating the Gregorian

---

Personal Reminiscences of Henry Irving, 2 vols., 1906, I, 226. The evidence is contradictory, but it seems likely that Irving used only four of the lines Tennyson provided. See, for example, the stage version in the Eversley Edition of *Becket and Other Plays*, 487.

melody 'Telluris ingens conditor'. There were ten separate sets, not all of them as lavish as Hawes Craven's Hall of Northampton Castle, but none skimped. Despite the confident front of the expenditure, the success took Irving by surprise. The play ran until the end of June, and could have run for longer. It became a stock piece for Irving, even more a breadwinner for him than Byron's *Werner* had been for Macready; and it was the play he acted in on the night he died, so that, as countless elegists remembered, the last words Irving spoke on stage were 'Into Thy hands, O Lord—into Thy hands!' Whereas *Queen Mary* had been butchered for the stage, *Becket* was treated as respectfully as Shakespeare's plays were treated in the nineteenth-century theatre. Probably it was improved. It was felt so at the time, and Henry Arthur Jones felt so still in 1912: 'Becket owed everything to Irving's arrangement and perfor-mance. Never was an author more indebted to an actor than was Tennyson to Irving in Becket, not merely for the acting of the chief part but for the shaping, arranging, and direction of the play. Will it ever be successful again? Will it ever be played again?'[1] Jones is praising Irving's playmaking. Irving, on the contrary, felt always in Tennyson's debt. The part of Becket stirred him deeply. That quality in his charac-ter which Craig called 'concentrated fanatical joy, bound tight under the control of his immense will'[2] was the quality he in his turn found and played in Becket. But there was a gentler expression, the 'sweet smile' Clement Scott remembered, for the reminiscence just before the arrival of the murdering knights:

> *There was a little fair-hair'd Norman maid*
> *Lived in my mother's house: if Rosamund is*
> *The world's rose, as her name imports her—she*
> *Was the world's lily.*

(V. ii: CPW, 691)

Irving doubted whether there was anything in Shakespeare better than those lines, and if the judgment is wayward, it attests to an experience not far from religious ecstasy. Laurence Irving states as unquestionable

---

[1] *The Shadow of Henry Irving*, 1931, 62. Jones wrote most of this book in 1912–13.
[2] Edward Gordon Craig, *Henry Irving*, 1930, 183.

that in *Becket* 'Irving established a closer affinity with his public than in any other piece he played', and goes on to record that he 'persuaded himself that in the performance of Becket, spanning the gulf between Church and Stage, he and his audience united in an act of worship'.[1] Unquestionably, Irving's performance of Tennyson's hero was an importantly representative Victorian event. To the younger members of the Lyceum audience it offered an opportunity to hear ancestral voices prophesying war.

Set against the historical trilogy, *The Cup* is static and unadventurous, solemn even where it comes closest to being felt. Tennyson found the story first in Lecky's *History of European Morals,* and checked it against its source in Plutarch's *Moralia.* It was only the demand of Irving's interest that carried it into dramatic form. It might to better advantage have supplied the material for a monologue. The development of character through dialogue is slight, and Tennyson relies on the story to define his protagonists. His moral discriminations are fatally over-simple. The Galatian hero Sinnatus and his loyal wife Camma are patriots. The lecherous Synorix who kills Sinnatus and who lusts after Camma is a quisling. Camma's revenge is spectacular but unaffecting, and even the restraint of the verse contributes to the lack of narrative urgency that must, in a longer play, have deterred the friendliest audience. Indeed, brevity is *The Cup's* strongest hold on dramatic tact.

In early December 1880 Tennyson read the play to Knowles, Irving, Terriss, Ellen Terry, and Ellen's daughter Edie, who giggled when Tennyson recited Camma's lines in wavering falsetto. Irving suggested a few additions, and the play went almost immediately into rehearsal. It opened on 3 January 1881 with the strong support of Boucicault's *The Corsican Brothers.* In money-per-minute terms *The Cup* was perhaps the most expensively produced play in the history of the English theatre. Irving had spent £2,370 on costumes and set—and the costumes and set won. Even the acting features less than the set in reviews of the production, though there is admiration for the processions and rituals devised by Irving, and for the beauty of the hundred priestesses of Artemis whom he and Bram Stoker had personally selected. Stoker supposes that it was

[1] Laurence Irving, *Henry Irving,* 560.

the ritual that brought an unusually high number of High Church clergy
to see *The Cup*. It does not occur to him that it might have been the
priestesses.[1]

The remaining three plays were produced at lesser theatres than the
Lyceum. The Kendals charmed audiences at the St. James's in *The
Falcon* during the 1879–80 season; nearly three years later *The Promise
of May* had its briefly notorious failure at the Globe; and in March 1892
The Foresters opened at Daly's Theatre, New York. Of *The Foresters*,
played or published, there is little good to say. Tennyson knew it to be
the unworthiest of his dramatic work. Presumably, the artistic appeal of
a chivalric subject counted for less than the hope of financial and
popular success in the decisions he made on the way to treat the Robin
Hood legends. *The Foresters* is an unresolved mixture of pastoral
romance, domestic melodrama, light opera, and heroic legend, with one
hand in history and the rest of its body firmly inside the theatre. George
Colman the Younger seems to have established the style almost a century
earlier with *The Battle of Hexham* (1789), but Colman and most of his
imitators wrote competently for a theatre they knew. Tennyson wrote
speculatively for a theatre he had glimpsed. *The Foresters* dithers between
prose and verse like the first draft of a play whose author has not yet
committed himself. Just over three-quarters of the lines are in verse, but
so intermingled with prose that the language never finds a level.
Sullivan's specially composed music had a lot to do with the play's
popularity in New York. Certainly it rescued the fairy scene, through
which Tennyson stumbles inelegantly. He was embarrassed by it, and
assured Daly that 'Irving suggested the fairies in my *Robin Hood*, else
I should not have dreamed of trenching on Shakespeare's ground in
that way' (*Mem.*, II, 390). Some of the writing is comically inept, as in
Titania's rebuke to the First Fairy:

> *I Titania bid you flit,*
> *And you dare to call me Tit.*
>
> . . . .
> *Pertest of our flickering mob,*
> *Wouldst thou call my Oberon Ob?*

(II. ii: CPW, 765)

[1] See Stoker, *Henry Irving*, I, 206.

Parody is not, I think, intended. Tennyson's humour in *The Foresters* is not so agile. His claim to have 'sketched the state of the people in another great transition period of the making of England . . .' (*Mem.,* II, 173) is a ridiculous one. He has not begun to do so.

The Falcon is much better. It is a one-act piece derived from Boccaccio, with the names and setting still Italian, but the feeling English. Made destitute by his extravagant courtship of the widowed Lady Giovanna, Count Federigo degli Alberighi is reduced to living in a cottage. Only his falcon remains to delight him. It is the task of the Count's opening speech to establish the force of the falcon in the play, and it does so with the kind of grace that did not come easily to Tennyson in the plays:

> *My Princess of the cloud, my plumed purveyor,*
> *My far-eyed queen of the winds—thou that canst soar*
> *Beyond the morning lark, and howsoe'er*
> *Thy quarry wind and wheel, swoop down upon him*
> *Eagle-like, lightning-like—strike, make his feathers*
> *Glance in mid heaven.*
>
> (CPW, 714)

When Giovanna visits the cottage unexpectedly, he is foodless and moneyless. He secretly orders the killing of the falcon to provide her meat, only to discover that she has come at the whim of her desperately sick son to beg the falcon from him. It might have been a mournful piece merely. Instead, Giovanna is won by the Count's sacrifice to confess her love for him, and, forgetting her dying son (a glaring fault—but what could Tennyson do without a second act?), ends the play in a chaste embrace. In Boccaccio the match is made only after the death of the son, a loss he treats without the slightest trace of melodramatic sorrow. The death of the boy would have unbalanced Tennyson's version. He omits it, and adds to his source a family feud to explain Giovanna's initial hesitance, and two household companions for the Count. *Romeo and Juliet* was in Tennyson's mind as he wrote, and these two invented characters are as Shakespearean as the commoners in Tennyson's plays usually are. With their departure the dialogue drifts a little towards mere translation, 'stately and tender' as Tennyson called it,[1] but lacking idiomatic equivalents for its original. It is not surprising that the Kendals chose to play this delicate and modestly inventive half-hour piece. Unlike Irving and Ellen Terry, they were picturesque portrayers of soulful love.

Tennyson's last play, *The Promise of May*, which he completed in 1882, did not share *The Falcon's* quiet acceptability. Erroll Sherson doubts whether the real story of its first night has ever been told. It opened at the Globe Theatre on 11 November 1882, with Vezin as Philip Edgar. This is Sherson's own account in a treatment of Mrs Bernard Beere, the play's producer and leading lady: 'She had to contend with a very bad play by the Poet Laureate; with the presence, in a private box, of Mr Gladstone whom the pit and gallery chose to regard with loud outspoken disfavour; with a most unfortunate *lapsus calami* on the part of Tennyson who had innocently allotted to the character played by Hermann Vezin a couple of lines with a double entendre that set the whole house (inclined to "guy" the piece) rocking with laughter. Moreover, the second night, that egregious person, the Marquis of Queensberry, stood up in the stalls and openly denounced certain lines also spoken by the unfortunate Vezin'.[2] *The Promise of May* is, whatever Tennyson may have thought, a domestic melodrama with the defect, common to its kind, of an overbearing solemnity in its analysis of human behaviour. During the negotiations over *Becket*, Irving had asked Tennyson to dramatise 'Enoch Arden', of which there were already some stage versions on the provincial round. They underline the fact that Tennyson's interest in a story tended to stir at the kind of emotionally charged situation that also attracted the journeyman melodramatists of the period. It is likely that Irving could have played an *Enoch Arden* dramatized by Tennyson into a popularity rivalling that of *The Bells*. He would have identified easily with the hero:

> *His large grey eyes and weather-beaten face*
> *All-kindled by a still and sacred fire,*
> *That burn'd as on an altar.*

(PT, 1131)

---

[1] See *Becket and Other Plays*, Eversley Edition, 1908, 527.
[2] Erroll Sherson, *London's Lost Theatres of the Nineteenth Century*, 1925, 245.

And the strength of Enoch Arden's silence may have reminded Irving of his magnificent Mathias in *The Bells*. *The Promise of May* was written towards Irving's interest in guilt-laden heroes, but Irving didn't want it. Neither did the Kendals, as W. H. Kendal hesitantly explained: 'It is full of dramatic incident and character, but it appears to me, if I may be allowed to say so, that the dramatic incident and character are so *strong*, the whole requires to be very much more fully developed!' (*Mem.*, II, 267). Tennyson may even have been gratified by the interest of Mrs Beere—at first.

The play begins with a happy chorus of 'farming men and women' assembled to celebrate the eightieth birthday of Farmer Steer. It is a day 'bright like a friend', but with the wind 'east like an enemy'. The contrasting stanzas of the song sung by Steer's elder daughter Dora initiate the ominous worm-in-the-bud mood that dominates Act One. In the first 'The hen cluckt late by the white farm gate' and 'The stock-dove cooed at the full of night'; in the second 'a fox from the glen ran away with the hen' and 'the stock-dove cooed, till a kite dropt down'. The refrain, too, shifts from 'joy for the promise of May' to 'grief for the promise of May'. During the clumsy courting of Dora by the neighbouring Farmer Dobson, the 'tragic' theme is introduced—the love of Dora's sister Eva for Philip Edgar, a stranger who 'weärs a Lunnun boot'. Edgar is, to borrow R. L. Stevenson's word, a 'squirradical', and it was his glibly expressed radical views that excited controversy during the play's run at the Globe. Andrew Lang states trenchantly that 'A man would give all other bliss and all his worldly wealth for this, to waste his whole strength in one kick upon this perfect prig'.[1] Edgar is certainly despicable, though Lang is reacting to a character much more complete than the one Tennyson has created. Tennyson's uncertainty about class is exposed both in his villainous gentleman and his simple farmer. Edgar is even made to bring blank verse into the play with him, as if it were as much a badge of class as an Oxford accent. Not only does he speak verse himself, but he is also the sole cause of verse in others, an unfortunate distinction that reduces his credibility. As for the political notions, they may owe their inadequacy to Edgar's ignorance or to Tennyson's,

[1] Lang, *Alfred Tennyson*, Edinburgh and London, 1904, 186. It is to Lang that I owe the reference to 'squirradicals'.

but they are anyway peripheral to the play. Edgar's dramatic function
is the familiar one of the heartless seducer of the simple maid, in this
case Eva:

> *I was just out of school, I had no mother—*
> *My sister far away—and you, a gentleman,*
> *Told me to trust you.*
>
> (I. i: CPW, 731)

In the jollity that brings Act One to an end Eva sits alone, dishonoured
and deserted. Five years have passed before the next rise of the curtain.
Eva has disappeared, believed drowned but known to have shamed the
family, and everything has changed for the worse. The note of continuing hope is sounded only by Dobson's persistent courtship of Dora,
who rebuffs him still: 'I have no thought of marriage, my friend. We
have been in such grief these five years, not only on my sister's account,
but the ill success of the farm, and the debts, and my father's breaking
down, and his blindness. How could I think of leaving him ?' The sudden
entrance of Philip Edgar, recalled mysteriously by the voice of Eva, and
claiming (a fatuously thin disguise) to be Philip Harold, a relation of the
dead Philip Edgar, requires effects-music if its impact is to be recap-
tured. Dora is immediately impressed by him:

> *How beautiful*
> *His manners are, and how unlike the farmer's!*
>
> (II. ii: CPW, 737)

Their long conversation is interrupted by a 'farming-man' with the
news that 'Dan Smith's cart hes runned ower a laädy i' the holler laäne,
and they ha' ta'en the body up inter your chamber'. Farmer Dobson,
suspicious of Edgar/Harold, ends the act in jealous soliloquy. The final
act takes place in Steer's house. Dora dispenses wages and heavy moral
advice to the few workers they can still afford to pay, and when they
have gone, the injured girl—Eva of course—talks out the blank five
years to Dora and to us. There follows the scene, deeply painful and in
its own terms entirely successful, in which Eva asks forgiveness of her
old, blind father. This is it in full:

Enter Steer led by Milly.
STEER. Hes the cow cawved?
DORA.   No, Father.
STEER. Be the colt deäd?
DORA.   No, Father.
STEER. He wur sa bellows'd out wi' the wind this murnin', 'at I
        tell'd 'em to gallop 'im. Be he deäd?
DORA.   Not that I know.
STEER. What hasta sent fur me, then, fur?
DORA (*taking Steer's arm*). Well, Father, I have a surprise for you.
STEER. I ha niver been surprised but once i' my life, and I went blind
        upon it.
DORA.   Eva has come home.
STEER. Hoäm? fro' the bottom o' the river?
DORA.   No, Father, that was a mistake. She's here again.
STEER. The Steers was all gentlefoälks i' the owd times, an' I worked
        early an' laäte to maäke 'em all gentlefoälks ageän. The land
        belonged to the Steers i' the owd times, an' it belongs to the
        Steers ageän: I bowt it back ageän; but I couldn't buy my
        darter back ageän when she lost hersen, could I? I eddicated
        boäth on 'em to marry gentlemen, an' one on 'em went an' lost
        hersen i' the river.
DORA.   No, Father, she's here.
STEER. Here! she moänt coom here. What would her mother saäy?
        If it be her ghoäst, we mun abide it. We can't keep a ghoäst
        out.
EVA (*falling at his feet*). O forgive me! forgive me!
STEER. Who said that? Taäke me awaäy, little gell. It be one o' my
        bad daäys.
Exit Steer led by Milly.
                                        (III. iii: CPW, 743)

Eva is helped back to bed, and Philip enters to the shaken Dora. He
confesses to some opinions 'which you would scarce approve of', but
denounces Socialism, Communism, and Nihilism as 'Utopian idiotcies':

> . . . *such rampant weeds*
> *Strangle each other, die, and make the soil*
> *For Caesars, Cromwells, and Napoleons*
> *To root their power in.*

                                        (CPW, 745)

All this is prefatory to a proposal of marriage, which Dora receives with
    They kiss, and a voice from the bedroom shouts 'Philip Edgar!'
There is a flurry of explanation, broken by the stage direction, *Eva opens
the door and stands in the entry*. She utters the single line, 'Make her happy,
then, and I forgive you', and falls dead. Tennyson, it must be admitted,
has read too many bad plays. This one comes to an end, after a scuffle
between Dobson and Philip, with Dora's chilling lines:

> *If you ever*
> *Forgive yourself, you are even lower and baser*
> *Than even I can well believe you. Go!*
> He lies at her feet. Curtain falls.

(CPW, 747)

The Promise of May, directed so openly towards the contemporary
theatre, illustrates well the limits of Tennyson's knowledge of that
theatre. It is crude and lifeless compared with the work of a practised
hand like Boucicault's; and it commits the error of underrating the concern for truth of the theatrical traditions that it plunders. Tennyson's
best plays—*Queen Mary* and, perhaps, *The Falcon*—work slightly against
the tide of the period's drama. *The Promise of May* is indistinct among
the undistinguished.

Tennyson: A Select Bibliography

LIONEL MADDEN

Note

Place of publication is London unless otherwise stated. The following abbreviations have been used:

CS	*Critical Survey*
EC	*Essays in Criticism*
ELH	*English Literary History*
JEGP	*Journal of English & Germanic Philology*
MLN	*Modern Language Notes*
New CBEL	*New Cambridge Bibliography of English Literature*
PMLA	*Publications of the Modern Language Association of America*
RES	*Review of English Studies*
TLS	*Times Literary Supplement*
UTQ	*University of Toronto Quarterly*
VP	*Victorian Poetry*
VS	*Victorian Studies*

I. TEXTS

Dates of publication of Tennyson's works are included in the Chronological Table at the front of this volume. For more detailed information see works listed in S 2 below and Ricks's edition of *Poems*.

Collected Works

The Works of Tennyson Annotated, ed Hallam, Lord Tennyson, 9 vol., 1907–8. The 'Eversley' edition. Carefully edited text with many notes by Tennyson himself.

The Works of Tennyson with Notes by the Author, ed with a memoir by Hallam, Lord Tennyson, 1913. One-volume edition based on Eversley with some modifications.

The Poems of Tennyson, ed Christopher Ricks, 1969. In the 'Longmans Annotated English Poets' series. Based on the Eversley text but includes manuscript poems and poems published since Eversley. Excludes the plays except *The Devil and the Lady.* The text of the plays is available in:

Tennyson: Poems and Plays, ed T. Herbert Warren, revised and enlarged by Frederick Page, 1953. In the 'Oxford Standard Authors' series. Published 1953 as *The Complete Poetical Works of Tennyson;* reprinted 1965 and later as *Tennyson: Poems and Plays.*

Selections

Auden, W. H., ed *Tennyson: An Introduction and a Selection,* 1946.

Blunden, Edmund, ed *Selected Poems of Tennyson,* 1960.

Buckley, Jerome Hamilton, ed *Poems of Tennyson,* Cambridge, Mass. 1958.

Burton, H. M., ed *Selections from Tennyson,* 1960.

Bush, Douglas, ed *Tennyson: Selected Poetry,* New York 1951.

Cecil, Lord David, ed *A Choice of Tennyson's Verse,* 1971.

McLuhan, H. M., ed *Tennyson: Selected Poetry,* New York 1956.

Palgrave, F. T., ed *Lyrical Poems of Tennyson,* 1885.

Southam, B. C., ed *Selected Poems of Lord Tennyson,* 1964.

Tennyson, Charles, ed *Poems of Tennyson,* 1954.

Letters

There is, as yet, no full-scale edition of Tennyson's letters, though one is in preparation by Edgar F. Shannon and Cecil Y. Laing. Some letters are printed in Hallam Tennyson's *Memoir* and in the following:'

Dyson, Hope and Tennyson, Charles, eds *Dear and Honoured Lady: The Correspondence between Queen Victoria and Afred Tennyson,* 1969.

Ellmann, Mary Joan, 'Tennyson: unpublished letters, 1833–6', *MLN* LXV, 1950, 223–8.

Mumby, Frank Arthur, ed *Letters of Literary Men: The Nineteenth Century,* 1906.

Pierce, L., ed *Alfred, Lord Tennyson and William Kirby: Unpublished Correspondence,* Toronto 1929.

2. BIBLIOGRAPHIES, DICTIONARIES & CONCORDANCE

Baker, Arthur Ernest, *A Concordance to the Poetical and Dramatic Works of Alfred, Lord Tennyson,* 1914. Supplement: *The Devil and the Lady,* 1931.

— *A Tennyson Dictionary,* 1916.

Campion, G. Edward, *A Tennyson Dialect Glossary with the Dialect Poems,* Lincoln 1969.

Hunt, John Dixon, Narrative bibliography in *English Poetry: Select Bibliographical Guides,* ed A. E. Dyson, 1971.

Johnson, E. D. H., Narrative bibliography in *The Victorian Poets: A Guide to Research,* ed Frederic E. Faverty, 2nd ed, Cambridge, Mass. 1968. Revision of the original contribution by P. F. Baum.

Luce, Morton, *A Handbook to the Works of Alfred Lord Tennyson,* 1895.

Marshall, George O., Jr., *A Tennyson Handbook,* New York 1963.

Paden, W. D. and Laurence, Dan H. Select bibliography in *New CBEL* Vol. III, ed George Watson, Cambridge 1969.

Smith, Elton E., 'Tennyson criticism 1923–1966: from fragmentation to tension in polarity', *Victorian Newsletter* No. 31, 1967, 1–4.

Tennyson, Charles and Fall, Christine, *Alfred Tennyson: An Annotated Bibliography* Athens, Georgia 1967.

Wise, Thomas J. *A Bibliography of the Writings of Alfred, Lord Tennyson,* 2 vol., 1908. For a list of Wise's forgeries see William B. Todd, 'A handlist of Thomas J. Wise' in *Thomas J. Wise: Centenary Studies,* ed W. B. Todd, Austin, Texas 1959.

3. DESCRIPTIONS OF SPECIAL COLLECTIONS

Campbell, Nancie, comp. *Tennyson in Lincoln: A Catalogue of the Collections in the Research Centre,* 1972. Planned in 3 vol. Vol. I lists the libraries of the Tennyson family.

Collins, Rowland L., 'The Frederick Tennyson Collection' [Lilly Library of Indiana University], *VS* VII, Christmas Supplement 1963, 56–76.

Gransden, K. W., 'Some uncatalogued manuscripts of Tennyson' [in Palgrave bequest to the British Museum], *Book Collector* IV, 1955, 159–62.

Ricks, Christopher, 'The Tennyson manuscripts at Trinity College, Cambridge', *TLS*, 21 August 1969, 918–22.

Shannon, Edgar F., Jr. and Bond, W. H., 'Literary manuscripts of Alfred Tennyson in the Harvard College Library', *Harvard Library Bulletin* X, 1956, 254–74.

Tennyson, Charles, 'J. M. Heath's "Commonplace Book"' [in the Fitzwilliam Museum, Cambridge], *Cornhill Magazine* CLIII, 1936, 426–49.

4. BIOGRAPHICAL STUDIES

Fausset, Hugh l'Anson, *Tennyson: A Modern Portrait*, 1923.

Knowles, James, 'Aspects of Tennyson, II: a personal reminiscence', *Nineteenth Century* XXXIII, 1893, 164–88.

Rawnsley, H. D., *Memories of the Tennysons*, Glasgow 1900, revised 1912.

Richardson, Joanna, *The Pre-eminent Victorian: A Study of Tennyson*, 1962.

Tennyson, Charles, *Alfred Tennyson*, 1949.

—'The Somersby Tennysons', *VS* VII, Christmas Supplement,1963, 7–55. See also 'The Somersby Tennysons: a postscript', *VS* IX, 1966, 303–5.

A bibliography of the writings of Sir Charles Tennyson, including many shorter biographical studies, is currently being compiled by Lionel Madden for publication by the Tennyson Society.

Tennyson, Hallam, Lord, *Alfred Lord Tennyson: A Memoir*, 2 vol., 1897,

—*Materials for a Life of A. T., Collected for My Children*, 4 vol., priv. pr., n.d. [1895–6].

—ed *Tennyson and His Friends*, 1911.

5. GENERAL CRITICAL STUDIES

Items which are reprinted in the important collections by Jump and Killham are indicated by [CH] or [K] after the entry.

Armstrong, Isobel, ed *The Major Victorian Poets: Reconsiderations*, 1969. Includes essays on Tennyson by M. Dodsworth, B. Bergonzi, A. Sinfield and A. S. Byatt.

Arnold, Matthew, in *On Translating Homer: Last Words*, 1862 [CH].

Baum, Paul F., *Tennyson Sixty Years After*, Chapel Hill, N.C. 1948.

Bradley, A. C., *The Reaction Against Tennyson*, 1917.

Brooke, Stopford A., *Tennyson: His Art and Relation to Modern Life*, 1894.

Buckley, Jerome Hamilton, *Tennyson: The Growth of a Poet*, Cambridge, Mass. 1960.

—'Tennyson: the two voices' in *The Victorian Temper: A Study in Literary Culture*, Cambridge, Mass. 1951.

Bush, J. N. D. in *Mythology and the Romantic Tradition in English Poetry*, Cambridge, Mass. 1937.

Carr, Arthur J., 'Tennyson as a modern poet', *UTQ* XIX, 1950, 361–82 [K].

Chesterton, G. K. and Garnett, R., *Tennyson*, 1903.

Davies, H. S., in *The Poets and Their Critics: Blake to Browning*, 1962.

Dodsworth, Martin, 'Patterns of morbidity: repetition in Tennyson's poetry' in *The Major Victorian Poets: Reconsiderations*, ed Isobel Armstrong, 1969.

Eidson, John Olin, *Tennyson in America: His Reputation and Influence from 1827 to 1858*, Athens, Georgia 1943.

Gibson, Walker, 'Behind the veil: a distinction between poetic and scientific language in Tennyson, Lyell, and Darwin', *VS* II, 1958, 60–8.

Green, Joyce, 'Tennyson's development during the "Ten Years' Silence" (1832–1842)', *PMLA* LXVI, 1951, 662–97.

Grierson, Herbert, J. C., 'The Tennysons' in *The Cambridge History of English Literature*, ed A. W. Ward and A. R. Waller, Vol. XIII, 1916.

Houghton, W. E., in *The Victorian Frame of Mind, 1830–1870*, New Haven, Conn. 1957.

House, Humphry, 'Tennyson and the spirit of the age' in *All in Due Time*, 1955.

Hutton, R. H., in *Literary Essays*, 1888 [CH].

Johnson, E. D. H., in *The Alien Vision of Victorian Poetry: Sources of the Poetic Imagination in Tennyson, Browning, and Arnold*, Princeton 1952.

Joseph, Gerhard, *Tennysonian Love: The Strange Diagonal*, Minneapolis 1969.

Jump, John D., ed *Tennyson: The Critical Heritage*, 1967. Reprints 35 evaluations of Tennyson written between 1831 and 1891.

Ker, W. P., *Tennyson*, Cambridge 1909.

Killham, John, ed *Critical Essays on the Poetry of Tennyson*, 1960. Includes essays by G. M. Young, A. J. Carr, H. M. McLuhan, G. R. Stange, E. H. Waterston, L. Stevenson, W. W. Robson, E. J. Chiasson, C. Brooks, G. Hough, L. Spitzer, T. S. Eliot, J. Killham and F. E. L. Priestley.

Kissane, James, *Alfred Tennyson*, New York 1970.

Lang, Andrew, *Alfred Tennyson*, 1901.

Langbaum, R., in *The Poetry of Experience: The Dramatic Monologue in Modern Literary Tradition*, New York 1957.

Leavis, F. R., in *The Common Pursuit*, 1952.

—in *New Bearings in English Poetry: A Study of the Contemporary Situation*, 1932.

—in *Revaluation: Tradition and Development in English Poetry*, 1936.

—in '"Thought" and emotional quality: notes in the analysis of poetry', *Scrutiny* XIII, 1945, 53-71.

McLuhan, H. M., 'Tennyson and picturesque poetry', *EC* I, 1951, 262-82 [K].

—'Tennyson and the romantic epic' [K].

Mayhead, Robin, 'The poetry of Tennyson' in *The Pelican Guide to English Literature, Vol. 6: From Dickens to Hardy*, ed Boris Ford, 1958.

Nicolson, Harold, *Tennyson: Aspects of his Life, Character and Poetry*, 1923.

Paden, W. D., 'Tennyson and the reviewers, 1829-35', *University of Kansas Publications, Humanistic Studies* VI, 1940, 15-39.

Pitt, Valerie, *Tennyson Laureate*, 1962.

Ricks, Christopher, 'Tennyson's methods of composition', *Proceedings of the British Academy* LII, 1966, 209–30.

Ryals, Clyde de L., *Theme and Symbol in Tennyson's Poems to 1850*, Philadelphia 1964.

Shannon, Edgar, Finley, Jr. *Tennyson and the Reviewers: A Study of his Literary Reputation and of the Influence of the Critics upon his Poetry 1827–1851*, Cambridge, Mass. 1952.

Smith, Elton Edward, *The Two Voices: A Tennyson Study*, Lincoln, Nebr. 1964.

Southam, B. C. *Tennyson*, 1971.

Steane, J. B. *Tennyson*, 1966.

Stevenson, Lionel, in *Darwin among the Poets*, Chicago 1932.

—'The "high-born maiden" symbol in Tennyson', *PMLA* LXIII, 1948, 234–43 [K].

Tennyson, Charles, *Six Tennyson Essays*, 1954.

Waterston, Elizabeth Hillman, 'Symbolism in Tennyson's minor poems', *UTQ* XX, 1951, 369–80 [K].

Willey, Basil, in *More Nineteenth Century Studies: A Group of Honest Doubters*, 1956.

Wolfe, Humbert, *Tennyson*, 1930.

Yeats, W. B. in *Autobiographies*, 1926.

—'The symbolism of poetry' in *Essays and Introductions*, 1961. Essay first published in *The Dome*, 1900, and reprinted in *Ideas of Good and Evil*, 1903.

Young, G. M., 'The age of Tennyson', *Proceedings of the British Academy* XXV, 1939, 125–42 [K].

6. STUDIES OF INDIVIDUAL WORKS AND GROUPS

Early Poems to 1842

Chiasson, E. J., 'Tennyson's "Ulysses": a re-interpretation', *UTQ* XXIII, 1954, 402–9 [K].

Hallam, A. H., '*Poems, Chiefly Lyrical* (1830)', *Englishman's Magazine* I, 1831, 616–28 [CH].

Hunt, Leigh, '*Poems* (1842)', *Church of England Quarterly Review* XII, 1842, 361–76 [CH].

Mill, John Stuart, '*Poems, Chiefly Lyrical* (1830) and *Poems* (1833)', *London Review* I, 1835, 402–24 [CH].

Mitchell, Charles, 'The undying will of Tennyson's Ulysses', *VP* II, 1964, 87–95.

Paden, W. D., *Tennyson in Egypt: A Study of the Imagery in his Earlier Work*, Lawrence, Kan. 1942.

Pettigrew, John, *Tennyson: The Early Poems*, 1970.

Pyre, J. F. A., *The Formation of Tennyson's Style: A Study, Primarily, of the Versification of the Early Poems*, Madison, Wis. 1921. Concentrates on early poems but includes some discussion of later work.

Robson, W. W., 'The dilemma of Tennyson', *Listener* 13 June 1957, reprinted in *Critical Essays* 1966. On 'Ulysses' [K].

Spedding, James, '*Poems* (1842)', *Edinburgh Review* LXXVII, 1843, 373–91 [CH].

Stange, G. Robert, 'Tennyson's garden of art: a study of "The Hesperides"', *PMLA* LXVII, 1952, 732–43 [K].

Sterling, John. '*Poems* (1842)', *Quarterly Review* LXX, 1842, 385–416 [CH].

The Princess

Assad, Thomas J., 'Tennyson's use of the tripartite view of man in three songs from *The Princess*', *Tulane Studies in English* XV, 1967, 31–58.

Bateson, F. W., 'Romantic schizophrenia: Tennyson's "Tears, idle tears"' in *English Poetry: A Critical Introduction*, 1950, revised 1966.

Bergonzi, Bernard, 'Feminism and femininity in *The Princess*' in *The Major Victorian Poets: Reconsiderations*, ed Isobel Armstrong, 1969.

Brook's Cleanth, 'The motivation of Tennyson's weeper' in *The Well Wrought Urn: Studies in the Structure of Poetry*, New York 1947 [K].

Hough, Graham, 'Tears, idle tears', *Hopkins Review* IV, 1951, 31–6 [K].

Killham, John, *Tennyson and 'The Princess': Reflections of an Age*, 1958.

Marston, J. W., '*The Princess*', *Athenaeum* XXI, 1848, 6–8 [CH].

Millhauser, Milton, 'Tennyson's *Princess* and *Vestiges*', *PMLA* LXIX, 1954, 337–43.

Ryals, Clyde de L., 'The "Weird Seizures" in *The Princess*', *University of Texas Studies in Language and Literature* IV, 1962, 268–75.

Spitzer, Leo, '"Tears, idle tears" again', *Hopkins Review* V, 1952, 71–80 [K].

In Memoriam

Bradley, A. C., *A Commentary on Tennyson's 'In Memoriam'*, 1901, revised 1902, 1930.

Eliot, T. S., '*In Memoriam*' in *Essays Ancient and Modern*, 1936 [K].

Gransden, K. W., *Tennyson: 'In Memoriam'*, 1964.

Hough, Graham, 'The natural theology of *In Memoriam*', *RES* XXIII, 1947, 244–56.

Hunt, John Dixon, ed *Tennyson, 'In Memoriam': A Casebook*, 1970.

Johnson, E. D. H., '*In Memoriam*: the way of the poet', *VS* II, 1958, 139–48.

Mattes, E. B., '*In Memoriam': The Way of a Soul. A Study of Some Influences that Shaped Tennyson's Poem*, New York 1951.

Moore, Carlisle, 'Faith, doubt and mystical experience in *In Memoriam*', *VS* VII, 1963, 155–69.

Rosenberg, John D., 'The two kingdoms of *In Memoriam*', *JEGP* LVIII, 1959, 228–40.

Sinfield, Alan, *The Language of Tennyson's 'In Memoriam'*, Oxford 1971.

—'Matter-moulded forms of speech: Tennyson's use of language in *In Memoriam*' in *The Major Victorian Poets: Reconsiderations*, ed Isobel Armstrong, 1969.

Svaglic, Martin J., 'A framework for Tennyson's *In Memoriam*', *JEGP* LXI, 1962, 810–25.

Maud

Basler, Roy Prentice, in *Sex, Symbolism and Psychology in Literature*, New Brunswick, N.J. 1948.

Byatt, A. S., 'The lyric structure of Tennyson's *Maud*' in *The Major Victorian Poets: Reconsiderations*, ed Isobel Armstrong, 1969.

Johnson, E. D. H., 'The lily and the rose: symbolic meaning in *Maud*', *PMLA* LXIV, 1949, 1222–7.

Killham, John, 'Tennyson's *Maud*: the function of the imagery' [K].
Mann, Robert James, *Tennyson's 'Maud' Vindicated: An Explanatory Essay*, 1856 [CH].
Rader, Ralph Wilson, *Tennyson's 'Maud': The Biographical Genesis*, Berkeley 1963.
Shannon, Edgar Finley, Jr., 'The critical reception of Tennyson's *Maud*', *PMLA* LXVIII, 1953, 397–417.
Smith, Goldwin, 'The war passages in *Maud*', *Saturday Review* I, 3 November 1855, 14–15 [CH].
Stokes, Edward, 'The metrics of *Maud*', *VP* II, 1964, 97–110.

Enoch Arden
Assad, Thomas J., 'On the major poems of Tennyson's *Enoch Arden* volume', *Tulane Studies in English* XIV, 1966, 29–56.
Bagehot, Walter, in 'Wordsworth, Tennyson, and Browning: or, pure, ornate, and grotesque art in English poetry', *National Review* NS I, 1864, 27–66 [CH].
Scott, P. G., *Tennyson's 'Enoch Arden': A Victorian Best-Seller*, Lincoln 1970.

Demeter and Persephone
Dahl, Curtis, 'A double frame for Tennyson's Demeter?' *VS* I, 1958, 356–62.
Stange, G. Robert, 'Tennyson's mythology: a study of "Demeter and Persephone"', *ELH* XXI, 1954, 67–80 [K].

Idylls of the King
Bagehot, Walter, '*Idylls of the King*', *National Review* IX, 1859, 368–94 [CH].
Eggers, J. Philip, *King Arthur's Laureate: A Study of Tennyson's 'Idylls of the King'*, New York 1971.
Gladstone, William Ewart, '*Idylls of the King*', *Quarterly Review* CVI, 1859, 454–85 [CH].
Gray, J. M., *Tennyson's Doppelgänger: 'Balin and Balan'*, Lincoln 1971.
Jones, Richard, *The Growth of the 'Idylls of the King'*, Philadelphia 1895.

Kozicki, Henry, 'Tennyson's *Idylls of the King* as tragic drama', *VP* IV, 1966, 15–20.

Palmer, David, 'The Laureate in Lyonesse', *Listener* LXXVII, 1967, 815–17.

Priestley, F. E. L., 'Tennyson's *Idylls*', *UTQ* XIX, 1949, 35–49 [K].

Reed, John R., *Perception and Design in Tennyson's 'Idylls of the King'*, Athens, Ohio 1969.

Ryals, Clyde de L., *From the Great Deep: Essays on 'Idylls of the King'*, Athens, Ohio 1967.

Swinburne, Algernon Charles, in *Under the Microscope*, 1872 [CH].

Tillotson, Kathleen, 'Tennyson's serial poem' in Geoffrey and Kathleen Tillotson, *Mid-Victorian Studies*, 1965.

Plays

Granville-Barker, Harley, 'Tennyson, Swinburne, Meredith—and the theatre' in *The Eighteen-Seventies: Essays by Fellows of the Royal Society of Literature*, ed H. Granville-Barker, Cambridge 1929.

James, Henry, 'Tennyson's drama' in *Views and Reviews*, Boston, Mass. 1908.

Knight, G. Wilson, in *The Golden Labyrinth: A Study of British Drama*, 1962.

December 1971

Index

Compiled by Mrs Brenda Hall MA